New Proclamation

NEW PROCLAMATION

YEAR C, 2001

EASTER THROUGH PENTECOST

EDITED BY MARSHALL D. JOHNSON

EASTER

BARBARA R. ROSSING

PENTECOST

HOWARD CLARK KEE

JANET L. WEATHERS

EDGAR KRENTZ

FORTRESS PRESS

MINNEAPOLIS

NEW PROCLAMATION
Year C, 2001
Easter through Pentecost

Cover and book design: Joseph Bonyata
Illustrations: Tanja Butler, *Graphics for Worship,* copyright © 1996 Augsburg Fortress.

Library of Congress Cataloging-in-Publication Data

New proclamation year C, 2001 : Easter through Pentecost / Barbara R. Rossing . . . [et al.].
    p. cm.
  Includes bibliographical references.
  ISBN 0-8006-4244-9 (alk. paper)
    1. Catholic Church—Liturgy. 2. Church year. I. Rossing, Barbara R.

  BX1970 .N48 2000
  251'.6—dc21
            00-051403

Manufactured in the U.S.A.   AF 1-4244

05   04   03   02   01   1   2   3   4   5   6   7   8   9   10

Contents

THE SEASON OF PENTECOST
JANET L. WEATHERS

The Season of Pentecost
Edgar Krentz

FOREWORD

Nᴇᴡ *Proclamation* continues the venerable Fortress Press tradition of offering a lectionary preaching resource that provides the best in biblical exegetical aids for a variety of lectionary traditions.

Thoroughly ecumenical and built around the three-year lectionary cycle, *New Proclamation* is focused on the biblical text, based on the conviction that those who are well equipped to understand a pericope in both its historical and liturgical contexts will be stimulated to preach engaging and compelling sermons. For this reason, *New Proclamation*—like its predecessor, *Proclamation*—invites the most capable North American biblical scholars and homileticians to contribute to the series.

- *New Proclamation* retains the best of the hallmarks that made *Proclamation* so widely used and appreciated while introducing changes that make it more user-friendly.

- *New Proclamation* is published in two volumes per year, designed for convenience. The volume you are holding covers the lections for approximately the second half of the church year, Easter through Pentecost, which culminates in Christ the King Sunday.

- This two-volume format offers a larger, workbook-style page with a lay-flat binding and space for making notes.

- Each season of the church year is prefaced by an introduction that offers insight into the background and spiritual significance of the period.

- There is greater emphasis on how the preacher can apply biblical texts to contemporary situations. Exegetical work ("Interpreting the Text") is more concise, and thoughts on how the text addresses today's world and our personal situations ("Responding to the Texts") have a more prominent role.

- Although they are not usually used as preaching texts, brief comments on each assigned psalm ("Responsive Reading") are included so that the preacher also can incorporate reflections on these readings in the sermon.
- Boxed quotations in the margins help signal important themes in the texts for the day.
- The material for Year C is here dated specifically for the year 2001, for easier coordination with other dated lectionary materials.
- These materials can be adapted for uses other than for corporate worship on the day indicated. They are well suited for adult discussion groups or personal meditation and reflection.

We are grateful to our contributors, Barbara R. Rossing, Howard Clark Kee, Janet L. Weathers, and Edgar Krentz, for their insights and for their commitment to effective Christian preaching. We hope that you find in this volume ideas, stimulation, and encouragement in your ministry of proclamation.

Marshall D. Johnson

THE SEASON OF EASTER

BARBARA R. ROSSING

The fifty days of Easter are a time of rejoicing, a time to see and celebrate the risen Christ alive in the world today. The Emmaus encounter (Luke 24) and other stories of appearances provide paradigms for the church's ongoing encounters with Jesus: We find Christ in the Scriptures and breaking bread. We find him in shattered hopes and deep fears, coming through locked doors and meeting us when we flee. Our hearts are set on fire with the "Aha" of recognizing Christ's presence with us on our Emmaus journeys.

The Easter appearance stories are "master narratives" into which the preacher can invite all Christians to place their own stories.[1] During the seven weeks of Easter we discover the diverse ways the risen Jesus speaks our name and invites us to touch and see him. Stories of Jesus' appearances to Mary Magdalene and the disciples provide a narrative framework by which everyone "who has not seen" may also "come to believe" (John 19:35; 20:31). The task of the preacher is to give voice to the resurrection, to name the living Christ who accompanies us as *Rabbouni* ("teacher," John 20:16), as "Lord and God" (John 20:28), as Shepherd, and as Lamb.

In a remarkable study of the Easter stories as master narratives, Robert Schreiter sets the resurrection story alongside stories of victims of violence and torture in Chile, South Africa, and around the world. He suggests a reading of the Easter stories as narratives of reconciliation in which both victim and oppressor experience the power of new creation. Thus, for example, "the wounds of Thomas' heart can be placed in the larger and deeper wounds of Jesus' hands and side." Mothers of the Plaza de Mayo in Argentina whose children had been "disappeared" create a "circle of love around death," breaking the power of evil through the power of reconciliation.[2] Reconciliation becomes possible for them and for us because God's new creation has dawned.

In commenting on the Easter lections, I will focus especially on new creation themes, beginning with Mary's encounter with the risen Jesus in the garden (John 20). The lessons from the book of Revelation for six Sundays lead us also into a rich metaphorical world of creation imagery: the quartet of zoological living creatures who sing hallelujahs; the lamb that is the light of the city; a wondrous river of life; a healing tree; a tabernacling God who dwells in and with creation and desires to wipe away all its tears. These profound and vivid Easter images proclaim God's love for the entire created world, a theme to emphasize for each day, especially Earth Day, April 22 (Second Sunday of Easter). The Easter season provides the preacher with six Sundays to introduce the book of Revelation in a way that is Christ-centered and hope-filled, countering fundamentalist and literalist readings.

Easter is not simply a resuscitation or renewal of the created world. Resurrection holds profound political significance, overturning injustice and heralding God's new reign. With its critique of Roman imperial violence and injustice, the book of Revelation can aid also in unmasking such violence and injustice in the world today. Jesus' proclamation, "Peace be with you" (John 20:19, 21, 26; John 14:27; Acts 10:36) subverts all false declarations of peace—both the first-century imperial "Pax Romana" (Roman peace) as well as today's "Pax Americana." The true and just peace that Jesus proclaims is the peace of new creation—nothing less.

I write from Jerusalem, a paradoxical and holy city under disputed control and occupation, a city beloved by three faiths—Christians, Jews, and Muslims. In this city where Jesus was crucified and raised, people's hopes for a just peace and a shared future seem as impossible today as they did in the first century under Roman occupation. But it is in such landscapes of shattered hopes and division, in the stones of people's demolished homes and the fragile living stones of their lives, that we discover anew the face of resurrection in our world. Unexpectedly we glimpse the transforming power of Christ's presence, hope reborn in landscapes where no reconciliation seemed possible. This is the face of Easter's new creation, for which we sing and pray.

THE RESURRECTION OF OUR LORD—EASTER DAY

APRIL 15, 2001

REVISED COMMON	EPISCOPAL (BCP)	ROMAN CATHOLIC
Acts 10:34-43	Acts 10:34-43	Acts 10:34a, 37-43
or Isa. 65:17-25	or Isa. 51:9-11	
Ps. 118:1-2, 14-24	Ps. 118:14-29	Ps. 118:1-2, 16-17, 22-24
	or 118:14-17, 22-24	
1 Cor. 15:19-26	Col. 3:1-4	Col. 3:1-4 or 1 Cor. 5:6-8
or Acts 10:34-43	or Acts 10:34-43	
John 20:1-18	Luke 24:1-10	John 20:1-9
or Luke 24:1-12		

FIRST READING

ACTS 10:34-43 (RCL/BCP);
ACTS 10:34a, 37-43 (RC)

During the Easter season in many traditions, texts from the Acts of the Apostles replace the Old Testament as the first lesson. The goal is to see and proclaim Christ as alive in the world and the church today, just as in the immediate post-Easter period of Acts.

Peter's speech from Acts 10 is taken from the larger story of Peter's and Cornelius's visions that will be read again on the Fifth Sunday of Easter. Summoned to the house of the God-fearing Gentile Cornelius, Peter comes to realize the radical message of his vision of the sheet full of unclean animals: God "shows no partiality" between Gentiles and Jews. Taken out of this narrative context, the sermon gives a short creedal summary about Jesus. Like all the speeches in Acts, it shows Luke's careful shaping. Peter's speech and the bold joy with which it was delivered can provide a model sermon for us: God came "preaching peace by Jesus Christ" (10:36); Jesus "went about doing good and healing all who were oppressed" (10:38); they put Jesus to death "on a tree," but God raised him up on the third day. We are witnesses to the fact that Jesus "ate and drank" with people (a probable reference to the issue of table fellowship with Gentiles, Acts 10:41). In Jesus' name, God grants forgiveness to everyone who believes. What more could one preach in an Easter sermon than this?

ISAIAH 65:17-25 (RCL alt.)

Congregations that did not have an Easter Vigil service with readings from the Old Testament would do well to use this wonderful text from Isaiah. The proclamation of God's new creation, of a new heaven and a new earth, is one of the most powerful apocalyptic visions of this postexilic prophet. "Joy" and "gladness" appear six times in vv. 18 and 19, and even become the name of the new city. The city itself will be created and named "as a joy" and its people as a "delight." God will rejoice. Rooted on the land, the people's days shall be lengthened "like the days of a tree." This imagery of newness, drawing from creation, speaks to the Easter promise of God's presence and new creation, a link to the garden theme of John 20.

ISAIAH 51:9-11 (BCP alt.)

This opening section of a larger unit (extending through Isa. 52:3) begins with a community lament addressed to God, contrasting God's former great acts to God's apparent nonintervention. The goal of the lament is to rouse God to action once again, in preparation for the people's exit from Babylon to return to their homeland.[3] The pair of imperatives, "Awake, awake," is a typical construction of Second Isaiah (recall "Comfort, comfort," Isa. 40:1; "Rouse yourself, rouse yourself," Isa. 51:17; "Awake, awake," Isa. 52:1).

Addressed as questions to God, these verses review salvation history by weaving together powerful themes of creation, exodus, and the return from exile. Verse 9 borrows heavily from the Babylonian creation myth of the victory over the chaos dragon (Rahab, the dragon, is also mentioned in Ps. 89:10; Job 9:13; 26:12). Verse 10 celebrates the cosmological deliverance of the redeemed people through the dry bed of the Red Sea. Verse 11 (identical to Isa 35:10) shifts to the present situation of exile, proclaiming that the "ransomed of the Lord" will be brought out of Babylon in a manner reminiscent of the Exodus.

RESPONSIVE READING
PSALM 118:1-2, 14-24 (RCL);
PS. 118:14-24 or 118:14-17, 22-24 (BCP);
PS. 118:1-2, 16-17, 22-24 (RC)

Psalm 118, a community song of thanks sung by Jews at the Passover Seder, is also "the Church's Easter psalm par excellence," sung at the Easter Vigil and the Easter morning liturgy in all three years of the lectionary.[4] Martin Luther said that he "fell in love with this Psalm" and prized it above all others.[5] Repetition gives the psalm its power, with the ever-intensifying declaration that God's "steadfast love (*ḥesed*) endures forever!" Verses 10-13 (omitted here, sung during Holy Week) describe the trauma of torture and death. But God has triumphed over death, leading the psalmist to proclaim, "I shall not die, but I shall live, and recount the deeds of the Lord" (Ps. 118:17). For Christians, Jesus Christ is the stone rejected by builders who has become the cornerstone, and he is marvelous in our sight.

SECOND READING
1 CORINTHIANS 15:19-26 (RCL)

In 1 Corinthians 15, Paul concludes the letter with a carefully argued theological statement on resurrection, responding to doubts among some members of the Corinthian church. The primary question Paul addresses is how we Christians will share in Christ's resurrection. In these verses he develops two metaphors for our participation in Christ's resurrection: "first fruits" and the typology of Adam/Christ.

First fruits is a favorite image for Paul, both in reference to the first Christians in a community (the household of Stephanas as the "first fruits of Achaia," 1 Cor. 16:15) and as the first item in various series. In describing Christ as the "first fruits of those who have fallen asleep"(1 Cor. 15:20, 23), Paul is presenting Christ as a down payment toward a resurrection in which we will all share (similar to Rom. 8:23, where he speaks of the Holy Spirit as a first-fruits gift to us). First fruits is harvest imagery, anticipating the imagery of seeds and sowing by which Paul will describe the resurrection body in vv. 35ff. Having been raised as the first fruits, Jesus is "a divine guarantee that the entire harvest would follow."[6]

There is an "order" (*tagma*, 1 Cor. 15:23) to the sequence of the resurrection of the dead: Christ first; then at his parousia those who belong to Christ; then will come the *telos* or end, when he will destroy all enemies, including death. Victory over death, however, could be won only by victory over sin, since death is the consequence of sin. Here Paul develops his second major image, the Adam/Christ typology. The whole human situation now has been changed by Christ's taking upon himself Adam's legacy of sin and death in order to rescue us from that legacy. Just as sin came to us through the one human, Adam, so now resurrection has come to us through one human being, Jesus Christ (1 Cor. 15:21-22). Thus, on Easter, we proclaim the good news of resurrection, that "all will be made alive in Christ."

COLOSSIANS 3:1-4 (BCP/RC)

Easter invites us to turn our minds to the "things that are above," ordering our lives in light of the resurrection we have experienced with Christ. This passage from Colossians sets the context for the lengthy ethical exhortation that will occupy most of the second half of this epistle. Colossians was probably not written by Paul, as evidenced by the frequent occurrence of words used nowhere else in the Pauline corpus, and by the "realized eschatology" perspective of today's text. The statement that "you have been raised with Christ" (Col. 3:1) conflicts with Paul's own careful formulations in Romans 6 in which he states that we have been "buried with Christ" but stops short of proclaiming that we have been raised with Christ. Pauline or not, the soaring eschatological proclamation of Colossians 3 that we have been raised with Christ can set a basis for the transformed ethic for Easter Christians. The declaration that our lives are "hidden with Christ in God" locates our life, through Christ's resurrection, in the very heart of God.

1 CORINTHIANS 5:6-8 (RC alt.)

The "paschal lamb" imagery for Christ is the reason for this text's selection for Easter morning (or Easter Eve in some lectionaries). In its First Corinthians narrative context, however, the passage fits less well with Easter, since Paul uses the imagery of a lump of dough to express outrage at incest in the community. Paul images the man who has sinned as "old leaven" who must be excised because he poses a danger to the community, imaged as the "new lump." (Paul cites the same parable about the danger of a little leaven leavening the whole lump also in Gal. 5:9, again warning the community about associating with evildoers.)

THE GOSPEL
JOHN 20:1-18 (RCL); JOHN 20:1-9 (RC)

The Gospel of John narrates vivid stories of Jesus' Easter appearances to individual disciples as models of faith for the entire community. They are written "so that you may come to believe that Jesus is the Christ . . . and that through believing you may have life in his name" (John 20:31). Familiar phrases from the Synoptic Gospels, such as "he is risen," do not appear in this text. Rather, the Johannine focus is on "seeing" and "believing."

Mary Magdalene is the disciple whose story frames this episode (vv. 1-2, 11-18). Having stood with the other women and the beloved disciple at the foot of the cross (John 19:25), Mary is now the first person at the tomb. All four canonical Gospels as well as the Gospel of Peter and other Christian Gospels attest to Mary Magdalene's primacy among Easter witnesses, a tradition celebrated in the Easter Proper Preface for Holy Communion: "Therefore *with Mary Magdalene* and Peter, with all the witnesses of the resurrection, with earth and sea and all their creatures, . . . we praise your name and join their unending hymn."

Sandwiched into Mary Magdalene's story is the narrative of Peter and the beloved disciple running to the tomb. Shifts in the verbs used for "seeing" may reflect stages on the way toward faith in John 20.[7] Initially, Mary "sees" (*blepei*, 20:1) that the tomb is empty and fears that grave robbers have taken Jesus' body. The same verb describes the beloved disciple's "seeing" the grave cloths in 20:5—sight that is not yet faith. Peter also "sees" (*theōrei*) the grave cloths, just as Mary's "sees" the two angels in 20:12, but this is still not faith. Only the "seeing" marked by the verb *horan*, first achieved by the beloved disciple upon entrance into the tomb, is perfect sight that leads to faith: "he saw (*eiden*) and believed" (John 20:8; see also Mary's statement, "I have seen the Lord," John 20:18).

> ALL FOUR CANONICAL GOSPELS AS WELL AS THE GOSPEL OF PETER AND OTHER CHRISTIAN GOSPELS ATTEST TO MARY MAGDALENE'S PRIMACY AMONG EASTER WITNESSES.

The "garden" setting for Jesus' tomb (*kēpos*, John 19:41) and for the Lord's appearance to Mary Magdalene is unique to the Fourth Gospel. Paradise traditions may lie behind this garden encounter, if the irony in Mary's identification of Jesus as the "gardener" is a deliberate allusion to God as gardener in Gen. 3:8. Some ancient commentators and feminist scholars hear echoes also of the garden of the Song of Solomon in John 20:11-18, as Mary searches for her beloved ("Have you seen him whom my soul loves?" Song of Sol. 3:3); Mary "peers into" into the tomb (*parakyptō*, John 20:11—the same word as the Greek text for Song of Sol. 2:9); her beloved has "gone to the garden" (Song of Sol. 6:2); and when Mary finds Jesus there she "holds him and would not let him go"(Song of Sol. 3:4).[8]

If John has composed this garden scene in allusion to the Song of Solomon, the connection underscores the love and intimacy between Mary and Jesus. The command not to cling to Jesus (John 20:17) is not necessarily a rebuke but an indication that Jesus' resurrected body is now transformed. Mary's relationship to her beloved is to be expressed not through touch but through speech.[9] In her desire to hold on to the Lord, Mary may be a representative for the Johannine community that feels "orphaned" (John 14:18) and longs for an ongoing intimate relationship to Jesus.

Sandra Schneiders divides the episode of Mary's encounter with Jesus in 20:11-18 into three sections, each governed by a verbal participle about Mary: her "weeping" (vv. 11-15), "turning" (v. 16), and "announcing" (vv. 17-18).[10]

Only when Jesus speaks her name does Mary turn a second time and recognize him as her risen Lord. In speaking Mary's name, Jesus fulfills the description of the good shepherd who "calls his own by name," and they recognize his voice (John 10:3-4).

Jesus commissions Mary to go to the disciples with news of his appearance. He also tells her of his new familial relationship with them: For the first time in the Gospel, Jesus refers to his followers as "brothers and sisters" (John 20:7; the Greek *adelphoi* includes the feminine). Mary is to proclaim that Jesus' God and Father is now "my God and your God" (a pattern familiar from Ruth 1:16).[11]

LUKE 24:1-12 (RCL alt.); LUKE 24:1-10 (BCP)

Interpreting the Text

Easter is a day to celebrate the "idle tale" (Luke 24:12) that God raised Jesus from the dead. Luke's story of the women at the tomb was appointed for the Easter Vigil, but congregations may also wish to use it on Easter morning.

The many women "who had followed Jesus from Galilee" serve as pivotal characters in the transition from Jesus' crucifixion to his resurrection in Luke's Gospel. These women stood at the cross, watching Jesus' public execution (Luke 23:49). They kept vigil as Jesus' body was laid in a rock-hewn tomb. Immediately after his burial, on that same Friday, they began to prepare spices and ointments to anoint Jesus' dead body (Luke 21:55).[12]

After the obligatory Sabbath day's rest, the women who kept vigil in death now bring their spices to the tomb, expecting to anoint the dead body of Jesus. Instead, two dazzling angels greet them with the astounding news of life, in the form of the question, "Why do you seek the living among the dead?" Jesus is not to be found among the tombs, for he is now alive. "He is not here," the angel adds. (This statement and "he has been raised," from the first half of v. 6, are not found in all manuscripts.) But where, then, is Jesus? Faith is not yet possible for the women in the face of such absence. Their initial reaction to the news that "He has been raised" is not joy but bewilderment. Resurrection for us, too, is so totally unexpected as to be incomprehensible.

The command to "remember" and the Lukan sense of necessity (*dei*) guide our journey toward comprehension in the Lukan resurrection stories. The angels aim to trigger the women's recollection of the scriptures and of all that Jesus taught in advance of his death. "It was necessary" (*dei*, Luke 24:7, 26) for Jesus to be handed over for crucifixion and on the third day to rise. Nothing happened that was contrary to scripture, even though it was "sinful people" who crucified Jesus (24:7).

The women *do* remember Jesus' words. Verbs of "proclaiming" (Luke 24:9) and "telling" (Luke 24:10) underscore their witness to the eleven and all the rest. The Lukan account even names three of these women witnesses, beginning with Mary Magdalene and Joanna (a list similar to that of the women patrons who had funded the apostles' ministry, Luke 8:2). But the disciples do not believe the women. Their witness to resurrection seemed to them an "idle tale."

Many manuscripts add v. 12, the account of Peter's trip to the tomb to verify for himself the women's story of the empty tomb and the linen cloths, and his return home in amazement. Not until later that same evening, however, after Cleopas and his companion return to Jerusalem with news of actually having seen Jesus on the road to Emmaus, will the disciples truly begin to comprehend that Jesus has been raised and is now alive (Luke 24:33-35).

Responding to the Text

The task of the preacher is to tell the resurrection story in such a way that each person hears the risen Jesus calling them by name, intimately and lovingly. John 20 offers different models of people coming to faith, embodied in the diversity of characters at the tomb—Mary, Peter, and the beloved disciple.

The garden encounter of Jesus with Mary Magdalene in John 20 is a favorite for many Christians. In Jerusalem, Protestants have created a "garden tomb" site for this encounter, because the more probable historical burial site, the Church of the Holy Sepulchre, no longer looks like a garden. While a sentimental "Jesus and me in the garden" piety can be a danger, the text does not permit such a privatizing of the Easter experience. Mary does not hold on to Jesus but goes forth in faith to proclaim to the disciples, who had returned to their homes, "I have seen the Lord." Christianity owes its existence to Mary's witness, to her model of faith that responds to Jesus' speaking of her name and goes out from the garden into the world in public proclamation.

JOHN 20 OFFERS DIFFERENT MODELS OF PEOPLE COMING TO FAITH, EMBODIED IN THE DIVERSITY OF CHARACTERS AT THE TOMB—MARY, PETER, AND THE BELOVED DISCIPLE.

Other characters in John 20 remind us that not all Christians can expect such intimate and personal encounters in the garden as a basis for faith. The beloved disciple is the first person to "believe," although he himself does not meet the risen Jesus. Peter models a faithfulness that heeds the words of Mary and runs to accompany the beloved disciple to the tomb, but does not yet fully understand the scriptures.

John's Gospel, like all the Easter Gospels, acknowledges the difficulty of faith in the risen Jesus. In the combining of these different experiences of resurrection—

Mary's, Peter's and the beloved disciple's—the text places value on each one. Understanding of the Easter event builds piece by piece in John 20, progressively for the individual characters and progressively for the community of faith. This valuing of different experiences and ways of coming to faith can be a source of strength for us, both as individuals and as the community of faith, as we seek to recognize Christ's transformative presence alive in the world.

EASTER EVENING

APRIL 15, 2001

REVISED COMMON	EPISCOPAL (BCP)	ROMAN CATHOLIC
Isa. 25:6-9	Acts 5:29a, 30-32 or Dan. 12:1-3	Acts 10:34a, 37-43
Ps. 114	Ps. 114 or 136 or 118:14-17, 22-24	Ps. 118:1-2, 16-17, 22-24
1 Corinthians. 5:6b-8	1 Cor. 5:6b-8 or Acts 5:29a, 30-32	Col. 3:1-4 or 1 Cor. 5:6-8
Luke 24:13-49	Luke 24:13-35	Luke 24:13-35

FIRST READING
ISAIAH 25:6-9 (RCL)

The banquet of abundant food links this text to the meal setting of the Emmaus encounter (Luke 24). God sets for us a rich table on Mount Zion and then, in a final course, God "swallows up death forever." Such an Old Testament reference to the end to death is very rare. Tenderly, God will wipe away all tears and will destroy the shroud of death that was cast over us. Easter celebrates that "this is our God," who invites us to the great eschatological feast and destroys our death.

ACTS 5:29a, 30-32 (BCP)

Peter's speech before the Sanhedrin after the escape from prison sum-marizes the Easter kerygma. Characteristic Lukan themes include the Holy Spirit and allusions to scripture. The reference to "hanging on a tree" draws on Deut. 21:22-23 (see the comments on Acts 5:27-32, Second Sunday of Easter), while God's "right hand" where Jesus is exalted alludes to Psalm 110 (see Ascension Day comments).

DANIEL 12:1-3 (BCP alt.)

Daniel 12 formulates the first biblical glimpse of the idea of resurrection that will come to full development in the New Testament. God will raise the martyrs from the dead as vindication of their righteous cause. Daniel was written not at the time of Nebuchadnezzar, as it purports, but during the Seleucid period (167 B.C.E.). In the apocalyptic scenario, the battle against the evil emperor Antiochus Epiphanes is also viewed as God's cosmic battle against the powers of evil. After the battle, a person's fate will be determined by whose name is in the book of life. In this dualistic resurrection scenario, the "wise ones" (*maśkilim*) will be raised to shine like bright stars, while the wicked will be raised to everlasting shame.

RESPONSIVE READING

PSALM 114 (RCL); PS. 114 or PS. 136 or PS. 118:14-17, 22-24 (BCP alt.); PS. 118:1-2, 16-17, 22-24 (RC)

The Easter Eve psalms celebrate the Exodus story. Psalm 114, one of the Hallel psalms sung at Passover (Psalms 113–118), praises God for redemption from Egypt. Water imagery roots the people's liberation in creation motifs. In personified metaphors, the sea "looks" around and then flees in terror, the Jordan River reverses its direction, the mountains and hills skip for joy, and the psalmist taunts them all with the wonderful rhetorical question, "Why?" God's victory not only liberates the people from Egypt but also reshapes the entire cosmos.

Psalm 136 moves through each step of the Exodus with the refrain that God's "steadfast love endures forever."

SECOND LESSON

1 CORINTHIANS 5:6b-8

See Easter Day.

THE GOSPEL

LUKE 24:13-49 (RCL); LUKE 24:13-35 (BCP and RC)

Interpreting the Text

The journey to Emmaus offers the moving and challenging story of accompaniment and breaking of bread, a "master narrative" of reconciliation through which Christians through the centuries have discovered Jesus' presence in their own journeys. Journeys and meals are two favorite Lukan settings, with the entire second half of the Gospel structured around Jesus' journey to Jerusalem. Both the Emmaus journey and Jesus' bread breaking at the meal recapitulate key Lukan themes.

Evidence that the circle of Jesus' disciples included many more than the twelve can be seen in this story of Jesus' appearance to "Cleopas" and an unnamed companion, and again in the reference of v. 22 to "some women from our group." The two dejected disciples are walking away from Jerusalem, away from the terrible events of the past week. Along the journey they discuss all that had happened, but without comprehension. The phrase "we had hoped" (Luke 24:21) sums up their situation. They are walking to Emmaus to flee the pain of despair. Their hope is extinguished.

A stranger joins them, listening. The disciples pour out their hearts about all that has happened, even referring to Jesus as a "prophet mighty in deed and word before God and all the people" (Luke 24:19) and acknowledging that the tomb was empty, "just as the women had said" (Luke 24:24). But this is not a confession of faith. The two disciples are stuck in their inability to put the pieces of the narrative together. Robert Schreiter compares their storytelling to that of trauma survivors, who "can get all the words right, but something still is missing. . . . We struggle to find the one thing that will help us overcome the pain, transform the memory, allow us to get on with our lives."[13]

The stranger provides the transformative key by shifting the disciples' perspective on the events in Jerusalem. He places their story about the Lord's death into the larger story of God's action in the world, as recorded in the prophets and the scriptures. It was "necessary" (*dei*, v. 26) for the Christ to suffer, but death was not the end of the story.

The second part of this event, the meal, completes their breakthrough to recognition that began on the road. In Luke's Gospel, breaking of bread is often the setting for divine encounters, whether at the homes of Pharisees, at the feeding of the thousands, or at the last supper. As Jesus breaks bread once again, the disciples' eyes that were kept from recognizing him on the road (Luke 24:16) are now opened. This is an "Aha" moment of recognition, of sacramental sharing, transforming the disciples' memory and sight. Now they can look back with burning hearts, and recognize that Jesus had been walking with them all along.

Responding to the Text

The Emmaus story is foundational for the church. From now on, God's people will experience the risen Jesus as the two disciples did that first Easter Eve, in the scriptures and in bread breaking. The preacher's call is to help individuals and the community of faith view their own life journey in light of the Emmaus journey. We can evoke recognition of the living Christ in our midst, sharing bread with us today, as articulated in the disciples' question, "Did not our hearts burn within us while he talked with us on the road?"

A sculpture in the Monastery of Silos, on the pilgrimage route to San Jacques de Compostela in Spain, contextualizes the Emmaus road encounter for medieval pilgrims. Jesus is depicted in traditional pilgrim cap and garb, carrying in his hand the pilgrim shell, walking with the pilgrims. In the same way, the Emmaus story invites us to envision Jesus depicted in our contexts, accompanying us on the roads of our lives today. In Chicago, where I teach, we can say with the disciples, "Did not our hearts burn within us as Jesus walked with us on 55th Street, as he opened to us the scriptures?"

THE EMMAUS STORY INVITES US TO ENVISION JESUS DEPICTED IN OUR CONTEXTS, ACCOMPANYING US ON THE ROADS OF OUR LIVES TODAY.

Walking and bread breaking—central to the recognition of God's presence in this story—remind us to leave our cars and take time to walk, to be willing to greet the unexpected stranger. The presence of Jesus in the shared meal points to the sacred dimension in all our meals.

The concept of "accompaniment," modeled by Jesus in Luke 24, has become a central model for cross-cultural ministry, a gift from the Christian community in Latin America. A recent document of the Evangelical Lutheran Church in America envisions mission as walking together with global churches in a "journey where the presence of God is revealed to us. . . . We journey side by side, with neither companion ahead or behind, above or below, the other. . . . Accompaniment implies companionship of mutual respect and signals mutuality in our relationships...The accompaniment model holds the potential to create a radical shift in power within today's global relationships."[14]

SECOND SUNDAY OF EASTER

APRIL 22, 2001

REVISED COMMON	EPISCOPAL (BCP)	ROMAN CATHOLIC
Acts 5:27-32	Acts 5:12a, 17-22, 25-29 or Job 42:1-6	Acts 5:12-16
Ps. 118:14-29 or Ps. 150	Ps. 111 or Ps. 118:19-24	Ps. 118:2-4, 13-15, 22-24
Rev. 1:4-8	Rev. 1:(1-8), 9-19 or Acts 5:12a, 17-22, 25-29	Rev. 1:9-11a, 12-13, 17-19
John 20:19-31	John 20:19-31	John 20:19-31

Arrest in Jerusalem, exile in Asia Minor—today's texts situate the Easter proclamation within a tense political context. The author of Revelation writes against a backdrop of Roman imperial injustice. In John 20, terrified disciples huddle together in a locked room. But God's word of life cannot be fettered.

Today is also Earth Day, the anniversary of a day that underscores our connection to the earth. Just as Easter celebrates Jesus' bodily resurrection as the first-born of creation, so today an emphasis on the renewal of creation—drawing on ancient Christian Easter imagery of the tree and Jesus' scarred body—can be a way to enflesh our Easter proclamation within a contemporary context that includes violence against the earth. Today's texts proclaim that Jesus who was put to death "on a tree" is now alive, breathing the new life of the spirit into the whole creation, and commissioning us to serve as "priests" (Rev. 1:6) in God's renewed world.

FIRST READING
ACTS 5:27-32 (RCL);
ACTS 5:12a, 17-22, 25-29 (BCP)

For a second time, Peter and the other disciples are arrested for preaching and teaching. The Sanhedrin and the high priest before whom the disciples stand trial were Roman-appointed leaders, governing Jewish life within the larger framework of Roman rule.[15] Thus, the seeming anti-Judaism of this passage ("*you* killed him") must be nuanced by an awareness of the reality of Roman occupation under which Palestine lived in the first century.

While scholars once thought that the sermons in Acts reflected the most ancient material, most now agree that the speeches are compositions in which we see Luke's own artistry and theological perspective most clearly.[16] As in his other speeches in the early chapters of Acts, Peter summarizes the essentials of early Christian proclamation: (1) The promises of scripture to our ancestors are fulfilled in Jesus Christ. (2) Opponents ("you") killed Jesus but God raised him up. (3) Repentance and forgiveness are given in Jesus' name. Peter has preached these same essential elements in Acts 2:14-39; 3:13-36; 4:8-12; and will cover them again in 10:34-43 (see Easter Day). Paul's speeches in Acts will follow a similar pattern in proclaiming the gospel to Gentile audiences.

Noteworthy is Peter's use of the word "tree" (*xylon*) in Acts 5:30 and 10:39 to describe Jesus' crucifixion. Similarly, Paul's speech in Acts 13:29 narrates how "they took him down from the tree (*xylon*) and laid him in a tomb." References to the tree in these sermons from Acts probably reflects a very early exegetical tradition of applying Deut. 21:22-23 ("Cursed is anyone who hangs on a tree") to Jesus. Such a christological reading of the curse from Deuteronomy could explain how Jesus' ignominious death on the cross fulfilled scripture. Whereas Paul invokes this Deuteronomy tree tradition in Galatians to argue that Jesus became a curse in place of us ("Christ redeemed us from the curse of the law by becoming a curse for us—for it is written "Cursed is everyone who hangs on a tree," Gal. 3:13), Acts emphasizes rather Jesus' innocence and unjust execution.[17] God vindicated Jesus by raising him from the dead rather than applying the curse. First Peter makes a similar reference to Jesus' death "upon the tree," also proclaiming Jesus' innocence (1 Pet. 2:24).

The tree of Jesus' crucifixion in these texts quickly became conflated with the "tree of life" (Genesis 2–3; Rev. 2:7; 22:2, 14, 19) in patristic Christian exegesis, yielding a whole rich exegetical tree tradition around Jesus' crucifixion and resurrection. The Eucharistic Proper Preface for Holy Week echoes this tree tradition, with the proclamation that Christ "who by a tree once overcame should by a tree be overcome." In Jerusalem, frescoes in the Monastery of the True Cross trace the mythological lineage of the tree of Jesus' cross back to the staffs of the three angels who visited Abraham and Sarah (Genesis 18), which Abraham's kinsman, Lot, planted and tended.

Perhaps the most marvelous example of this tree tradition in art is the twelfth-century apse mosaic in the basilica of San Clemente in Rome, depicting Christ's crucifix as a life-giving tree for nesting birds and other creatures, from which flows a stream of water giving drink to two deer, symbolizing both paradise and baptism.[18] The tradition is also present in the "green cross" of the stained glass windows at Chartres cathedral, with the color green symbolizing the life-giving power of the cross and the tree of life in Eden.[19] The christological tree tradition is clearly ancient and offers wonderful ecological possibilities for Easter preaching of this Acts 5 text.[20]

ACTS 5:12-16 (RC)

This is the third summary of the idyllic life of the early Christian community in Acts, where growing numbers of people flock to the apostolic community of generosity and faith. Prayer and economic sharing (*koinōnia*) were central to the other two summaries (Acts 2:42-47; 4:32-35), but here the emphasis is more on signs and wonders, specifically on the apostles' miraculous healing powers. The apostles are held in such "high esteem" that even Peter's shadow is believed to cure diseases. Such legendary power will be paralleled only by the handkerchiefs and aprons by which Paul can effect cures in Acts 19:12.

Acclamation for the growing Christian community and its leaders causes public controversy. The high priest and Sadducees order the apostles imprisoned. But God's word of "life" cannot be fettered (Acts 5:21). An angel releases the apostles to return to the Temple, where they once more heal the sick and proclaim the good news. Brought up again on trial, Peter responds by declaring the necessity of God's mission by means of the Lukan *dei*: "It is necessary (*dei*) for us to obey God rather than humans!"

JOB 42:1-6 (BCP alt.)

This text from the end of Job seems to present Job as the model of perfect penitence and submission, confessing his folly in seeking his own vindication. The link between Job and the Easter Gospel is the recognition that comes from "seeing" in v. 5. Like Thomas who insisted on seeing Jesus in order to believe, Job tells God, "I had heard of you by the hearing of the ear, but now my eye *sees* you."

RESPONSIVE READING

PSALM 118:14-29 (RCL);
PS. 118:19-24 (BCP alt.);
PS. 118:2-4, 13-15, 22-24 (RC)

See Easter Day.

PSALM 150 (RCL alt.);
PS. 111 (BCP)

"Praise the Lord!" is the theme for the Psalm today, celebrating the resurrection with all variety of musical instruments and with all creation. Psalm 150 is the final psalm of the Psalter. As a bookend to Psalm 1, with its emphasis on the wise person's keeping of God's law, Psalm 150 lifts up unqualified praise as our response to God. In praising God, there is hope for us and for all creation. If one chooses to observe the Earth Day theme today, v. 6 is especially appropriate: "Let everything that breathes praise the Lord!"

SECOND READING

REVELATION 1:4-8 (RCL);
REV. 1:(1-8), 9-19 (BCP);
REV. 1:9-11a, 12-13, 17-19 (RC)

For the next six Sundays the second lesson will be from the book of Revelation. I highly recommend that pastors preach at least one sermon on this book! If we don't preach on it, others will—from Hollywood disaster movies to the fundamentalist "Left Behind" novels and millennialist Web sites. I therefore want to set a framework for this oft-misunderstood book. While the meaning of this book has long been contested, there is no rapture, and the word "Armageddon" is mentioned only once (Rev. 16:16). Revelation is a wonderful Christ-centered book, liturgically rich, full of liberation imagery that is especially suitable for the Easter season. The "Alpha and Omega" of Rev. 1:8 (also Rev. 21:6 and 22:13), inscribed on churches' paschal candles, can be a starting point for congregations to enter this book during the Easter season.

As an apocalypse (Rev. 1:1), Revelation takes us on a journey—a journey to the throne of God, a journey into the heart of the universe, a journey of radical hope and transformation. It uses apocalyptic language to present an alternative world of vision, centered in Jesus Christ. The preacher's task is to help people enter the visionary imagery, to go on the journey. We should resist efforts to try to "figure out" the symbols of Revelation as if they are equations to be solved. Rather, we can help parishioners enter Revelation as we would a work of poetry or music. As essayist Kathleen Norris writes,

> This is a poet's book, which is probably the best argument for reclaiming it from fundamentalists. It doesn't tell, it shows, over and over again, its images unfolding, pushing hard against the limits of language and metaphor, engaging the listener in a tale that has the satisfying yet unsettling logic of a dream.[21]

Revelation has an alternative vision for our world. The author uses vivid language and pictures to critique injustice and exhort faithfulness. The insights of marginalized people today are especially important, and they can help us bypass the interpretations of Revelation by fundamentalists and millennialists. Central to this interpretation of Revelation is God's descent to earth in Rev. 21:1, one of the most hope-filled moments in all of Scripture. The good news of Revelation is that God comes to live with us on earth. This is a vision that can speak to today's observance of Earth Day (April 22).

A sense of literary genre can help us navigate through Revelation. At least three genres are named in the opening verses of Revelation. In addition to "apocalypse" (the first word of the book, Rev. 1:1), Revelation is "prophecy" (Rev. 1:3), in the biblical tradition of prophecy—not as a predictive script for end-time events but rather as proclamation of God's salvation and judgment. Much of Revelation's predictive-sounding language should be read rather as a prophetic wake-up call, exhorting repentance so that destruction will *not* happen (in the same way that the prophet Jonah's "prediction" that God would destroy Nineveh in forty days did not come to pass because Nineveh repented).

Revelation also employs the genre of pastoral letter, in the tradition of Pauline letters. From the island isolation of Patmos, John communicates with Christian communities in cities of Asia Minor (Turkey) by writing a letter to them. The epistolary framework at the beginning and end (Rev. 1:4-6, 22:10-12) underscores the book's identity as a prophetic letter. Unlike other apocalypses, it is not a secret message to be sealed up until the end (contrast Dan. 12:4). Rather, as a public letter, Revelation is to be "read aloud" in the communities to which it is addressed (Rev. 1:3).

The book sets a tone of hard-hitting political polemic with the introduction of Jesus Christ in Rev. 1:5 as the "ruler of the kings of the earth." Countering Rome's claims to rule over nations of the earth, John's Apocalypse attributes authority over kings to Jesus Christ alone. The message of the imminent end of the Roman Empire and the dawn of God's alternative reign of justice will be proclaimed in every chapter of Revelation.

Revelation 1:6 introduces the wonderful theme of the priesthood of all God's people that will recur throughout the book (Rev. 5:10; 20:6). This is baptismal and liberation imagery, drawing on the Exodus tradition that God liberated Israel from Egypt to be a "priestly kingdom" (Exod. 19:6).[22] Isaiah, too, proclaimed the priesthood of all God's people in the return from exile in Babylon (Isa. 61:6). The three-fold proclamation that Christ loves us, has liberated us, and has installed us to kingship as priests (Rev. 1:6) is similar to the "royal priesthood" baptismal proclamation of 1 Pet. 2:5 and 2:9, from which Martin Luther drew his doctrine of the priesthood of all believers. Like the old Imperial margarine television commercials, in which a crown appeared on the head of someone breakfasting on toast with margarine, Revelation invites us to think of ourselves as royalty and priests, wearing crowns and serving God.

Revelation's concept of a democratized priesthood as well as the book's valuation of prophecy demonstrate the great diversity of early church structures. John's first-century churches in cities of western Asia Minor do not seem to have had pastoral offices such as presbyters (pastors), deacons, or bishops. Rather, they recognized only the office of "prophet" and viewed all Christians as priests. Such a lay-focused ecclesiology can offer the preacher an opportunity to teach about baptism as our "ordination" into the priesthood of all believers in which we all share.

Revelation is written in intimate conversation with the Old Testament, but without ever citing biblical texts directly. Revelation 1:8 conflates Zech. 12:10 and Dan. 7:13 in announcing Christ's return. The longer selection of the Episcopal and Roman Catholic lectionaries extends into John's call narrative, based on the call narrative of Daniel and its vision of "one like a son of humanity" (Rev. 1:13; Dan. 7:13).

The Gospel

JOHN 20:19-31

Interpreting the Text

Each year the Gospel for this day situates the Christian community in relationship to Thomas, the disciple who finds faith difficult. In John 20:30-31, the narrator speaks directly to us as readers (recall John 19:35, "so that *you also* may believe"), blessing us and inviting us to enter into the Easter story as we journey toward faith.

Although Jesus' appearance to the disciples takes place on the same day as the morning's empty tomb appearance, neither Mary's proclamation nor the beloved disciple's faith (John 20:8) seems to have had any impact on the disciples. We find them huddled together in a locked room "out of fear of the Judeans." (This translation of *ioudaioi* reflects the geographical sense of the term elsewhere in John—

"He did not wish to go about in Judea because the Judeans were looking for him," John 7:1—and it avoids anti-Judaism by underscoring that Jesus and his Galilean disciples were foreigners in the Judean city of Jerusalem.)[23]

Jesus appears to the disciples in compassion and love, with the greeting, "Peace to you." In showing his hands and side to the disciples, Jesus identifies himself in terms of his wounded body that shows the visible marks of his torture. Were his scars still tender? Jesus may pass through locked doors, but his risen body still bears the marks of the nails. Like our own scars, these scars inscribe Jesus' bodily history.

Jesus "breathes" on the disciples, an echo of God's breath that brought creation to life in Gen. 1:2; 2:7; and Ps. 104:29-30 ("When you send forth your breath they are created; and you renew the face of the ground"). Jesus' breath at Easter brings forth new creation. Raymond Brown underscores the strong creation grounding of John's Gospel: "The Gospel opened with the theme of creation in the Prologue . . . and the theme of creation returns at the end."[24] Similarly, Ernst Käsemann portrays the Johannine community as living from its "ever-new experience of the first day of creation." The presence of Jesus is the presence of the Creator.[25] Such an emphasis on creation can be an important corrective to docetic readings of John. Just as God breathed new life into the dry bones in the desert of Ezekiel (Ezekiel 37), so on Easter the risen Jesus now breathes new life into the disciples and into the world.

With this breath Jesus bestows the Holy Spirit. Rather than harmonizing John's understanding of the giving of the Spirit with the Pentecost account of Acts, we can seek to enter John's own rich symbolic world. Several recent scholars have revived the intriguing suggestion that the Spirit is first given in John 19:35, when Jesus "hands over the spirit" from the cross.[26] The flow of blood and water from Jesus' side on the cross not only proved that Jesus was dead but also "revealed that through death Jesus was the fountainhead of the life-giving Spirit."[27] Other vivid imagery for the promise of the Spirit throughout the Gospel (the water of life, John 7: 38-39; the Paraclete, John 14:16) has prepared readers for the full bestowal of the Spirit in John 20:22.

Thomas is famous as the disciple who doubted, having missed out on the Easter meeting with the risen Jesus. An individual character in John's Gospel, Thomas may also represent an entire community in early Christianity who cherished his unique memory.[28] As the disciple who was willing to risk admitting, "We don't know," at Jesus' farewell discourse (John 14:5; see also John 11:16), Thomas brings an honesty and longing for proof that many Christians can relate to. Thomas is a "Twin" to us all (John 20:24).

Jesus does show his wounded body to Thomas, in love, eight days later. Thomas's confession of faith, "My Lord and my God," is one of the most powerful confessions in the entire Gospel (comparable to Martha's "I believe that you are the Christ, the Son of God," John 11:27).

Responding to the Text

All the Easter Gospels focus on Jesus' risen body, on his bodily presence, and on people's physical experience of him in material things such as food. The resurrection of the body is God's ultimate "yes" to creation. That God raised Jesus from the dead as the first-born of all creation has profound ecological implications. My approach to these texts for Earth Day aims at such a creation-focused proclamation of the resurrection. But, regardless of such recent designation of a day for the earth, these Easter texts speak profoundly about our embodied life within creation, and on God's valuing of embodied creation.

> THE RESURRECTION OF THE BODY IS GOD'S ULTIMATE "YES" TO CREATION.

In the same way that Jesus invites Thomas to touch and feel his scarred body ("Reach out your hand and put it in my side," John 20:27), so the Easter texts invite us to touch and feel the scars of Christ's wounded world today. Building on Paul's metaphor of the church as Christ's body (1 Corinthians 12), some recent theologians have proposed extending the "body" metaphor further, to speak of the earth itself as God's "body."[29] Even if we do not go this far, the world is certainly *a* body, a body that God loves, but a body now with scars: the scars of the ozone hole, of once-beautiful agricultural fields scarred by land mines, of clear-cut forests, of missing species. The preacher can invite worshipers to touch and feel these scars, the marks of deep wounds. And we can proclaim God's Easter promise of healing and resurrection for our bodies and for all creation.

THIRD SUNDAY OF EASTER

APRIL 29, 2001

REVISED COMMON	EPISCOPAL (BCP)	ROMAN CATHOLIC
Acts 9:1-6 (7-20)	Acts 9:1-19a	Acts 5:27b-32, 40b-41
	or Jer. 32:36-41	
Ps. 30	Ps. 33 or Ps. 33:1-11	Ps. 30:2, 4-6, 11-13
Rev. 5:11-14	Rev. 5:6-14	Rev. 5:11-14
	or Acts 9:1-19a	
John 21:1-19	John 21:1-14	John 21:1-19
		or John 21:1-14

Today's texts are epiphanies. The crucified Jesus appears to Paul, to John of Patmos, and to the disciples as their risen Lord. Paul's question on the Damascus road, "Who are you, Lord?" is echoed in the question the disciples dare not voice in John 21 ("Who are you?") and is also heard in the book of Revelation's question, "Who is worthy?" The amazement expressed by these witnesses to Jesus' presence confronts us also with the question of Jesus' identity in the world. In all three texts, "seeing" Jesus is not the final goal, but rather sight that leads to commissioning for service and witness.

FIRST READING
ACTS 9:1-6 (7-20) (RCL);
ACTS 9:1-19a (BCP)

Interpreting the Text

This is the first of three accounts in Acts of Paul's transforming epiphany on the Damascus road (see also Acts 22:3-21; 26:9-23). Paul's dramatic reversal is best described not as a conversion from one religion to another but rather as a call, in the tradition of the biblical prophets.[30] What Paul experiences is a commissioning for God's mission to the Gentiles. Paul the Jew continues to be Jewish, but now with a new mission to "the ends of the earth" (Acts 1:8). The double address, "Saul, Saul," is typical of prophetic calls such as that of Samuel (1 Sam. 3:4) and Moses (Exod. 3:4).

One aspect of Paul's transformation that can speak to our increasingly violent world is Paul's call away from violence to nonviolence. Paul's former violence in persecuting the church was notorious. As a young person he had participated in the murder of Stephen (Acts 7:58) and forcibly invaded homes in order to drag believers ("both women and men" Acts 8:3) into imprisonment. As the scene opens in today's text, Paul is once again "breathing threats and murder" (Acts 9:1), seeking to extend the persecution from Jerusalem to Damascus. The Acts of the Apostles presents Paul in his former life as a violent persecutor, a portrait that many people in our world (both perpetrators and victims) can relate to.

ONE ASPECT OF PAUL'S TRANSFORMATION THAT CAN SPEAK TO OUR INCREASINGLY VIOLENT WORLD IS PAUL'S CALL AWAY FROM VIOLENCE TO NONVIOLENCE.

In a powerful vision, the risen Jesus appears to Paul as one of his own victims, confronting him with the question "Why are you persecuting me?" Blinded, Paul falls to his knees. "Who are you, Lord?" Now Jesus reveals himself as One whom Paul has been persecuting. This encounter with a victim of his own violence is life-transforming for Paul. Reconciliation and courageous proclamation will take the place of violence in Paul's life in subsequent narratives in Acts.

But first, Paul must be reconciled with those Christians whom he has terrorized. Ananias, a disciple in Damascus, also has an epiphany of the risen Jesus. Only such a vivid encounter and direct command from the Lord himself could assure Ananias and other believers that their former violent tormenter was now to become God's "instrument whom I have chosen to bring my name before Gentiles" (Acts 9:15).

Responding to the Text

One element that a preacher can draw on in this text is Jesus' word to Paul that Jesus himself was present in those whom Paul persecuted (Acts 9:5). If Easter is a season to see the appearances of the living Christ in our world today, then this text suggests that Jesus continues to be present in a special way in the lives of victims of violence (similar to Jesus' proclamation in Matt. 25:40-45 that he is present in "the least of these").

Another aspect of this text that invites proclamation is the wonderful model of reconciliation between Paul and Ananias. Ananias unconditionally embraces his former enemy, calling Paul "brother" from the first moment he sees him (Acts 9:17). During his imprisonment in the 1980s, Pastor Simon Farisani of the Evangelical Lutheran Church in Southern Africa was brutally tortured. Upon his release from prison he returned to his pastoral ministry of preaching and anti-apartheid work. One day Pastor Farisani found himself serving Holy Communion to one of his former torturers.

Ananias's baptism of Paul is a similar sacramental moment of reconciliation, when the power of Jesus achieves a remarkable reversal in the life of an enemy. The history of the church is full of such stories, and we need to tell them. The overwhelming message of Acts is that God can effect transformation in the lives of people who encounter the presence of the risen Jesus in the world. Violence can give way to the active nonviolence of love.[31]

JEREMIAH 32:36-41 (BCP alt.)

This oracle is God's response to Jeremiah's prayer on the eve of the fall of Jerusalem. As Jerusalem's populace faced capture and deportation, God unexpectedly commanded Jeremiah to purchase his cousin's field at Anathoth as a tangible sign that the exiles would one day return. The prophet undertook a "public, concrete economic act" to symbolize God's promise of hope and return.[32] As the siege ramps surround the city, Jeremiah prays to God. God responds in the form of a lawsuit, first reminding Jeremiah of all the evil the city's inhabitants had done (Jer. 26:30-35), but also promising restoration.

This text from Jeremiah 32 details that wondrous future restoration: God will gather the people once again and make an everlasting covenant with them in which "they shall be my people, and I will be their God" (Jer 32:38). The people will once again flourish on the land, and God will rejoice in doing good to them.

ACTS 5:27b-32; 40b-41 (RC)

See Second Sunday of Easter.

RESPONSIVE READING
PSALM 30 (RCL);
PS. 30:2, 4-6, 11-13 (RC)

This psalm of thanksgiving for recovery from grave illness sings in personal terms of God's rescue of an individual and also invites the community to join in that person's praise. This is the concrete song of an unnamed and marginalized person, "who had no recourse but to 'take it to the Lord in prayer.'"[33] Verses 9-10 recall the sufferer's lament to God with a desperate series of rhetorical questions intended to motivate God to action. Verse 11 narrates how God heard the plea and responded with healing and transformation, turning the psalmist's mourning into dancing and praise. Verses 4-5 summon the community ("you saints") to join in praising God who brings about such wondrous transformation. The personal lament psalm thus becomes a community song for the dedication of the temple. The invitation is extended to all of us to give thanks for healing and to join in the psalmist's praise of God in whom "Weeping may tarry for the night, but joy comes with the morning" (Ps. 30:5).

PSALM 33 or 33:1-11 (BCP)

This psalm of praise introduces the theme of "new song" (Ps. 33:3) that will be sung also in Revelation's song of the lamb who was slain (Rev. 5:9). Verses 4 and 5 start and end with the name of the Lord, forming a "little credo."[34] The statement that "the earth is full of the steadfast love of the Lord" introduces creation "by the word of the Lord." The majestic central section of the psalm praises God as enthroned on high, another link to Revelation's throne room vision. The strong antimilitaristic message of vv. 16 and 17 indicts every nation's armaments and trust in military might, for weapons are a "vain hope for victory." Finally, the psalm ends with the evocative prayer that God's steadfast love will remain upon us "even as we hope in thee" (Ps. 33:22).

SECOND READING

REVELATION 5:11-14 (RCL/RC);
REV. 5:6-14 (BCP)

Epiphanies evoke worship. Revelation 5 introduces the risen Jesus as the slain lamb whose worship is joined by "every creature in heaven and on earth and under the earth and in the sea" (Rev. 5:13). All heaven breaks loose in singing as the lamb is found worthy to open the scroll. Revelation is rich in such worship scenes. The hymns of Revelation are familiar—from Handel's "Messiah," "This Is the Feast of Victory for Our God," "Holy, Holy, Holy," and other hymns. No book of the Bible has had more influence on Western music and art than Revelation.

John of Patmos envisions a liturgy where animals and all living creatures join in cacophonous singing. This vision can serve as a corrective to our anthropocentric tendencies to neglect the truly cosmic dimension of God's praise. The Easter liturgical Proper Preface underscores this witness of all creation: "Therefore with Mary Magdalene and Peter, with all the witnesses of the resurrection, *with earth and sea and all their creatures,* . . . we praise your name and join their unending hymn."

In order to understand the full significance of this worship scene, we must view it in context—both the literary context of ancient apocalypses and the first-century context of Roman imperial theology. Beginning in chapter 4, Revelation follows the typical genre of "apocalypse" (the first word in Rev. 1:1), in which a representative seer goes on a journey up into heaven, encountering vivid colors, numbers, strange creatures, and other apocalyptic imagery along the way, and then returns with an urgent message to the community.

On this journey up into heaven (Revelation 4–5), John sees the divine throne and God as "the one seated upon it," surrounded by heavenly worshipers. The clear message is political: Only God is worthy of our worship, not the Roman emperor or any imperial power. This radical message is transformative for John and for his first-century communities in Asia Minor.

The political role of this worship scene becomes even more apparent if we consider the root meaning of the word "apocalypse"—*apo,* "from," and *kalypsis,* "covering" or "curtain." John's Apocalypse is an exposé, a pulling back of the curtain to expose the truth about the Roman Empire. In a role analogous to that of Toto in the climactic scene of the film *The Wizard of Oz,* Revelation pulls back the curtain to expose the fact that Rome is not the great eternal power it claims to be. Rome must not be worshiped.

As preachers, we can invite worshipers to savor the liturgy and join in the hymn of all creation, even while we also observe that radical liturgy demands saying no to false allegiances and claims. As Elisabeth Schüssler Fiorenza has shown, Revelation's frequent use of hymns, doxologies, hallelujahs, amens, and descriptions of heavenly liturgies serves "not for the sake of persuading his audience to participate in the daily or weekly liturgy," but rather "for the sake of moving the audience to political resistance." "If the author would write today, he might say: 'Don't salute the flag, salute God'; or 'Don't pledge allegiance to the state, pledge it to God.'"[35]

Revelation does not slavishly follow the genre of apocalypse but throws in some surprises. Most surprisingly, Revelation introduces Jesus not as the expected apocalyptic lion (Rev. 5:5) but rather as a "lamb" (literally the diminutive word, "little lamb"). Jesus Christ is God's Passover lamb, vulnerable and slain, who has been raised and now is worthy of our worship.

The powerful metaphor of Jesus as "the lamb who was slain" will become the central christological symbol of the entire book. This scripting of Jesus as a lamb is an obvious signal not to interpret the imagery of Revelation literally, but rather metaphorically. Just as Jesus was not literally a four-legged sheep or lamb, so Revelation's other symbols and numbers should not be read literally.

THE GOSPEL
JOHN 21:1-19 (RCL/RC);
JOHN 21:1-14 (BCP/RC alt.)

Interpreting the Text

This Easter breakfast epiphany (chapter 21) is probably an epilogue to the Gospel of John, written either by the same author or by someone else at a later date. From a narrative analysis standpoint, chapter 21 "undermines" the message of John 20 in that the Gospel that has just prepared readers for Jesus' *absence* ("blessed are those who have *not* seen and yet believe," John 20:29) now makes Jesus *present* once more.[36] Yet, unlike the dubious endings of Mark, chapter 21 is found in all manuscripts of John's Gospel.

Jesus is vividly present in this scene, sharing food with the disciples and commissioning them for service. As in the Lukan story of the Emmaus road, the disciples seem to be trying to forget the traumatic events that have taken place in Jerusalem. Back home in Galilee, back at their fishing jobs, they appear unaffected by the multiple resurrection appearances that they have just witnessed in Jerusalem (John 20).

The disciples fail to recognize the risen Jesus until he fills their nets with fish— 153 fish! It is the "disciple whom Jesus loved" (John 21:7), not Peter, who first recognizes the Lord. Rivalry between Peter and this beloved disciple in the Gospel of John probably represents ongoing differences among first century Christian communities. Although chapter 21 gives legitimacy to Peter, the Johannine Gospel's clear preference is for the "community of the beloved disciple" over the "apostolic Christianity" represented by the figure of Peter.[37]

THE CATCH OF FISH IS A MOVING PICTURE OF RECONCILIATION AND TRANSFORMATION.

The catch of fish that the disciples "draw" (*helkō*, John 21:6, 11) to the shore harks back to Jesus' promise that he will "draw" all people to himself (*helkō*, John 6:44; 12:32). The net does not tear, despite the great abundance of fish. This catch is an allegory for the church, with the number 153 possibly representing the inclusion of the whole world (symbolized in all the known species of fish).[38]

But the scene does more than allegorize. It is a moving picture of reconciliation and transformation, especially for Peter. In analyzing the resurrection appearances as narratives of reconciliation, Robert Schreiter identifies four steps of reconciliation that Jesus takes toward the disciples in John 21: accompaniment, hospitality, reconnecting, and commissioning.[39] Jesus fills the disciples' nets and then extends hospitality to them by sharing food, cooking it, and also inviting them to bring their contributions of fish.

The charcoal fire (*anthrakian*) on which Jesus cooks the breakfast fish recalls the charcoal fire (*anthrakian*, John 18:18) where Peter warmed himself outside the high priest's courtyard before denying Jesus three times. Jesus questions Peter in a three-fold ritual that restores him to community and commissions him for service.[40] The deep wound that Peter carried now finds healing through this public, three-fold pledge of love (using both the Greek words *agapaō* and *phileō*, although there seems to be no significance to the different words).[41] If Peter truly loves Jesus, he must "shepherd" and "feed" the flock. This commissioning for concrete service is part of Peter's healing, reconnecting him to ministry in the community. While some scholars have observed that John's Gospel seems to exhibit little concern for the poor or hungry,[42] the command to "feed" in this scene evidences concern for the hunger of the world in a literal as well as a figurative way.

Peter's rehabilitation and commissioning in John 21 is no less dramatic than that of the Apostle Paul in the Acts text. For both, to "follow Jesus" will mean suffering and martyrdom (John 21:19; Acts 9:16). For all of us, this text is a three-fold reminder that to "love Jesus" means loving and caring for those whom Jesus loves in the world today.

Responding to the Text

Where can we hear the lamb's "new song" (Rev. 5:9) being sung in the world today? Our texts make vibrant connections between worship and justice, between liturgy and political transformation. Singing is a profound source of hope in the book of Revelation, as Kathleen Norris writes:

> I am attracted to the Revelation also because it was Emily Dickinson's favorite book of the Bible, and because it takes a stand in favor of singing. In fact, it proclaims that when all is said and done, of the considerable noises human beings are capable of, it is singing that will endure. A new song—if you can imagine—and light will be what remains. I find this a cause for hope.[43]

During the 1980s, when South Africa was in the grip of apartheid, Alan Boesak listened for the "new song" in the songs of black people struggling for freedom. He commented on Rev. 5:11-14 as follows:

> It is a wonder that the twenty-four elders and the thousands around the throne are not struck dumb with wonder. But they break out in joy, singing a new song. It is a song of jubilation and of newfound certainty. They know the strife is not over yet. The battle is only about to begin. Deep valleys of pain and suffering lie ahead. And God's people are still in the midst of the struggle. Yet they sing. . . . "Worthy is the Lamb who was slain, to receive power and wealth and wisdom and might and honour and glory and blessing!"

On a Sunday afternoon young black Christians pick up this ancient song and make of it a new song as they dance around a police vehicle just after a student has been arrested at our church service. "Akanamandla, akanamandla, akanamandla uSataani! Sim'swabisile, Alleluia!". . . In translation it goes something like this: ". . . We have disappointed Satan, his power is broken. Alleluia!" As we sing, the song is picked up by others. The police, somewhat confused, somewhat bewildered, somewhat scared, release our friend. Others join us as we march, singing and dancing, back into the church. This is a new song, a freedom song, and the power of it, the sheer joy of it, the amazing truth in it captivate and inspire thousands upon thousands throughout South Africa.

For although the seals of the scroll must still be opened, the scroll is not in the hands of Caesar but in the hands of the Lamb. And we will sing this new song until "every creature in heaven and on earth and under the earth and in the sea, and all therein" will say (5:13): "To the one who sits upon the throne and to the Lamb be blessing and honour and glory and might for ever and ever!" Indeed: Akanamandla uSatani! Alleluia![44]

FOURTH SUNDAY OF EASTER

MAY 6, 2001

REVISED COMMON	EPISCOPAL (BCP)	ROMAN CATHOLIC
Acts 9:36-43	Acts 13:15-16, 26-33 (34-39) or Num. 27: 12-23	Acts 13:14, 43-52
Ps. 23	Ps. 100	Ps. 100:1-3, 5
Rev. 7:9-17	Rev. 7:9-17 or Acts 13:15-16, 26-33 (34-39)	Rev. 7:9, 14b-17
John 10:22-30	John 10: 22-30	John 10:27-30

The Fourth Sunday of Easter is Good Shepherd Sunday. While last week's Gospel invited us to feed Christ's sheep, this week's texts reverse the role: We are ourselves to become sheep, experiencing the protection of a loving shepherd. Adults are not always as good as children at pretending to be animals. Yet to fully savor the salvation promised in the good shepherd texts, we must imaginatively enter into the world of sheep, enjoying nature's gifts, such as green pastures (Ps. 23:2), springs of living water (Rev. 7:17), shelter from the scorching sun (Rev. 7:16), and safety from predators (John 10:28). Most of all, by becoming sheep we learn complete trust in our loving shepherd, Jesus.

FIRST LESSON
ACTS 9:36-43 (RCL)

Thanks to significant revisions of the Revised Common Lectionary, stories about women are now more frequent among the Sunday readings. The healing of the bent woman of Luke 13 (Pentecost 12, August 26) and the stories of Tabitha and Lydia (Acts 16, Sixth Sunday of Easter) are among the new texts included. The RCL also shifts away from Acts' speeches to more stories about the early church, a shift that narrative-oriented preachers may welcome.

Even if the story of Tabitha is a "local legend," as some scholars have claimed, it is noteworthy that Joppa's local Christians remembered a woman as their pre-eminent witness. The story takes place in the large coastal town that is now Tel

Aviv, on the Mediterranean. In a typical Lukan pattern, the author pairs the healing of a woman, Tabitha, with that of a man, Aeneas (Acts 9:32-35).

Only Tabitha is called a "disciple" (the feminine form, *mathētria*). She is a bene-
factor of the community, "full of good deeds and works of mercy which she did"
(Acts 9:36). If we are looking for a shepherd figure in this text, it is Tabitha, who
tends and cares for the widows of Joppa, providing clothing and alms. When
Tabitha falls ill and dies, she is mourned by everyone. The widows testify to
Tabitha's leadership by showing Peter the garments Tabitha has donated, an
important feature of the narrative. As Brazilian Yvoni Richter Reimer describes,
"God affirms Tabitha's work by making it possible, through the mediation of
Peter, for Tabitha to renew her life in community with the saints and widows."[45]

The healing of Tabitha parallels the healings by Elijah and Elisha (1 Kings
17:17ff.; 2 Kings 4:32ff.) and Jesus' healings of the widow's son at Nain (Luke
7:11-17) and the centurion's daughter (Luke 8:40-56). The same word as was
used of the widow's son in Luke 7:15, for example, is used to describe how
Tabitha "sat up." This parallelism establishes a continuity of the early church's
healing ministry to both Jesus' miraculous healings and the biblical prophets. One
difference is that Acts places more emphasis on prayer in healing stories. Peter
kneels down and prays before commanding Tabitha to "rise up," an allusion to
resurrection. Peter gives Tabitha his hand and "caused her to stand up (*anistanai*),"
also a verb of resurrection.

The statement that Peter "presented her alive" to the saints and widows in
Joppa echoes the description of Jesus who "presented himself alive" to the disciples (Acts 1:3).[46] No sermon follows the healings of either Tabitha or Aeneas in
Acts 9, unlike Peter's first healing of the lame man in Acts 3:1ff. Large crowds living in the entire coastal plain area believe in the Lord simply through hearing of
the miraculous healing of their beloved leader Tabitha. Thus, the prophecy of the
spread of the gospel in Acts 1:8 "from Jerusalem to Judea" is coming to fulfillment in the narrative of Acts. The stage is set for the mission to the Gentiles, and
to the "ends of the earth."

ACTS 13:15-16, 26-33 (34-39) (BCP)

Beginning with chapter 13, the second half of Acts tells the story of
Paul, set in parallelism to Peter.[47] In his speeches as well as in miracles and other
events, Paul's missionary career in Acts bears a striking similarity to Peter's. Today's
speech, the first of Paul's six major missionary speeches, echoes notes from Peter's
speech in Acts 2.

After their successful mission on the island of Cyprus, Paul and Barnabas move
on to the mainland of Asia Minor (modern-day Turkey), to the central city of
Pisidian Antioch. In contrast to the missionary strategy Paul describes in his own

letters, Acts presents Paul as first seeking out the Jewish synagogue in each city, and turning to Gentiles only after rejection by the Jews. Paul delivers his first missionary speech on the Jewish Sabbath, to an audience of Jewish religious leaders (the *archisynogōgoi*) who have invited him to speak a word of exhortation or comfort (*paraklēsis*).

Paul's speech reviews salvation history in a somewhat more positive tone than Peter's, drawing on Psalm 2 and other scriptures to argue that after Jesus was crucified on a "tree" God raised him from the dead (Acts 13:29; for the "tree" in the speeches of Acts, see comments on Acts 5:27-32 for April 22). Paul "brings good news" (Acts 13:32) that the scriptures and promise of God to the ancestors are now fulfilled in Jesus. Many people in Pisidian Antioch come to believe this good news.

ACTS 13:14, 43-52 (RC)

Acts 13 narrates the watershed event in the history of Christian mission, God's turning to the Gentiles. Whereas Acts 10–11 told the story of Peter's conversion to the Gentile mission, Acts 13 is the Pauline parallel. This week's text continues the story of the mission to the Jewish community in Pisidian Antioch. Paul's first Sabbath sermon in the synagogue was so successful that Paul and Barnabas were invited back on the next Sabbath (Acts 13:42-43). This second time the reception is hostile. So now, in obedience to Isa. 49:6, a text that Paul and Barnabas take to be God's commandment addressed to them, the missionaries turn to the Gentiles. Paul gives a theological justification to this Gentile turn with the word *dei*, "it was necessary" (Acts 13:46). Understanding themselves as a "light for the Gentiles," the missionaries will now take their message of salvation to the uttermost parts of the earth. On Good Shepherd Sunday, this text can be a reminder that God's flock is not limited by ethnic boundaries, but extends to the "ends of the earth" (Acts 1:8).

NUMBERS 27:12-23 (BCP alt.)

The Good Shepherd Sunday theme is rooted in this strong Old Testament shepherd lection. God shows the promised land to Moses, but because he rebelled against God he will not be permitted to enter this land. Moses asks God to appoint a shepherd (Joshua) so that the people are not "sheep without a shepherd." The image of sheep without a shepherd becomes a biblical formula for Israel without a leader, repeated by the prophet Micaiah in 1 Kings 22:17 (see also 2 Chron. 18:16) and in the New Testament by Jesus in Mark 6:34 (see also Matt. 9:36).

RESPONSIVE READING
PSALM 23 (RCL)

Psalm 23 develops the element of trust from the typical lament psalm, building on the shepherd image. One way to enter the psalm's richness is to trace shifts in its use of pronouns and references to God. The psalmist begins and ends by speaking *about* God in the third person ("Yahweh" is named in vv. 1 and 6), but shifts in the very center of the psalm to addressing God directly, in the second person ("you," v. 4). This "you" is the theological anchor of the psalm, expressing heartfelt trust and gratitude to God that "you are with me." Throughout the psalm, the use of the first person singular ("I," "my," "me") also gives a feeling of personal intimacy that makes this a favorite psalm for the church.

PSALM 100 (BCP); PS. 100:1-3, 5 (RC)

Psalm 100 also uses strong shepherd imagery.[48] Psalm 100 affirms that we are created to be the sheep of God's pasture. As God's well-tended flock, we are called to respond in praise. A strong series of imperatives ("make," "serve," "come," "enter," "give thanks") in vv. 1, 2, and 4 summons all lands and peoples to praise God, and to enter into God's presence in the temple courts. The reason for praise is that "the Lord is good," and God's steadfast love endures to all generations.

SECOND LESSON
REVELATION 7:9-17 (RCL/BCP);
REV. 7:9, 14B-17 (RC)

Revelation 7 is a wonderful "salvation interlude" between the opening of the sixth and seventh seals. Following the heavenly throne room vision of Revelation 4–5, the lamb began to open the first six seals on the scroll. The seals and the two other numbered sequences in the middle of Revelation—the seven trumpets and bowls—are modeled on the plagues of the Exodus story. For Revelation, a dramatic new Exodus is being undertaken "not in Egypt but in the heart of the Roman Empire."[49] God calls Christians to "come out" of Rome (Rev. 18:4), just as the Israelites came out of Egypt. A further Exodus connection can be seen with the sealing of God's saints in Revelation 7 (probably a baptismal reference), similar to the sealing of the Israelites' doorposts to protect them from the angel of death in the Exodus story.

Elisabeth Schüssler Fiorenza has pointed out the important function of Revelation's salvation interludes between the sixth and seventh element in each of the series of sevens (seals, trumpets, and bowls). Even in the most difficult sections, God's judgment is not unrelenting. Chapter 7 "interrupts the seal septet" to proclaim the "protection and salvation of the people of God."[50] (The millennial vision of Revelation 20, in her view, is another salvation interlude.) Only after the interlude of sealing all God's saints does judgment resume in Rev. 8:1 with the opening of the seventh seal.

Today's text portrays the multitude of God's people standing before the throne of God, who are "sheltered" by God's tabernacling presence. The scene divides into two sections, a heavenly vision (Rev. 7:9-12) and its interpretation (7:13-17). Worship and praise are central to both sections. Since those who belong to the lamb are said to be a multicultural multitude "that no one could count" (Rev. 7:9), literalist interpreters' fixation on the number 144,000 is thus undermined. Palm branches in the hands of these worshipers are a possible allusion to the Feast of Tabernacles, another Exodus link (Lev. 23:40-43). Everyone joins in acclaiming God and the lamb, to whom salvation belongs.

After the vision, one of the elders gives its interpretation, a typical apocalyptic question-and-answer format. People who belong to the lamb's multitude are those who have come out of the great *thlipsis* ("tribulation"). This word, which recurs throughout Revelation, is key to understanding the situation that John shares with his communities (Rev 1:9). The tribulation (*thlipsis*) of Revelation's audience was probably not state-sponsored persecution but rather the social, economic, and religious marginalization of those who refused to participate in first-century Roman imperial economic life by eating food sacrificed to idols (Rev. 2:20) or offering sacrifice to the emperor (Rev. 14:9-11).

Those who come through the tribulation now serve God. Like a shepherd, God tenderly cares for the people. The verb "shelter" (*skēnosei*) invokes tabernacle imagery, the sense of God's radiant presence or dwelling (see Ezek. 37:27) as a canopy or tent over us. In the New Jerusalem vision of Revelation 21, God's sheltering presence will be located in a city (Rev. 21:3), but here in Revelation 7 the setting is rural or wilderness-oriented. The longest of Revelation's hundreds of Old Testament allusions draws from Isa. 49:10, the call to return home from exile: God's people will not hunger or thirst on their journey through the wilderness, nor will any scorching wind or sun touch them (Rev. 7:16, a contrast to the sun's scorching of evildoers in Rev. 16:7). In an amazing combination of imagery, the lamb now becomes also the shepherd, tending the flock, leading people to springs of water, and wiping away all their tears (a quote from Isa. 25:8). Led by their shepherd-lamb, God's people will come through the tribulation into God's new promised land.

THE GOSPEL

JOHN 10:22-30 (RCL/BCP);
JOHN 10:27-30 (RC)

Interpreting the Text

The wonderful image of Jesus as a shepherd from John 10, Jesus' final public discourse, speaks to us on many levels. "Shepherd" was a political term for rulers in both Israelite and Greco-Roman traditions. Often the biblical shepherd image was positive (David, 1 Sam. 17:15) but Israel's prophets also lamented the bad shepherd-politicians who exploited their flock (Ezekiel 34; Jeremiah 23; Zechariah 11). For Gentile hearers, too, shepherd imagery would have been familiar from a long tradition of iconography and literature beginning already with Plato's *Republic* 343–345.[51] "Shepherd" was clearly a rich image that appealed to a broad spectrum of readers.

Yet, paradoxically, the good shepherd discourse of John 10 "exceeds the other discourses in difficulty."[52] Far from concluding on an idyllic or pastoral note, the section of the chapter assigned for today is divisive, even alienating. John 10 ends with a high level of conflict as well as a very high christology, proclaiming Jesus' "equality" (*hen*) to God in terms that provoke people to try to stone Jesus.

> FAR FROM CONCLUDING ON AN IDYLLIC OR PAS-
> TORAL NOTE, THE SECTION OF THE CHAPTER
> ASSIGNED FOR TODAY IS DIVISIVE, EVEN ALIENAT-
> ING. JOHN 10 ENDS WITH A HIGH LEVEL OF CON-
> FLICT AS WELL AS A VERY HIGH CHRISTOLOGY.

The temporal and spatial markers of "the festival of Dedication," "it was winter," and "walking in Solomon's Portico" suggest the beginning of a new section in John 10:22-23, not a strict continuation of the shepherd discourse of vv. 1-21. The authorities bring Jesus for questioning in a public trial-like setting, following up on his shepherd discourse. The question they pose to Jesus is similar to that of the Synoptic Gospels' trial before Pilate: Do you claim to be the messiah or not? (see Luke 22:67). In typical Johannine fashion, Jesus turns the tables on his questioners by judging *them* ("You do not believe because you are not of my sheep," 10:26), reframing their question to ask who belongs to his flock.

Verses 28-38 introduce a very high christology in the claim not only that Jesus is the messiah and shepherd, as in vv. 24-27, but that he is equal to God ("The Father and I are one," John 10:30; compare John 5:18), thus provoking charges of blasphemy (John 10:33). Jesus is equal to God in his power over death—both his own death ("I have power to lay it down, and I have power to take it up," John 10:18) and that of his followers ("I give them eternal life, and they will never perish," 10:28).[53] Eternal life is the gift of God, and here it is Jesus who presents it to his followers, thereby underscoring his identity and unity with God.

John's setting of this scene at the time of the Jewish Feast of Dedication, with its connection to the Temple, may help to explain why Jesus' claim to divinity was considered so provocative. The middle section of John's Gospel is organized around a series of Jewish festivals (Passover, John 2:13, 23; an unnamed feast, 5:1; a second Passover, 6:4; Tabernacles, 7:2; Dedication, 10:22; and a third Passover to follow in 11:55) in which Jesus is presented as personifying and perfecting the Jewish feasts (see John 2:21 for his claim to replace the temple). Dedication (Hanukkah) was the festival celebrating the rededication of the temple after its desecration in 167 B.C.E. (1 Macc. 4:52-59; 2 Macc. 10:5-8). James VanderKam compares Jesus' claims of divinity in John 10:30 to the recent memory of Emperor Antiochus Epiphanes' own divine claims:

> It should be recalled that Antiochus IV . . . imposed new forms of worship which included veneration of himself as a god in Jerusalem's temple. Jesus' strong assertions that he and the Father are one (10:30), that he was the Son of God (10:36) and that the Father was in him as he was in the Father (10:38) were uttered at a time when the blasphemous pretensions of Antiochus IV to be a god would have been particularly fresh in the minds of Jewish people.

Set against the backdrop of temple rededication, negative reactions of "the Jews" to Jesus' bold claims of divinity may become more understandable.[54] On the other hand, that Jesus is willing to give his life for the people also could invoke other, more positive Dedication-related memories of Judas Maccabaeus and the martyrs who gave their lives for the Temple.

The closing verses of the good shepherd discourse of John 10, like the closing verses of the bread discourse of chapter 6 and the Tabernacles of chapter 7, precipitate conflict and division between Jesus and the religious leaders. Jesus draws a stark contrast between true followers who acknowledge his equality to God, and all others who "do not belong to my sheep" (John 10:26). Some scholars think these provocative statements may be less reflective of Jesus' own words than of the painful separation taking place between the Johannine churches and Judaism at the end of the first century C.E. The highest christological statements may have aimed to force crypto-Christians who were still part of the synagogue (characterized by Nicodemus) to come out into the open, even at the risk of alienation from Judaism. The difficulty for the preacher today is that this high strand of Johannine christology, with its important emphasis on Jesus' gift of eternal life, is so closely tied to John's "conflictive context and its function to divide, dismiss, and condemn."[55] For all its invitational imagery, the good shepherd discourse concludes on a surprisingly combative note.

Not only are there good and bad shepherds, but true and false sheep. Given the contentiousness of the closing verses of the Good Shepherd discourse in John 10, it may be worthwhile for the preacher to spend some time with the notion of being "true sheep" of the good shepherd—sheep who know the shepherd's voice, rejoice in it, and trust the rich measure of grace the shepherd supplies to the sheep.

For the Moravian Church the image of Jesus as shepherd is central.[56] Hymns such as "Jesus makes my heart rejoice" by Henriette Louise van Hayn (1776) can help us enter into both the faithful sheep and the good shepherd imagery:[57]

> Jesus makes my heart rejoice,
> I'm his sheep and know his voice.
> He's a Shepherd, kind and gracious,
> And his pastures are delicious;
> Constant love to me he shows;
> Yea, my very name he knows.
>
> Trusting his mild staff always,
> I go in and out in peace;
> He will feed me with the treasure
> Of his grace in richest measure;
> When athirst to him I cry,
> Living water he'll supply.

Psalm 23 and its proclamation that sheep of the shepherd's flock need fear no evil (23:4) gives a definition of trusting, freeing faith, even in the presence of those who wish us harm. Revelation's allusion to the Exodus and wilderness sets the shepherd and flock imagery in the context of the most formative and liberating event of Israel's history.

The author of John's Gospel may have chosen the shepherd imagery of John 10 in order to appeal to a broad spectrum of hearers—Samaritans and Gentiles as well as Jews, all of whom brought rich associations of their own to the imagery and could enter it at many levels.[58] Today, too, the preacher can draw on the shepherd's expansive invitation to help people from diverse backgrounds enter into sheep-like faith and trust in the risen Christ.

FIFTH SUNDAY OF EASTER

MAY 13, 2001

REVISED COMMON	EPISCOPAL (BCP)	ROMAN CATHOLIC
Acts 11:1-18	Acts 13:44-52	Acts 14:21b-27
	or Lev. 19:1-2, 9-18	
Ps. 148	Ps. 145 or 145: 1-9	Ps. 145:1, 8-13
Rev. 21:1-6	Rev. 19:1, 4-9	Rev. 21:1-5a
	or Acts 13:44-52	
John 13:31-35	John 13:31-35	John 13:31-33a, 34-35

Newness is the unifying theme of this week's texts: a new boundary-crossing mission to the Gentiles; a new heaven and a new earth as the location for God's new city, Jerusalem; and a new commandment to love. This is a Sunday to proclaim God's grace dawning "new every morning" (Lam. 3:23). As the church continues to face new challenges and mission opportunities today, Peter's question in defense of the Gentile mission propels and guides us into God's new future: Who are we that we could withstand God? (Acts 11:17)

FIRST LESSON
ACTS 11:1-18 (RCL)

Interpreting the Text

The "conversion" of Peter and the early church to welcome Gentiles constitutes the great turning point in the book of Acts. In Acts it is Peter, not Paul, who inaugurates this Gentile mission. The conversion is dramatic, accomplished by a pair of visions from God and the dawning of the Holy Spirit. In a carefully structured parallelism, Acts 10–11 narrates how a God-fearing Gentile, Cornelius, comes to faith in the gospel of Jesus at the same time that the apostle Peter comes to the realization that God does not discriminate between Jews and Gentiles. Their two conversion stories mirror and complement one another, with Cornelius and Peter drawing on each other's visions in order fully to comprehend God's new mission. The outline of Acts 10–11 by Beverly Roberts Gaventa underscores the Cornelius/Peter parallelism:[59]

VISION SCENE	Cornelius (10:1-8)
	Peter (10:9-16)
JOURNEY AND WELCOME	Cornelius (10:17-23)
	Peter (10:23b-29)
PROCLAMATION	Cornelius (10:30-33)
	Peter (10:34-43)
CONFIRMATION	Holy Spirit (10:44-48)
	Community (11:1-8)

Peter's own conversion can be tracked by the word "discriminate" (*diakrinō*), used three times in this incident (and again in the controversy about Gentiles in Acts 15:9; obscured in most English translations). As Peter pondered the vision of the sheet full of unclean animals, God's Spirit told him to follow the three messengers to Cornelius' house "without discriminating" (Acts 10:20). Hearing of Peter's scandalous table fellowship with Gentiles, the circumcision party in Jerusalem "discriminated against him" (Acts 11:2). Now, in his speech before them in today's text, Peter recounts his vision and the Spirit's message to him that he should go to Cornelius' house "without discriminating" (Acts 11:12). God's radical new message is that the church must obey God by not discriminating between Jews and Gentiles.

Peter's speech in Acts 11:1-18, the final episode in this story, functions to provide the community's confirmation of the dramatic events in Caesarea. God has already given the Holy Spirit unconditionally to Cornelius and his household, but Peter must now justify this event to the skeptical Jerusalem community.

Peter presents the case for Gentile inclusion not by theological argument but by narrative, retelling his personal experience of the vision and the messengers from Cornelius. Especially powerful in favor of the Gentiles is the evidence that the "Holy Spirit fell on them just as on us," even before their baptism, thus fulfilling Jesus' ascension promise (Acts 1:5). Peter then asks the rhetorical question that leads the church to ratify his experience: If then God gave the same gift to the Gentiles as to us when we believed in the Lord Jesus Christ, who was I, even I (the *egō* is emphatic), that I could withstand God?

The community's deliberation and its glorification of God for granting "repentance unto life" to the Gentiles are the climax of the story in Acts 11:18. Not until this ratification of Peter's account by the assembled community is the narrative complete.[60] Such community confirmation is a key element in other scenes in Acts as well, where the Christian community receives a report of amazing new acts of God and ratifies with joy the new working of the Spirit.

What are analogous situations today in which God's Spirit may be leading the church to embrace new forms of boundary-crossing inclusivity, even when it seems contrary to scripture? As ethnic and racial divisions continue in the church today, the Peter/Cornelius story and its critique of discriminating can be a powerful resource for anti-racism training. Luke Timothy Johnson has proposed that the early church's decision for unconditional acceptance of Gentiles might be a tool for the church in addressing homosexuality.[61] If Acts 10–11 offers criteria for decision making, we should both listen to the personal narratives of individuals testifying to the new work of God in their lives and also seek confirmation by the assembled community in identifying this as the authentic work of God's spirit. Acts proclaims that God continues to do radical new things in the world, and that God's Spirit can work in the lives of those whom the church has long excluded.

> ACTS PROCLAIMS THAT GOD CONTINUES TO DO RADICAL NEW THINGS IN THE WORLD, AND THAT GOD'S SPIRIT CAN WORK IN THE LIVES OF THOSE WHOM THE CHURCH HAS LONG EXCLUDED.

ACTS 13:44-52 (BCP)

See the Roman Catholic lection for the First Lesson for May 6, 2001.

LEVITICUS 19:1-2, 9-18 (BCP alt.)

This reading introduces the theme of "holiness," which will also characterize God's holy city, New Jerusalem (Rev. 21:2). The grammar is ambiguous as to whether this is an indicative statement or a command—"You *are* holy" or "You are to *be* holy."[62] The laws that follow in vv. 9-18 spell out Israel's life as holiness as including love for neighbor and justice and care for the poor. The magisterial "I am the LORD" (repeated in vv. 10, 12, 14, 16, 18) grounds these laws and commandments in God's unique relationship to Israel.

ACTS 14:21b-27 (RC)

At the end of their first mission journey, Paul and his colleagues return home to Antioch in Syria, having "evangelized" and "discipled" many towns (Acts 14:21). On their way home they stop in each city to strengthen and encourage the new Christian communities and to install leaders (*presbyteroi*, probably a "Lukan anachronism,"[63] because Paul never uses this term to refer to church leaders in his own letters).

Upon their arrival in Antioch, Paul and his colleagues report to the community "all that God had accomplished with them," including the door that has been opened to the Gentiles (Acts 14:27). This summoning of the whole church to receive their report is an important element in the confirmation of the Pauline mission, similar to Peter's report to the community in Acts 11. Early Christian missionaries were not lone rangers, but were accountable to a home Christian community. The report of "all that God has done" brings mutual upbuilding and joy to all.[64]

RESPONSIVE READING
PSALM 148 (RCL)

Summons to praise God is the essence of this psalm, as the psalmist calls upon the entire created world to join in glorifying God. One by one, the created elements become part of the worshiping congregation. Mountains, fruit trees, stars, weather, and water—the joyous sound builds as all join with humans in praising their creator. The final stanza gives thanks for God's chosen people, Israel.

PSALM 145 (BCP); PS. 145:1–9 (BCP alt.); PS. 145:1, 8–13 (RC)

This is an alphabetical (acrostic) psalm, praising God from A to Z (from *'aleph* to *tav*). The comprehensiveness of God's blessing is signaled not only in the successive use of every letter of the alphabet, but also in the repetition of "all." Beginning with v. 13, attention turns to God's special care for the needy.

SECOND READING
REVELATION 21:1–6 (RCL); REV. 21:1–5a (RC)

The New Jerusalem vision of Revelation 21–22 is one of the most wonderful visions in all of scripture, fulfilling Isaiah's promises of newness ("I am about to do a new thing," Isa. 43:19; "For I am about to create new heavens and a new earth," Isa. 65:17). Belief in a heavenly Jerusalem, often personified as a feminine figure or "mother" (because the word "city" is feminine in both Greek and Hebrew; see Gal. 4:26, "Jerusalem above . . . is our mother") was widespread in biblical times. Especially after the destruction of the Jerusalem temple by the Romans in 70 C.E., dreams of a heavenly city flourished among Jews and

Christians (see Heb. 12:26; and Dead Sea Scrolls texts such as 5Q15). What is striking in Revelation is that this heavenly city descends from heaven down to earth.

Contrary to popular apocalyptic thinking, there is no "rapture" or a future snatching of Christians from the earth in Revelation.[65] Instead, God is "raptured" down to earth to take up residence among us. Revelation declares God's commitment to the earth as the location of salvation. God's bridal city (*polis*) will descend to earth, and God will "tent" there (*skēnē, skēnoō*, Rev. 21:3), in the midst of the city. With great tenderness God wipes away people's tears and takes away sorrow, a quotation of the Isaiah text that was used also in Rev. 7:17 (Isa. 25:8).

Revelation's vision of New Jerusalem, the city with the gleaming golden street and pearly gates, where death and tears are no more, has given form and voice to the dreams of God's people through the ages. From Augustine's "City of God" through William Blake's "Jerusalem," Revelation's holy city has promised life and healing, reconciliation and justice. African-American spirituals and gospel songs invoke imagery of the golden holy city and its river of life.

New Jerusalem is the contrast-city to evil "Babylon," John's name for the Roman empire (Revelation 17–18). The vision of Revelation 21–22 fulfills promises to the seven churches (Revelation 2–3), including the promise to the Philadelphians of citizenship in the "city of my God, the new Jerusalem which comes down from my God out of heaven" (Rev. 3:12), and to Ephesus of the "tree of life" (Rev. 2:7). All God's promises now come to fulfillment in this culminating vision of the entire book.

For the first time since Rev. 1:8, God speaks not through angelic intermediaries but directly, reiterating, "I am the Alpha and the Omega." God offers the promise of water of life for all who thirst, free of charge. The word *dōrean*, "without price" (Rev. 21:6; 22:17), underscores a key economic contrast between God's political economy and the Roman Empire. Unlike the unjust commerce of Babylon/Rome, God's New Jerusalem is a city where life and its essentials are given as a free gift, "without money," even to those who cannot pay for them. In our time when too many of the world's poor are being left behind by a globalized economy, this vision of participation for all, even those without money, can be important for preachers to proclaim.

New Jerusalem is a profoundly urban vision, renewing our vision for urban ministry. "God wills to restore this world to a beauty we can scarcely imagine. It is a city, not a solitude, an important distinction in the narcissistic din of American culture."[66] The

NEW JERUSALEM IS A PROFOUNDLY URBAN VISION, RENEWING OUR VISION FOR URBAN MINISTRY.

city that descends from heaven invites us all to enter as citizens and to "inherit" (Rev. 21:7) its blessings, as God's own sons and daughters.

After the fall of Babylon/Rome in Revelation 18, all heaven breaks loose in singing. Four jubilant "Hallelujahs" by the elders and living creatures in heaven celebrate the vindication of God's judgment. The text gives us the first glimpse of New Jerusalem, radiantly dressed as a bride, prepared for her marriage to the lamb. Dressed in white linen (signifying the "righteous deeds of the saints"), this woman is a contrast-figure to evil Babylon.[67] Her appearance is similar to that of the feminine figure of wisdom or sophia in wisdom literature. The fourth of Revelation's seven beatitudes (see also Rev. 1:3; 14:13; 16:15; 20:6; 22:7, 14) invites us to be guests at her wedding, "Blessed are those who are invited to the feast of the marriage of the Lamb" (Rev. 19:9).

THE GOSPEL
JOHN 13:31-35 (RCL/BCP);
JOHN 13:31-33a, 34-35 (RC)

Interpreting the Text

The theme of newness continues in today's text with the new commandment. For the next three Sundays the Gospel lessons will be from Jesus' final discourse, John 13–17, the Johannine last supper. Roughly one-fifth of the entire Gospel is devoted to this lengthy discourse. Jesus' speech employs the genre of testament, a typical pattern in the ancient world for a hero's speech before death. Jesus uses both words and deeds to prepare his followers for his absence, washing their feet and then giving instructions and a prayer for their future.

In several ways chapter 13 fits the Johannine pattern of a sign followed by dialogues or discourses interpreting that sign. Foot washing is the principal sign or "example" (hypodeigma, John 13:15) that today's text interprets. Jesus' question to the disciples after washing Peter's feet, "Do you know what I have done to you?" (John 13:12), sets the context for his teaching about love and about his death in today's text. Jesus' gift of the morsel of bread to Judas in John 13:26 is a further sign-action that Jesus interprets in vv. 31-35.[68] This morsel demonstrates Jesus' eucharistic hospitality even toward his betrayer, a final expression of love. In the broadest use of the Johannine sign/discourse pattern, the final and overarching sign-act of the Gospel is Jesus' own death and resurrection—his glorification— for which the entire farewell discourse (chaps. 13–17) provides advance interpretation.

Judas' departure sets in motion the glorification of Jesus. Calling his disciples "little children" (13:33, the only occurrence of this term in the Gospel), Jesus announces that his departure is "Now" (13:31) and begins by speaking about his death as a glorification.

Jesus repeats to the disciples what he previously told the Judeans (John 7:33; 8:21), that they cannot come where he is going. From a narrative or reader-response perspective, the disciples' lack of understanding of Jesus' words and actions throughout chapter 13 (note Peter's response in vv. 8-9, 36-38) aims to trigger in us as readers a desire to be less obtuse than the disciples.[69]

The disciples will participate in Jesus' glorification through participation in his love.[70] This is the meaning of the love commandment, the most important verse of this text. What is "new" is not the commandment itself, but its relationship to Jesus. If the disciples want to be faithful followers of Jesus, they must show this by their love for one another. This commandment parallels the foot washing "just as . . . so also," although the translation is somewhat difficult. Just as Jesus has loved the disciples, so they now are to love one another. This commandment will be repeated almost verbatim in 15:12 (without the reference to "new"). The link of love and commandment-keeping is found also in John 14:15, 21; 15:10.

THE DISCIPLES WILL PARTICIPATE IN JESUS' GLORIFICATION THROUGH PARTICIPATION IN HIS LOVE. THIS IS THE MEANING OF THE LOVE COMMANDMENT.

The relationship of "knowing" and "doing" is another key theme throughout this chapter.[71] It is significant that the way the world will "know" Jesus' followers is by their love for one another. During the time when Jesus is absent from the world, his followers are to live a life of love and thus make known his own lifestyle.

Responding to the Text

What does God's new eschatological world, the New Jerusalem, look like? Where does Jesus' new commandment of love take root in our lives? This is a day for preachers to make connections between the vision of a heavenly city and all the cities of our lives. The dreams of Dr. Martin Luther King Jr. for renewal of America were shaped and articulated in light of the New Jerusalem vision:

> It's alright to talk about "streets flowing with milk and honey," but God has commanded us to be concerned about the slums down here, and his children who can't eat three square meals a day. It's all right to talk about the new Jerusalem, but one day, God's preacher must talk about the New York, the new Atlanta, the new Philadelphia, the new Los Angeles, the new Memphis, Tennessee. This is what we have to do.[72]

In the same spirit, God's vision of the New Jerusalem should turn our eyes also to the present-day Jerusalem. The situation in today's *earthly* Jerusalem, which is

closed off to most Palestinian Christians and Muslims since 1967, makes the longing for the holy city expressed in Revelation 21 especially poignant. Most Palestinians have no permit to enter their holy city of Jerusalem since Israel annexed
the entire city. The recent observance of Holocaust Remembrance Day (April
19, 2001) and Israel's Independence Day (April 26), and this week's observance
of Palestinian "Al Naqba" Day ("The Catastrophe," May 15, when Palestinians
became refugees in their own land in 1948) offers an occasion for Christians of
the world to pray and advocate for a shared Jerusalem, an international city, holy
and open to all.[73]

In the city of Jerusalem, and in every city where people search for signs of
hope for a future, God's vision of a New Jerusalem can function both to expose
injustice and to nurture the promise of renewal for life in God's *polis*.

SIXTH SUNDAY OF EASTER

MAY 20, 2001

REVISED COMMON	EPISCOPAL (BCP)	ROMAN CATHOLIC
Acts 16:9-15	Acts 14:8-18	Acts 15:1-2, 22-29
	or Joel 2:21-27	
Ps. 67	Ps. 67	Ps. 67:2-3, 5, 6, 8
Rev. 21:10, 22—22:5	Rev. 21:22—22:5	Rev. 21:10-14, 22-23
	or Acts 14:8-18	
John 14:23-29 or 5:1-9	John 14:23-29	John 14:23-29

Today's first and second lessons center on imagery of the river and the nations. Water flows through these texts, extending the geography of God's life-giving river to the world. In Revelation 22 the river of the water of life flows from the throne of God through the center of New Jerusalem, welcoming all nations. In Acts 16 the life-giving river flows through Philippi, where Lydia and all her household were baptized. These glimpses of the life-giving waters of resurrection connect the rivers of our cities and our lives to the church's celebration of the Easter season. The preacher's task today is to help each person find and follow God's river of life flowing through our life.

FIRST LESSON
ACTS 16:9-15 (RCL)

Today's text tells the story of the first conversion in Europe, that of Lydia and her household. Still today, Christians in Philippi, in northern Greece, celebrate Lydia as their founder and as the first Christian in Europe.

Lydia's story frames the narrative of Paul's mission in Philippi, as seen in his return to her house in 16:40. She is a woman of means, a Gentile merchant from the city of Thyatira in Asia Minor, and the head of her household. The description of Lydia as a "God-fearer" (*sebomenē*) situates her as a sympathizer or proselyte to Judaism, a broad category of adherents in the ancient world. She takes part in an organized group of women who gather for worship at a "place of prayer," a typical Greek term for a Jewish synagogue building. The women welcome Paul and the other missionaries into their prayer service. There, beside the river, the women hear the news of Jesus Christ and receive baptism.

Lydia's hospitality toward Paul extends beyond worship to welcoming the missionaries into her home and becoming a benefactor of the early Christian house church. The word describing how Lydia "prevailed" upon Paul to stay at her house is the same word used in Luke 24:29, when the disciples "prevailed" upon Jesus to stay with them on the journey to Emmaus. Lydia's welcome may have aimed to protect the missionaries from the Roman authorities in Philippi, a danger evidenced by their arrest only a few days later.[74] In agreeing to stay at Lydia's house, Paul for the first time agrees to stay at the home of a Gentile, thus crossing the same ethnic boundary that Peter had already crossed in Acts 10.

Lydia's house serves as a base for Paul's missionary work in Philippi. The synagogue by the river ("place of prayer") where the missionaries worshiped with the women is Paul's destination a few days later, in Acts 16:16. After his release from prison, Paul again returns to Lydia's house in 16:40 before leaving for Thessalonica.

The preacher can draw on this wonderful text from Philippi in inviting all Christians to join with Lydia and her household, in the words of the great gospel hymn, to "gather with the saints by the river that flows from the throne of God."

ACTS 14:8–18 (BCP)

The strange incident at Lystra shows the difficulty of cross-cultural evangelism. To the distress of the apostles, the people of Lystra misinterpret the miraculous healing of a disabled man by trying to worship Paul and Barnabas as the Greek gods Hermes and Zeus. Paul nevertheless makes the positive connection between our shared human nature (14:15) and a common life in the created order of God. Paul uses the goodness of creation as evidence of God's faithfulness to the nations, arguing that even while the nations were allowed to walk in their own ways, God also "did good and gave you from heaven rains and fruitful seasons, satisfying your hearts with food and gladness" (14:17).

JOEL 2:21–27 (BCP alt.)

Creation imagery expresses the promise of restoration in this text, corresponding to the creation-focused laments of Joel 1:16-20. There the land and animals had groaned in anguish from the locust plague. Joel now addresses the first two joyous imperatives directly to the land and to the animals, comforting them with "Fear not." With the early rain that heralded the people's vindication, the prophet's third imperative summons all to celebrate God's faithfulness: "Be glad, O children of Zion, and rejoice." After the terrible calamity to the land, God promises overflowing abundance and restoration, with the twice-repeated proclamation that "my people shall never again be put to shame."

ACTS 15:1-2, 22-29 (RC)

Acts 15 is the Lukan version of the first apostolic synod council in Jerusalem, narrated also by Paul in Galatians 2. At issue was whether and to what extent Gentiles had to become Jews in order to be Christian. This was surely the most divisive and revolutionary issue the church of God has ever faced. Both Peter and Paul already welcomed Gentiles into the church without circumcision (we are not told whether any requirements were laid upon women), but this caused great division and controversy.

Historically, Paul's own account of the council meeting in Galatians 2, written several generations earlier than Acts, is probably more accurate than Acts. There Paul gives no indication of agreeing to "abstain from what has been sacrificed to idols and from blood and from what is strangled" (Acts 15:29). In Galatians, the only condition Paul accepts for Gentiles is to "remember the poor" (Gal. 2:10). The difference between Acts and Galatians on this watershed event probably reflects both the irreconcilable chasm over this issue in the early church and also a desire to harmonize by the time Acts was written. In wonderful Lukan fashion, the Acts account underscores the role of the Holy Spirit in discerning the path the church should take (Acts 15:28, "It seemed good to the Holy Spirit and to us").

RESPONSIVE READING
PSALM 67 (RCL/BCP);
PS. 67:2-3, 5, 6, 8 (RC)

International blessing and the universal goodness of creation are also the themes of today's psalm, a psalm of thanksgiving for harvest and a call for God's face to shine upon the entire earth. Psalm 67 appears frequently in the lectionary. During the Easter season, its call to "let all nations praise you" is an especially appropriate topic in light of the emphasis on the nations in Revelation 21–22 and the Gentile mission embodied in the conversion of Lydia. Singing this psalm pledges us to share our blessings and open our doors to peoples and nations beyond our own.

SECOND LESSON

REVELATION 21:10, 22—22:5 (RCL/BCP); REV. 21:10-14, 22-23 (RC)

God's New Jerusalem descends for a second time in Rev. 21:9-27, an architectural tour modeled on the angel's tour of the new temple in Ezekiel 40—48. Revelation makes important changes that open up Ezekiel's priestly vision to everyone. One striking modification is that New Jerusalem has "no temple" (21:22). God's presence now extends to the entire city's landscape, with all of God's people serving and reigning with Christ as priests (Rev. 1:6; 5:10; 20:6; 22:3, 5).

New Jerusalem is a welcoming city, not a gated community. Whereas Ezekiel's temple gate was shut so that "no one shall enter by it" (Ezek. 44:1-2), the gates into New Jerusalem are perpetually open—they are "never shut by day and there will be no night there" (Rev. 21:26). Even foreigners are invited to enter into this radiant city, whose lamp is the lamb, Jesus. The "nations" will walk by its light, streaming in through its pearly gates (21:24, 26). In our time when nations and neighborhoods seek to secure themselves against outsiders, the church needs to proclaim Revelation's vision of openness and multicultural welcome for Jerusalem and for all our cities.[75]

The final verse of the chapter (Rev. 21:27) is another prophetic wake-up call, exhorting faithfulness so that our names are written in Jesus' book of life and we may enter as citizens into God's New Jerusalem. Exhortation, not prediction, is the function of such verses.

Green space and God's river of life fill out the final description of the city. Revelation 22:1-5 recreates the garden of Eden in the center of a thriving urban landscape, drawing on Ezekiel's vision of a wondrous tree-lined river flowing out from the temple:

> Water was flowing from below the threshold of the temple toward the east.
> . . . On the banks, on both sides of the river, there will grow all kinds of trees
> for food. Their leaves will not wither nor their fruit fail, but they will bear
> fresh fruit every month, because the water for them flows from the sanctu-
> ary. Their fruit will be for food, and their leaves for healing. (Ezek. 47:1, 12)

In Revelation the river of life flows not from the temple but from the throne of God and the lamb, through the center of the processional street of the city. Ezekiel's fruit-trees on both banks become the wondrous "tree of life" in Revelation (Rev. 22:2), invoking Eden and paradise traditions. The fruit of the ever-bearing tree of life satisfies the hunger of everyone who is faithful (Rev. 2:7), overcoming the prohibition of Gen. 3:22.

The tree's leaves, as well as its fruit, offer blessing and healing. Revelation universalizes Ezekiel's already lavish vision by adding the "healing of the *nations*" to the tree's medicinal leaves (Rev. 22:2; compare Ezek. 47:12). In the award-winning movie "As Good as it Gets," Helen Hunt plays a waitress with a chronically ill child who cannot afford health insurance or medical care. For parents such as she, the tree of life with its medicinal leaves offers a vision of an alternative political economy in which the essentials of health and life are available for all children, even for those who cannot afford them.

As we live into the new millennium, Revelation's vision of God's life-giving river in the center of our cities can renew our hope for our future. We need New Jerusalem. We need the trees of life, the healing of the nations. These glimpses of a renewed earth can inspire and motivate us. Through each of our cities, by whatever name, there is a river flowing from the heart of God and the lamb, a life-giving river into which each of us was baptized and by which each of us is renewed.

> AS WE LIVE INTO THE NEW MILLENNIUM, REVELATION'S VISION OF GOD'S LIFE-GIVING RIVER IN THE CENTER OF OUR CITIES CAN RENEW OUR HOPE FOR OUR FUTURE.

THE GOSPEL
JOHN 14:23-29

The Gospel text prepares us for the Ascension we will celebrate on Thursday. In anticipation of his departure, Jesus teaches the disciples about the ways that he will remain with them. The farewell discourse circles around familiar constellations of themes with an "almost wavelike effect."[76] Building on the theme of love from chapter 13, this week's text also introduces new promises of peace and a Paraclete to insure Jesus' future presence with the community.

Jesus first promises to "make a home" (*monē*) with those who love him. This imagery is the same as that of the "many rooms" (*monē*, John 14:2) earlier in the chapter. In v. 2 Jesus said that he was going away to prepare such a place for his followers, but in v. 23 the emphasis is on Jesus and the Father coming toward his followers to make a home here in their midst.

Remembrance is another way Jesus will remain with his disciples. John's Gospel does not have the eucharistic words of institution "in remembrance of me," but it does have the Paraclete for whom a primary function is to "call to remembrance." Jesus' words in John 14:26 are a "key" to the Gospel of John, giving central importance to memory and remembrance in the life of the community.[77] Although the disciples do not understand Jesus' words until after his resurrection, the Spirit-Paraclete preserves the memory through which Jesus' sayings and deeds become the living kerygma of the church.

The Paraclete furnishes one of the most important images for Jesus' presence (John 15:25; 16:7). Introduced first in John 14:16 as the "Spirit of truth," the Paraclete is the Holy Spirit sent in Jesus' name (14:26), who will act as an advocate on the disciples' behalf. Anticipation of persecution by the Roman authorities may have been an element of the historical context for which the Johannine farewell discourse was shaped in the late first century. If so, translation of the word Paraclete as "Advocate" underscores this sense of juridical advocacy and encouragement. Besides calling to remembrance all that Jesus taught and witnessed, the Paraclete will assist Christians in making their own witness in time of trial.[78]

> THE SPIRIT-PARACLETE PRESERVES THE MEMORY THROUGH WHICH JESUS' SAYINGS AND DEEDS BECOME THE LIVING KERYGMA OF THE CHURCH.

Peace is Jesus' final gift to the disciples in this text—not the imperial peace of the Pax Romana but the true peace of God's *shalom*. When the risen Jesus first appears to the disciples he will greet them with "Peace be with you" (John 20:19, 20). Christians made the greeting of peace central to the liturgy, picking up on Jesus' parting gift of peace in our *Kyrie* ("In peace, let us pray to the Lord"), the greeting of peace, and the dismissal ("Go in peace").

JOHN 5:1-9 (RCL alt.)

This alternate Gospel selection recounting the paralyzed man's healing in the Pool of Siloam may be a wise choice if the preacher wants to sustain the theme of the river or water of life.[79] Following his second "sign" in Galilee (healing of the official's son at Capernaum, John 4:54), Jesus travels again to Jerusalem for a "feast of the Jews." The particular feast is not specified; we are told only that it is the Sabbath (John 5:9).

Near the Sheep Gate (or Sheep Pool) in the northeast corner of Jerusalem was the large pool of Bethesda, long associated with healing, where invalids gathered amid the porticoed stoas.[80] There they waited for the water to be "troubled," so that they might be healed (John 5:7). While Codex Alexandrinus and some other manuscripts include part or all of vv. 3b-4—the explanation that the first person into the water after it was troubled by the Lord's angel would be healed—this material is best omitted since it contains non-Johannine vocabulary and is not found in manuscripts such as Sinaiticus, Vaticanus, or the earliest papyri. It may, however, accurately reflect popular local tradition about the pool.[81]

At the pool Jesus "sees" a man whom he "knows" to have been waiting there for thirty-eight years, reflecting a sight and omniscience typical of the Johannine Jesus. Jesus asks the man, "Do you want to become healed [Greek *hygiēs*, the root of 'hygiene']?" The man responds not with yes or no, but with his helplessness over having no one to put him into the healing water. Instead of putting him into the water, Jesus commands the man to arise and walk, thereby healing him of his paralysis. The initiative for healing is entirely with Jesus. There is no indication that the man has faith beyond obedience, since in v. 13 he does not even know who healed him.

In the typical sign/discourse pattern of John's Gospel, this Sabbath healing will lead to a lengthy discourse and series of controversies, vv. 10-47. The paralyzed man receives no further mention after v. 16, as the controversy shifts to Jesus' claim to be "equal to God" (John 5:18). Such issues of contention between Jesus and the "Jews" in the rest of the chapter are probably more reflective of the separation between church and synagogue within Judaism in the late first century than of actual historical controversy at the time of Jesus. The paralyzed man was surely a Jew himself, a reminder to us not to read the discourse's anti-*ioudaioi* polemic as anti-Judaism.

Responding to the Texts

What does the watershed of God's river of life look like today? Where is that "river whose streams make glad the city of God" (Ps. 46:4)? With the Easter season's emphasis on baptismal renewal, the preacher may wish to dip into the life-giving river of God that flows from Genesis to Revelation, renewing the nations and our world in its healing waters, watering the trees of life.

It is the river that started east of Eden (Gen. 2:10-14), the fountain of life opened up in Zech. 13:1; it is the river for everyone who thirsts for cooling streams (Ps. 42:2), the river of Jesus' baptism at the Jordan, the river of Lydia's baptism in Philippi. This is the river that flows through our lives, by many names—the Amazon, the Colorado River, the Mississippi River—offering a glimpse of the river of life in each of our cities, flowing from the throne of God.

At times God's river of life may seem completely dried up. Someone in Chicago told me that there used to be a creek flowing through our neighborhood, but it has now been drained and paved over. "Follow the cottonwoods," the man told me, "and that's how you can see where the stream once was." Even where God's river has gone underground in our lives, it is still there. The preacher's task is to look for traces of the river—traces such as those cottonwoods—to call to memory the river of hope flowing under our feet.

THE SPIRIT-PARACLETE AWAKENS REMEMBRANCE OF JESUS' GIFT OF LIFE-GIVING WATER EVEN WHEN GOD'S PRESENCE SEEMS TO BE ONLY A DISTANT MEMORY.

The Spirit-Paraclete awakens remembrance of Jesus' gift of life-giving water even when God's presence seems to be only a distant memory.

But Revelation's waters of life are not just metaphorical waters, theological waters. They also can have something to say to the real rivers of our lives. In the Sahel Desert area of northern Africa, Lutheran World Relief and other development agencies help people construct wells and simple pumps that literally bring the "water of life" to local villages. Roman Catholic bishops in the Pacific Northwest have issued a pastoral letter on the Columbia River watershed, seeking an ecological approach that considers the needs of all residents, including salmon, who share in the "living waters in the sacramental commons of the Columbia Watershed."[82] This sense of a sacramental commons is one gift of Revelation's vision of the holy city, New Jerusalem, with the river flowing through its main street. It can become for us a vision of ecological renewal, of access to living waters for all, connecting the baptismal river of Philippi and all the wells and waters of our world to the future of God's river of life.[83]

THE ASCENSION OF OUR LORD

MAY 24, 2001

REVISED COMMON	EPISCOPAL (BCP)	ROMAN CATHOLIC
Acts 1:1-11	Acts 1:1-11 or 2 Kings 2:1-15	Acts 1:1-11
Ps. 47 or Ps. 93	Ps. 47 or Ps. 110:1-5	Ps. 47:2-3, 6-9
Eph. 1:15-23	Eph. 1:15-23 or Acts 1:1-11	Eph. 1:17-23 or Heb. 9:24-28; 10:19-23
Luke 24:44-53	Luke 24:49-53 or Mark 16:9-15, 19-20	Luke 24:46-53

The Revised Common Lectionary assigns the same texts for Ascension Day in all three years. Parishes that do not hold Ascension services on Thursday may want to use one or more of these texts on the Seventh Sunday of Easter.

FIRST LESSON
ACTS 1:1-11

The story of the Ascension forms a bridge from Luke into Acts, from the time of Jesus into the time of the church. Luke is the only Gospel writer to distinguish Jesus' ascension from his resurrection as a separate event.

Luke tells the story twice, at the end of the Gospel and again at the beginning of Acts. One interesting aspect of the two versions of the Ascension narrative is the chronological conflict between them. In Luke 24 Jesus ascends late on Easter day itself, whereas in Acts 1 his ascension is delayed until "after forty days" (reminiscent of Jesus' forty-day stay in the wilderness, Luke 4:2).

Luke uses the Ascension story not only to narrate Jesus' departure but also to discourage expectations and speculations about the timetable of Jesus' return. In response to questions of the chronology, such as the question posed by the disciples, Jesus replies with words that bear repeating today: "It is not for you to know the times or the seasons." Jesus specifically orders the disciples not to try to cal-culate the date of his return (see also Matt. 24:36 and Mark 13:32, "But about that day and hour no one knows").

Luke also uses this story to mark an end to Jesus' resurrection appearances on earth. No more can anyone claim to "see" the risen Jesus in the same way that Mary Magdalene and the other disciples saw him. The forty days of Easter appearances are over. In this sense, the Ascension exerts a degree of social con-trol against any enthusiasts who would still claim to "see" appearances of Christ. The importance of marking an end to Jesus' appearances can be seen, for exam-ple, in 1 Cor. 15:5-8, Paul's listing of eyewitnesses who saw the risen Jesus. It is noteworthy that Paul leaves out any mention of women from this list and says that he himself is the "last" person who can make the claim to have seen Jesus alive after his resurrection. (It is doubtful that Luke would agree in according even Paul the status of eyewitness, since Acts itself never accords Paul the title of "apostle.") Both Paul and the Ascension narratives mark a watershed: Henceforth, no one can claim to be an eyewitness, for Jesus is to be known only through the power of the Holy Spirit, in the scriptures and the church.

The Ascension is not about Jesus' absence, but about his presence in the world in a new way. A mosaic at the Church of the Ascension at Augusta Victoria Hos-pital on the Mount of Olives, one of the possible sites of Jesus' ascension, por-trays the ascending Jesus flanked by the two angels who tell the nostalgic disci-ples to stop gazing up into heaven. These two are depicted as ordinary-looking men, gazing lovingly down at us rather than up at the ascending Jesus. They point us in the most important direction of this text—not heav-enward but earthward: "Why are you stand-ing looking up toward heaven?" (The present-day presence of a Lutheran World Federation hospital at this particular holy site, attending to Palestinian people's earthly ills, is an apt successor to Ascension on the Mount of Olives.)

> THE ASCENSION IS NOT ABOUT JESUS' ABSENCE, BUT ABOUT HIS PRESENCE IN THE WORLD IN A NEW WAY.

Even on Ascension Day, Jesus calls us to direct our gaze not toward heaven but toward the world, where our mission is now to be his witnesses "in Jerusalem, in all Judea and Samaria, and to the ends of the earth" (Acts 1:8). The ten days between Ascension and Pentecost are a time to await with joy the promised "power" (*dynamis*) of the Holy Spirit that will come upon the church, to empower our mission.

2 KINGS 2:1-15 (BCP alt.)

Before the prophet Elijah ascends in the whirlwind, he hands on the mantle of prophetic succession to Elisha. Both Elisha's response to his master's departure and also his willingness to take up the prophetic mantle can guide the church's reflection on Jesus' ascension.

The vivid imagery of the chariot and horses of fire that transport Elijah away has a rich interpretive life in film and art. But the most powerful image in this story is surely Elijah's cloak or mantle. What did Elijah's mantle look like? This prophetic mantle must have been distinctive, for when fifty members of the company of prophets see Elisha wearing it from a distance, they know immediately that "The spirit of Elijah rests on Elisha" (2 Kings 2:15). Symbolically, the same prophetic mantle was laid on the shoulders of Jesus, Elijah's successor in the New Testament, who also ascended into heaven. Prophetic succession has not ceased today. The prophetic mantle that was worn by Elijah and Elisha, and also by Jesus, is still being placed on the shoulders of God's prophetic voices in our world.

RESPONSIVE READING

PSALM 47 or 93 (RCL); PS. 47:2-3, 6-9 (RC)

Enthronement psalms sweep us into a great procession, ritualizing God's royal rule over the earth with the enthronement formula, "Yahweh reigns" (Ps. 93:1) or "God reigns" (Ps. 47:7, 8). Enthronement Psalms reenact God's victory over enemies and God's installation as ruler. Psalm 93 describes the royal procession and God's victory over floods and storm. Psalm 47 uses imperatives to summon people to praise, describing how God has "gone up" to ascend the throne amid shouts of joy. Assigned for Ascension Day, these psalms interpret Jesus' ascension as his enthronement on high, at God's right hand.

PSALM 110:1-5 (BCP alt.)

A royal psalm, Psalm 110 is cited extensively in the New Testament to support christological claims about Jesus Christ. The newly enthroned king ("my lord") is invited by God ("the Lord") to ascend the throne. This reference to two "lords" was aptly applied to Jesus (Mark 12:36 and parallels; Acts 2:34). The twice-repeated image of God's right hand in Psalm 110:1, 5 also provides the background for the New Testament enthronement imagery of God making Christ "sit at his right hand" (Eph. 1:20; Heb. 1:13). The new king will rule also with priestly investiture, after the order of Melchizedek.

SECOND LESSON
EPHESIANS 1:15–23 (RCL/BCP);
EPH. 1:17–23 (RC)

While Luke and Acts speak of Jesus' ascension into heaven, only Ephesians speaks of his enthronement. This text is assigned for today because it portrays Jesus Christ as seated in the heavenly places at the right hand of God, as Lord of the church, presiding over its cosmic unity. Ephesians is the source of the church's creedal statements that Christ is "seated at the right hand of the Father."

Today's text comes from the opening thanksgiving section of the letter, consisting of two long, participle-rich Greek sentences. Unlike the authentic Pauline letters, Ephesians was probably not written to one specific church (since the reference to the saints of God "in Ephesus," Eph. 1:1, is not found in the best manuscripts). In this letter, we begin to see the concept of the "church" as encompassing multiple congregations united in Christ's oneness. The author (not Paul) prays with unceasing thanks for the whole church, for its faith and love. The prayer is grounded in cosmic praise of God, drawing on imagery of heavenly unity from Colossians.

Psalm 110 shapes Ephesian's description of Christ's journey to enthronement at God's "right hand" (v. 20) and the proclamation that God has "put all things under his feet" (v. 22). A royal coronation psalm, Psalm 110 projects extravagant hopes for the future messiah. Ephesians and other New Testament texts pick up these same hopes and ascribe them to Jesus Christ, who is seated high above any other authority, surpassing all political rulers and dominions in this age and in every age (v. 21).

No other New Testament letter speaks with such detail about the "heavenly places" (*epouraniois*, Eph. 1:20; 2:6; 3:10; 6:12). Especially striking is the declaration of Eph. 2:6 that *we*, too, have been raised already to "sit" with Christ in the heavenly places.

HEBREWS 9:24–28; 10:19–23 (RC alt.)

This text emphasizes the priestly role of Christ in his ascension into heaven. Entering the heavenly sanctuary, Christ offered "once for all" the sacrifice of himself (Heb. 9: 26). In Christ we now have a "great priest over the house of God" (10:21), so that we can be bold to draw near to God. This primacy for the priestly role of Christ in the Epistle to the Hebrews, grounded in the Jewish tradition of sacrifice, aims to demonstrate how Christ abolished the cultic sacrificial system by fulfilling it. The priestly imagery also emphasizes Christ's kinship with us.[84] The difficulty with such cultic imagery today is that since most of us lack familiarity with the whole sacrifice system, the preacher has to first draw attention to the system in order to explain how Jesus has overcome it.

The Gospel
LUKE 24:44-53 (RCL);
LUKE 24:49-53 (BCP); LUKE 24:46-53 (RC);
MARK 16:9-15, 19-20 (BCP alt.)

Interpreting the Texts

The Lukan Ascension narrative takes place on the same long Easter day that began at the empty tomb, then saw Jesus walking on the Emmaus road and finally appearing to the disciples in Jerusalem. Like the Emmaus conversation earlier in the day, Jesus' concern is to teach about fulfillment of scripture. He opens the disciples' minds to understand the law, the prophets, and the psalms—naming all three parts of the Bible—so that they might understand that his death and resurrection were all in accordance with God's word.

Jerusalem is the center from which Jesus' mission will go forth, the place where the disciples will receive "power from on high." In contrast to the post-Easter geography of Mark and Matthew, the disciples are not instructed to go to Galilee in Luke. They are to wait in Jerusalem for the Holy Spirit.

Jesus' last act on earth is to bless the disciples, a farewell gesture reminiscent of biblical prophets and priests (Num. 6:22-27; Sir. 50:20-21; Luke 2:34). As he is blessing them, Jesus is taken up from their sight. The preacher may want to emphasize the blessing that was Jesus' final gift to the disciples. After Jesus departs, his followers return to Jerusalem with great joy, where they too are continually "blessing" God (the same Greek word).

Responding to the Texts

The preacher faces several challenges in these Ascension texts: first, how to present Jesus' departure from the earth not as an occasion for sorrow but celebration; and second, how to translate the kingship and hierarchical language of the enthronement texts (Psalms 47, 93, 110; Ephesians 1) into imagery that speaks to a world no longer governed by kings and monarchs. Contemporary hymn writer Brian Wren explains why he does not use imagery of divine kingship in his lyrics: "Those who use such language doom themselves to thinking of God as influential only in their personal lives or in the life of the church. Though still colorful, this language doesn't resonate except at a very privatized level."[85]

If Jesus' ascension is to have meaning today, it must not be as a way of inscribing churchly hierarchy (the danger of Ephesians) but rather as a way of expressing Jesus' presence still among us in the world, inhabiting every time and place. Biblical descriptions of Jesus' enthronement in political terms can counteract tendencies to privatize faith today, but this political dimension, too, needs to be expressed in language and analogies that speak to our own *polis* or contemporary context.

In preaching the Ascension, we do well to follow the Lukan and Acts turning of our gaze earthward. Brazilian theologian Vitor Westhelle argues that this is the meaning of the statement of the angels in Acts 1:11—that just as we experienced Jesus first on earth, and then departing to heaven, so will we experience him coming again from earth.[86] Earth is the place to look for Jesus' presence. The disciples' response to Ascension can be ours as well, to return with great joy, "blessing God," and to set out in mission and ministry in the world.

IF JESUS' ASCENSION IS TO HAVE MEANING TODAY, IT MUST NOT BE AS A WAY OF INSCRIBING CHURCHLY HIERARCHY (THE DANGER OF EPHESIANS) BUT RATHER AS A WAY OF EXPRESSING JESUS' PRESENCE STILL AMONG US IN THE WORLD, INHABITING EVERY TIME AND PLACE.

SEVENTH SUNDAY OF EASTER

MAY 27, 2001

REVISED COMMON	EPISCOPAL (BCP)	ROMAN CATHOLIC
Acts 16:16–34	Acts 16:16–34 or 1 Sam. 12:19–24	Acts 7:55–60
Ps. 97	Ps. 68:1–20 or Ps. 47	Ps. 97:1–2, 6–7, 9
Rev. 22:12–14, 16–17, 20–21	Rev. 22:12–14, 16–17, 20 or Acts 16:16–34	Rev. 22:12–14, 16–17, 20
John 17:20–26	John 17:20–26	John 17:20–26

Comings and goings, prayers of farewell and promise of return: today's texts are especially timely against the background of Ascension, celebrated last Thursday. Jesus has ascended; the church cannot deny his departure. But the promise of his return, and the presence of the Spirit, bring Jesus near. "Surely I am coming soon," the risen Jesus declares (Rev. 22:7, 12, 20). In the interim until his return, love witnesses to Jesus' way of life present in the world.

FIRST LESSON
ACTS 16:16–34 (RCL/BCP)

Continuing the Philippi narrative from last week, this text lauds Paul's miraculous powers in two events, an exorcism and an earthquake. A prophetic slave girl with a "pythian" or mantic spirit (probably related to the Pythian Apollo oracle at Delphi) sets the story in motion.[87] Her plight is typical of slaves in the ancient world who had no rights, may have been owned by more than one "master" (*kyrios*), and were used strictly for financial gain. With her powers of prophecy she correctly proclaims that Paul and his companions are "slaves of the most high God who proclaim to you the way of salvation"(16:17). But because her persistence annoyed Paul, he exorcised her prophetic spirit from her.

This exorcism causes chagrin to the slave girl's owners, who charge Paul and Silas with anti-Roman subversion and have them beaten and imprisoned. The slaveowners' concern is not for the slave's wellbeing but for their financial loss.

We hear no more of Paul's relationship with the slave girl after v. 18, nor of how she lived after losing her spirit of prophecy. Absent any typical words of acclamation or thanksgiving after an exorcism, we can only hope that the Christian community embraced her.

By contrast, Paul shows great concern for the life and livelihood of his jailer in the second miraculous event, a story of rescue and reconciliation. An earthquake releases the prison doors and fetters, leading us to expect a jailbreak similar to Peter's miraculous deliverance from prison in Acts 12:6-11. Yet, out of concern for their jailer, Paul and Silas forgo escape, and they persuade all the other prisoners to remain as well. Converted by their witness, the jailer asks what he must do to be saved. In an ironic reversal of roles, the jailer is the one who receives release ("salvation") from the prisoners he held captive. The jailer washes the prisoners' wounds, receives baptism along with his whole household, and brings the missionaries into his house. The transformed relationship between prisoners and jailer is a testimony to the power of Christian reconciliation and compassion.

In a moving scene after their release, the missionaries stop at Lydia's house to bid farewell to her and the other sisters and brothers before leaving Philippi. The Philippian church remained Paul's favorite church (see Phil. 1:7, 4:15, and other passages in his letter to the Philippians).

1 SAMUEL 12:19-24 (BCP alt.)

The prophet Samuel granted the Israelites' request in anointing Saul as king. The people now regret that decision. First Samuel 12 marks the watershed between the end of the period of the judges and the beginning of the age of kingship.[88] There is no going back to pre-kingship days. After reviewing the past history of the judges, the text shifts to the present with the transitional "And now" (1 Sam. 12:14). Even if kingship is a mistake, Samuel promises to be faithful in prayer, always interceding to God and instructing the people, for "the Lord will not cast away his people." In vv. 24-25 Samuel cites the requirements of God's covenant, patterned in the typical format of blessings and curses: the people must fear the Lord and serve faithfully with all their heart, calling to mind the great things God has done for them. If not, both they and their new king will be swept away.

ACTS 7:55-60 (RC)

Stephen is the first Christian martyr, stoned in a lynching-like scene in which Saul also took part. In a lengthy and inflammatory speech, Stephen had interpreted the Hebrew scriptures to prove Jesus was the messiah, ending with his labeling of the Sanhedrin and Jewish high priest as "you stiff-necked people" (Acts 7:51). Stephen's death by stoning parallels the death of Jesus by crucifixion. Both Jesus and Stephen utter a loud cry before their death (Luke 23:46; Acts 7:60). Most importantly, both Jesus and Stephen pray for forgiveness for their executioners ("Father, forgive them, for they know not what they do," Luke 13:34, omitted in some manuscripts; "Lord, do not hold this sin against them," Acts 7:56). This Luke/Acts parallelism demonstrates the continuation of Jesus' ministry in his followers, including martyrdom.

RESPONSIVE READING
PSALM 97 (RCL); PS. 97:1-2, 6-7, 9 (RC)

Psalms 96–99 are all enthronement psalms, celebrating God's righteous governance in a processional liturgy of victory up to Mount Zion. Verses 1-6 tell of God's theophany, revealed in storm and lightning, and of all creation's glad response. Verses 7-12 describe the effect that theophany has on the Gentile nations. God's royal reign is bad news to those who have worshiped other gods, but good news to the righteous who long for God's deliverance (v. 10). Psalm 97 is also sung on Christmas morning in some traditions.

PSALM 68:1-20 (BCP)

This difficult psalm may be an "anthology of quotations," with a number of textual and translation problems.[89] It seems to have been sung at a festival liturgy, as evidenced by the liturgical instruction "Selah" that may have signaled liturgical interludes. Despite the apparent disunity, its stanzas laud God in wonderful imagery—as "protector of widows"; as "one who gives the desolate a home to dwell in" (vv. 5-6); as one who daily bears us up (v. 19); and as a God of our salvation (v. 19).

PSALM 47 (BCP alt.)

See Ascension Day.

SECOND LESSON

REVELATION 22:12-14, 16-17, 20-21 (RCL); REV. 22:12-14, 16-17, 20 (BCP/RC)

Revelation 22 concludes the prophetic letter with formulaic blessings, warnings, and exhortations. An eschatological urgency underlies this chapter, with the repeated proclamation that Christ will come "soon" (*tachy*, Rev. 22:6, 7, 12, 20) and the declaration that he is the first and the "last" (*eschatos*), the beginning and the end. It is probably important for preachers to address the issue of Revelation's eschatology, because premillennialist interpretations have so successfully monopolized American discourse that most parishioners are unaware of critical alternative interpretations. Literalist scripts for end-times events such as Hal Lindsey's *The Late Great Planet Earth* and the "Left Behind" novels by Tim LaHaye and Jerry Jenkins are recent inventions, growing out of nineteenth-century British and American fundamentalism.[90]

For the original first-century community, Revelation's proclamation of the impending "end" referred not so much to the end of the world as the end of Roman rule. The first century was a time of dueling eschatologies—of Roman propaganda claiming the empire's eternity (slogans such as "*Roma Aeterna*") versus Christian belief in a future reign of Jesus Christ. Against Rome's own eschatological claims that it would rule forever, Revelation proclaimed the good news that the end "soon" would take place (Rev. 1:1), thus offering comfort and assurance to God's saints who cried out, "How long, O Lord?" (Rev. 6:10). American fundamentalists today who transmute the sense of an "end" into their own chronology, or who locate literal fulfillment of Revelation in contemporary political events, deny this first-century historical and contextual dimension to Revelation. Now that the Roman Empire has ended, as John assured Christians that it would, the question is whether there are analogous situations of injustice or imperialism in the world today, to which Christians may be called to offer a similar pronouncement of an "end."

Revelation ends as it began, with a blessing, pronouncing everyone as "blessed" (*makarios*) who hears and keeps what is written. The blessings in vv. 7 and 14 are the last of Revelation's seven beatitudes, a typical form of speech used by Christian prophets (see Rev. 1:3; 14:13; 16:15; 19:9; 20:6; 22:7, 14). Recalling the promises to Ephesus and Philadelphia, the beatitude of Rev. 22:14 promises the tree of life and citizenship in the holy city as a reward to motivate Christian faithfulness ("so that they may have the right to enter the city by the gates"). Jesus is the bright

DRINKING AND EATING AT THE EUCHARISTIC TABLE TRANSPORT US IN SOME MEASURE INTO GOD'S FUTURE HOLY CITY, TO GLIMPSE THE THRONE OF GOD AND TASTE ITS LIFE-GIVING WATER.

morning star of Balaam's oracle in Num. 24:17, a text that was already interpreted messianically by the time of the New Testament.

Revelation's apocalyptic journey concludes with a liturgical dialogue. The antiphonal "Come" (Rev. 22:17) is a eucharistic liturgy in which the Spirit and the bridal New Jerusalem call the community to participate. The invitation to everyone who thirsts to "take the water of life" (Rev. 22:17) draws the New Jerusalem vision to a sacramental close. Drinking and eating at the eucharistic table transport us in some measure into God's future holy city, to glimpse the throne of God and taste its life-giving water. As in Rev. 21:6, God gives the water of life *dōrean* ("without cost"), contrasting the Lamb's gift-economy once again to the ruthless economies of all of our Babylons and Romes.

Revelation has invited us to drink deeply from its metaphors of promise and warning, vision and blessing. It is a book not of judgment but of justice, of radical hope for the world's future, where God's people gather around the throne and the Lamb. "Amen! Come, Lord Jesus!"

The Gospel
JOHN 17:20-26

Interpreting the Text

Each year, the Gospel for the Seventh Sunday of Easter, between Ascension and Pentecost, is taken from Jesus' great prayer in John 17, the conclusion of his farewell discourse. This prayer, like Jesus' other prayers (John 11:41-42 and 12:27-28), is meant to be overhead by us. It witnesses to Jesus' return to God (his "glorification") and to his deep love for his followers. Everything he has he now gives to us, as he is returning back to God.

In the third and final section of the prayer in John 17, beginning with v. 20, Jesus intercedes on behalf of all those who will come to believe through the disciples' word. It is a prayer for all of us. Jesus invites us into a "heavenly family conversation" between himself and God.[91]

While it has become fashionable to excerpt John 17:21 as an ecumenical program exhorting denominational unity, Jesus' words are more mystical than programmatic. We should read this text first of all as a prayer, a window into the very heart of God.

WE SHOULD READ THIS TEXT FIRST OF ALL AS A PRAYER, A WINDOW INTO THE VERY HEART OF GOD.

"In-ness" and "one-ness" flow back and forth, perhaps a play on the similarity of the two words in Greek (*en* and *hen*). In the mystical geography of God's love, we are now "in" Jesus and he is in us, just as he and the Father are in one another. The preposition "in" (*en*) occurs seven times, richly describing Jesus' indwelling in the disciples and in God, and the indwelling of his love in us (v. 26). The word "one" (*hen*, a neuter form; four occurrences in vv. 21, 22, 23) grounds the disciples' oneness in Jesus' prior mystical oneness and in-ness with the Father (v. 22). Horizontal unity among Jesus' followers is thus a (vertical) gift from God, not the result of their own action.

God's glory bathes this prayer. We are permitted to "behold Jesus' glory"—recall the reference to the Word become flesh whom we behold in John 1:14—a glory given to Jesus in love before the foundation of the world. This is a glory that Jesus now gives also to us (v. 22).

How powerful it is to know that Jesus has prayed to God on our behalf! There is no one for whom Jesus did not pray on his last night. Like the prayer of a parent overhead by the child for whom one intercedes, what this prayer reveals is Jesus' deep love for the disciples and his deep trust in God as he prepares for his death.

Love is at the heart of this prayer. In the logic of comparison (*kathos*, "just as," vv. 14, 16, 18, 21, 22, 23) that is so central to this entire prayer, Jesus proclaims in v. 23 that God will now love *us* with the very same love God had for Jesus. God's "name" which Jesus makes known in v. 26 is a name that he will continue to make known through love. Of love such as this one can only sing, in the words of the great spiritual, "What wondrous love is this, O my soul!"

Responding to the Texts

At least two elements invite proclamation in these texts: intercessory prayer and unity. Paul's prayer brought such joy to his fellow prisoners that they were persuaded to stay in jail—in the freedom of Christ—rather than escape to freedom. What made Paul's night in prison transformative for an entire jailhouse community was singing and praying together. Similarly, the great prayer of John 17 evokes longing in us to be fully "one" with Jesus, in the mystical communion of prayer, so that his prayer of love for us becomes not a farewell but rather a homecoming.

How do we learn to pray with such oneness in the heart of God? The poet George MacDonald draws on imagery from the leaves of the tree of life from Revelation 22: "Sometimes, hard-trying, it seems I cannot pray for doubt and pain and anger and all strife. Yet some half-fledged prayer-bird from the nest may fall, flit, fly, perch—crouch in the bowery breast of the large, nation-healing tree of life. Moveless there sit through the burning day, and on my heart at night a fresh leaf cooling lay."[92] In this Easter season, when so many of us long to pray, perhaps these texts and Revelation's tree of life can provide a canopy under which we can learn how to pray, in the spirit of Jesus who intercedes for us.

A second theme for preaching is the ecumenical vision "that they may all be one" of John 17:22-23. For those who want to preach on Jesus' prayer for unity in John 17 as a model for Christian unity today, several cautions by Johannine scholar Raymond Brown are appropriate. First, given the overall sectarian orientation of John's Gospel, "the Johannine outlook is not overly ecumenical." Second, "unity should allow for diversity, for the Father and the Son remain distinct persons despite their unity."[93]

Recent scholarship has highlighted the problem of Johannine sectarianism, the fact that John presents Jesus and the community in opposition to the world and even in opposition to more orthodox Christianity. Clearly, this Gospel reflects tensions in the early church, in which John's is a minority position.

Third, if we are to preach this text to exhort ecumenical unity, we need to lift up models of unity that can also embrace diversity—not sameness—as essential to ecumenical unity. David Rhoads suggests that one such model is the New Testament canon itself, in which diverse Christian authors with divergent perspectives and even disagreements are nonetheless laid alongside one another in the unity of the Christian biblical canon.[94] This model can help us celebrate differences and disagreements as part of the broad spectrum of Christian theology, resisting the tendency to harmonize for the sake of unity.

The geological image of a "braided stream," picking up on last week's river texts, is a favorite image of such unity in diversity for me. A braided stream is a type of river found especially in mountain settings, in which multiple strands of water come together and divide again, crisscrossing in a beautiful braided pattern that sparkles and shifts across the broad streambed. If the church is like a river, we can seek models of ecumenical unity that aim not to merge everyone into one monolithic main channel of the stream, but rather affirm the multiplicity of strands as they braid and crisscross and sparkle across the broad spectrum of God's river of unity.[95]

NOTES

1. Robert Schreiter, *The Ministry of Reconciliation: Spirituality and Strategies* (Maryknoll: Orbis, 1998) vi.

2. Ibid., 30.

3. Claus Westermann, *Isaiah 40–66,* trans. D. M. G. Stalker (OTL; Philadelphia: Westminster, 1969) 240.

4. Irene Nowell, *Sing a New Song: The Psalms in the Sunday Lectionary* (Collegeville, Minn.: Liturgical Press, 1993) 116.

5. *Luther's Works*, Vol. 14, ed. by Jaroslav Pelikan (St. Louis: Concordia, 1995) 45.

6. Paul Minear, "Adam and Christ: Death and Life in I Corinthians 15," in *Christians and the New Creation: Genesis Motifs in the New Testament* (Louisville: Westminster, 1994) 77.

7. This is not the case in John's Gospel as a whole, however, which employs verbs for "seeing" interchangeably. See Raymond E. Brown, *The Gospel According to John* (2 vols.; AB 29, 29A; New York: Doubleday, 1970) 1:501-2.

8. If the preacher wants to emphasize the garden connection, one possibility is to substitute Song of Sol. 6:1-3 for today's first reading.

9. Adele Reinhartz, "To Love the Lord: An Intertextual Reading of John 21," in *The Labour of Reading: Desire, Alienation, and Biblical Interpretation*, ed. Fiona Black, Roland Boer, and Erion Runions (Atlanta: Scholars Press, 1999) 66.

10. Sandra Schneiders, "John 20:11-18: The Encounter of the Easter Jesus with Mary Magdalene—A Transformative Feminist Reading," in *What Is John? Readers and Readings in the Fourth Gospel*, ed. Fernando Segovia (Atlanta: Scholars Press, 1996) 161.

11. Suggested by Brown, *John*, 2:1016.

12. These women of Luke's Gospel are described as the original "spice girls," in the Bible Study "The Original Spice Girls," by Stacy Kitahata, Hjamil Martinez-Vazquez, Paul Van de Berg, Rachel Bass, and Andrea Walker, ELCA Division for Congregational Ministries, 2000.

13. Robert Schreiter, *Ministry of Reconciliation,* 43.

14. "Global Mission in the Twenty-First Century," Evangelical Lutheran Church in America Division for Global Mission, 2000, p. 12.

15. Richard J. Cassidy, *Society and Politics in the Acts of the Apostles* (Maryknoll: Orbis, 1987) 15, 40.

16. For a summary of this argument see Mark Allan Powell, *What Are They Saying about Acts?* (New York: Paulist, 1991) 30-32.

17. See the discussion by Max Wilcox in "'Upon the Tree': Deut 21:22-23 in the New Testament," *Journal of Biblical Literature* 96 (1977) 85-99.

18. See description of the mosaic of "Triumph of the Cross" by Peter and Linda Murray, *The Oxford Companion to Christian Art and Architecture* (Oxford University Press, 1996) 450-51. See also p. 192 on the tree tradition in the paintings of the nineteenth-century German Romantic artist Caspar David Friedrich.

19. Malcolm Miller, *Chartres Cathedral* (New York: Pitkin Unichrome, 1996).

20. See the section on "Tree of Life" in Larry Rasmussen, *Earth Community, Earth Ethics* (Maryknoll: Orbis, 1996) 195-208.

21. Kathleen Norris, Introduction to *Revelation* (Pocket Canon Series; New York: Grove Press, 1999) ix.

22. Elisabeth Schüssler Fiorenza, *Revelation: Vision of a Just World* (Proclamation Commentary; Minneapolis: Fortress Press, 1991) 41-43.

23. For a discussion of Galilean-Judean tensions and the argument for translating *ioudaioi* as Judeans, see Richard Horsley, *Galilee: History, Politics, People* (Valley Forge: Trinity Press International, 1995) 13.

24. Brown, *John*, 2:1037.

25. Ernst Käsemann, *The Testament of Jesus according to John 17,* trans. G. Krodel (Philadelphia: Fortress Press, 1968) 54.

26. See most recently Francis J. Moloney, *Glory Not Dishonor: Reading John 13–21* (Minneapolis: Fortress Press, 1998) 151, 171–73.

27. Craig R. Koester, *Symbolism in the Fourth Gospel: Meaning, Mystery, Community* (Minneapolis: Fortress Press, 1995) 204.

28. See Gregory J. Riley, *Resurrection Reconsidered: Thomas and John in Controversy* (Minneapolis: Fortress Press, 1994).

29. Sallie McFague, *The Body of God* (Minneapolis: Fortress Press, 1993).

30. See the discussion by Krister Stendahl, in *Paul Among Jews and Gentiles* (Philadelphia: Fortress Press, 1976), especially the section on "Call, Not Conversion."

31. Responding to an appeal from the world's Nobel Peace Prize laureates, the United Nations General Assembly has declared the first ten years of the new millennium to be a "Decade for a Culture of Peace and nonviolence for the Children of the World." Churches and religious peace fellowships, including the ELCA, Lutheran Peace Fellowship, and the Fellowship of Reconciliation, have joined this effort and can provide materials for teaching Christian nonviolence during this decade. See www.nonviolence.org.

32. Walter Brueggemann, *To Build, to Plant: A Commentary on Jeremiah 26–52,* ITC (Grand Rapids: Eerdmans, 1991) 80.

33. Walter Brueggemann, *Israel's Praise: Doxology against Idolatry and Ideology* (Philadelphia: Fortress Press, 1988) 81.

34. Brueggemann, *The Message of the Psalms* (Minneapolis: Augsburg, 1984) 34.

35. Elisabeth Schüssler Fiorenza, *Revelation: Vision of a Just World,* 103.

36. Moloney, *Glory Not Dishonor,* 190–91.

37. Raymond Brown, *The Community of the Beloved Disciple* (New York: Paulist, 1979) 84: "The Johannine Christians, represented by the Beloved Disciple, clearly regard themselves as closer to Jesus and more perceptive than the Christians of the Apostolic Churches." The beloved disciple's privileged role in John's gospel is seen in his proximity to Jesus at table (John 13:23) and his embrace of Jesus' mother at the foot of the cross (John 19:26-27).

38. See Ernst Haenchen, *John,* trans. R. W. Funk (Hermeneia; Philadelphia: Fortress, 1984) 2:224, citing Jerome and Oppianus Cilix on the number of species of fish known to the ancient world.

39. Robert Schreiter, *Ministry of Reconciliation,* 87-94.

40. Ibid., 92.

41. Brown, *John,* 2:1103.

42. See for example Robert Smith, *Easter Gospels: The Resurrection of Jesus According to the Four Evangelists* (Minneapolis: Augsburg, 1983) 148.

43. Norris, Introduction to *Revelation*, vii.

44. Alan Boesak, *Comfort and Protest: The Apocalypse from a South African Perspective* (Philadelphia: Westminster, 1987) 60-62.

45. *Women in the Acts of the Apostles: A Feminist Liberation Perspective,* trans. L. M. Maloney (Minneapolis: Fortress Press, 1995) 61.

46. This parallel is noted by Ernst Haenchen, *The Acts of the Apostles,* trans. B. Noble and G. Shinn (Philadelphia: Westminster, 1971) 340.

47. See Charles Talbert, *Literary Patterns, Theological Themes, and the Genre of Luke-Acts* (SBLMS 20; Missoula, Mont.: Scholars Press, 1974).

48. See the lectionary-based commentary by Irene Nowell, *Sing a New Song*, 186-87.

49. Pablo Richard, *Apocalypse: A People's Commentary* (Maryknoll: Orbis, 1995) 77. Richard is a Chilean scholar whose liberation-theology commentary on Revelation is readable and insightful.

50. Schüssler Fiorenza, *Revelation*, 65-69.

51. Adele Reinhartz, *The Word in the World: The Cosmological Tale in the Fourth Gospel* (Atlanta: Scholars Press, 1992) 107-09.

52. Ernst Haenchen, *John,* 2:50.

53. Jerome Neyrey, *An Ideology of Revolt: John's Christology in Social-Scientific Perspective* (Philadelphia: Fortress Press, 1988) 65-72.

54. James VanderKam, "John 10 and the Feast of the Dedication," in *Of Scribes and Scrolls: Studies on the Hebrew Bible, Intertestamental Judaism, and Christian Origins,* ed. H. Attridge, J. Collins, and T. Tobin (Lanham, Md.: University Press of America, 1990) 211.

55. Neyrey, *Ideology of Revolt*, 109.

56. Lutherans and Moravians have recently concluded a full-communion agreement, "Following Our Shepherd to Full Communion," described in a document that is rich in Good Shepherd imagery. View the full text at www.elca.org/ea/fos.html, or www.moravian.org.

57. *Moravian Book of Worship* (Bethlehem, Penn.: Interprovincial Board of Publications and Communications, 1995).

58. Craig R. Koester, "The Spectrum of Johannine Readers," in *What Is John?*, 18. See also Koester's *Symbolism in the Fourth Gospel*, 18.

59. Beverly Roberts Gaventa, *From Darkness to Light: Aspects of Conversion in the New Testament* (Philadelphia: Fortress Press, 1986) 111-12.

60. See Linda M. Maloney, *All That God Had Done with Them* (New York: Peter Lang, 1991) 82.

61. See Luke Timothy Johnson's *Decisionmaking in the Church* (Philadelphia: Fortress Press, 1983).

62. Martin Noth, *Leviticus,* trans. J. S. Anderson (OTL; Philadelphia: Westminster, 1965) 139.

63. Joseph A. Fitzmyer, *The Acts of the Apostles* (AB 31; New York: Doubleday, 1997) 535.

64. See Maloney, *All That God Had Done with Them.*

65. The idea of the so-called rapture is found in only one biblical text, 1 Thess. 4:16-17, where Paul states that those who have died will meet Christ in the air, together with those who are alive. This gave pastoral assurance to Christians that their loved ones would *not* be left behind. Recent fundamentalists twist these verses into the opposite meaning, to threaten that some will be "left behind" when the rapture comes. (See the bestselling novels by Tim LaHaye and Jerry Jenkins in the "Left Behind" series.)

66. Kathleen Norris, Introduction to *Revelation*, xii.

67. See Barbara R. Rossing, *The Choice between Two Cities: Whore, Bride and Empire in the Apocalypse* (Valley Forge, Penn.: Trinity Press International, 1999).

68. Moloney, *Glory Not Dishonor*, 22-23; see also Moloney's "A Sacramental Reading of John 13:1-38," *Catholic Biblical Quarterly* 53 (1991) 254-55.

69. R. Alan Culpepper, "The Johannine *Hypodeigma*," *Semeia* 53 (1991) 138-41.

70. See Ernst Käsemann, *The Testament of Jesus*, 50.

71. Culpepper, "The Johannine *Hypodeigma*," 145.

72. Martin Luther King Jr., "I've Been to the Mountaintop," April 3, 1963, speech at the Masonic Temple, Memphis, Tennessee. Cited in *An Easter Source-book: The Fifty Days,* ed. G. Huck, G. Ramshaw, and G. Lathrop (Chicago: Liturgy Training Publications, 1988) 41.

73. One specific way churches can advocate for Jerusalem is by supporting the "Call for a Shared Jerusalem," sponsored by Lutherans, Episcopalians, Roman Catholics, and other U.S. denominations through Churches for Middle East Peace (110 Maryland Ave NE, Suite 108, Washington, DC 20002). The Call argues that Jerusalem is a sacred city for three faiths and two peoples, Palestinians and Israelis, and should not be exclusively controlled by Israel. See www.cmep.org.

74. Ivoni Richter Reimer, *Women in the Acts of the Apostles*, 122-25.

75. Justo Gonzalez argues that because Revelation deals with the issue of the coming together of a variety of peoples and cultures more specifically than any other book in the New Testament, it can be a resource for multicultural education today. See *For the Healing of the Nations: The Book of Revelation in an Age of Cultural Conflict* (Maryknoll: Orbis, 1999) 69.

76. Richard J. Cassidy, *John's Gospel in New Perspective* (Maryknoll: Orbis, 1992) 65.

77. Nils A. Dahl, "Anamnesis: Memory and Commemoration in Early Christianity" in *Jesus in the Memory of the Early Church* (Minneapolis: Augsburg, 1976) 28.

78. Cassidy, *John's Gospel in New Perspective*, 61.

79. Another possibility is to substitute John 7:37-39 as the Gospel, a text that images the gift of the spirit in terms of rivers of living water flowing from the heart of the one who believes.

80. Francis J. Moloney, *The Gospel of John* (Sacra Pagina; Collegeville, Minn.: Liturgical Press, 1998) 166.

81. Brown, *John*, 1:207.

82. "The Columbia River Watershed: Realities and Possibilities," signed by Archbishops Alex Brunett (Seattle) and John Vlazny (Portland), Bishops Thomas Connolly (Baker, Or.), Eugene Cooney (Nelson, British Columbia), Michael Driscoll (Boise), Carlos Sevilla (Yakima), William Skylstad (Spokane), and Rev. John Darragh (Helena), 1999. For the full text see www.columbiariver.org.

83. See Barbara Rossing, "River of Life in God's New Jerusalem: An Ecological Vision for Earth's Future," *Currents in Theology and Mission* 25 (1998) 487-99.

84. Cynthia Briggs Kittredge, "Hebrews" in *Searching the Scriptures,* Volume 2: *A Feminist Commentary,* ed. Elisabeth Schüssler Fiorenza (New York: Crossroad, 1994).

85. Interview in *The Christian Century* (May 3, 2000) 506.

86. Vitor Westhelle, unpublished Ascension sermon, Chicago, May 16, 1999.

87. Reimer, *Women in Acts*, 154-56.

88. P. Kyle McCarter Jr., *1 Samuel* (AB 8; New York: Doubleday, 1980) 220.

89. Artur Weiser, *The Psalms,* trans. H. Hartwell (OTL; Philadelphia: Westminster, 1962) 481.

90. Even premillennialists do not agree about the chronology of final events, debating whether the so-called rapture will occur before or after the seven-year tribulation. See the excellent overview of the interpretation of Revelation and its use in recent American political discourse by Paul Boyer, *When Time Shall Be No More: Prophecy Belief in American Culture* (Cambridge: Harvard Univ. Press, 1992).

91. Brown, *John*, 2:747.

92. George MacDonald, *Diary of an Old Soul: 366 Writings for Devotional Reflection* (Minneapolis: Augsburg, 1994), entry for January 14.

93. Brown, *John*, 2:775.

94. David Rhoads, *The Challenge of Diversity* (Minneapolis: Fortress Press, 1996).

95. I want to thank Revs. Susan and Michael Thomas, pastors at Lutheran Church of the Redeemer in Jerusalem, and the W. F. Albright Institute in East Jerusalem for generous hospitality during my work on this project. I am grateful also to Lutheran Brotherhood for a sabbatical grant and to the Lutheran School of Theology at Chicago for a sabbatical leave.

THE SEASON
OF PENTECOST

HOWARD CLARK KEE

The word *Pentecost*, from the Greek term for "fifty," is used in the Jewish scriptures for the day that follows the seven weeks of grain harvest, "the day after the seventh sabbath" (Lev. 23:15-16) = 49 + 1 = the fiftieth day. This festival was the celebration of God's provision of what was essential for the sustaining of the people, as demonstrated by the harvest. This period began with the Passover, when a sheep was killed and its body consumed by a family in a sacred meal (Exodus 12–13), and it concluded with the celebration of the harvest. Thus both these festivals were established as acts of gratitude to God for the continuing productivity of the crops and the herds, but they soon came to function symbolically as testimony to the ways in which God has established and continues to support the covenant people. The Passover symbolized the dramatic escape of the people of Israel from slavery in Egypt as they safely crossed the Red Sea and their enemies were destroyed by its waters. The harvest symbolized God's provision for the people's understanding of their place and responsibility in the divine purpose, as most dramatically disclosed when God gave them the Torah through Moses on Mount Sinai. The annual celebrations of these feasts not only recalled what God had done for them in the past but also embodied continuing commitment on their part to the covenant that had been established by and was being sustained by God. The two festivals were linked by Jews at the turn of the eras, as is attested in the writings of Philo of Alexandria and Josephus. The pilgrims' departure from home and their journey to Jerusalem, where they shared the Passover meal, were seen as symbols and experience of the opening to them of a new world and a new experience of life as God's people.

Features of both sacred meals appear in the Gospel accounts of the Last Supper. The first three Gospels depict Jesus as eating the Passover meal with his disciples (Mark 14:15-16), while John 13:1 states that Jesus' last meal with them was "before the Passover." For John, the sacrifice of "the Lamb of God" (1:29) who is to take away "the sin of the world" takes place on the next day, at Jesus' crucifixion. The import of his death is the same, but the Passover imagery is employed in different ways, the first three Gospels picturing present participation in the covenant people and John emphasizing its timeless significance for the community who are still in "the world."

The opening paragraphs of Acts describe the divine purpose that was being inaugurated by the risen Christ and would be accomplished through the work of the Holy Spirit operative in those whom he has called to be witnesses to him and to what God was doing through him. Their testimony would begin there in Jerusalem, but would reach out "to the ends of the earth" (Acts 1:8). When he was taken up from them, they were given assurance that he "will come in the same way as you saw him go into heaven" (1:11). What follows in Acts gives specifics of the resources available to the messengers: the scriptural basis for the divine program in which they are to be engaged and the God-given power of the Spirit by which they would be guided and enabled to carry out their mission.

The range and diversity of participants in this work are indicated from the outset: there is no place for those whose aim is personal gain (1:15-20), as is dramatically indicated in the fearful death that strikes down Judas, who had been paid to guide the authorities to Jesus in order to seize and execute him. The central leadership group of the apostles is to number twelve, obviously corresponding to the number of the tribes of Israel and of the circle of disciples who were witnesses of Jesus. The one chosen to replace Judas must have had continuing experience of Jesus from his baptism to his resurrection and ascension (1:21-26). Matthias was designated to join these pioneers who were called and empowered to carry out this mission to the wider world. They were now no longer designated as "disciples"—which means learners, or those receiving instruction—but are now "apostles"—those authorized, commissioned, empowered, and informed so as to carry out the mission to which they had been called (1:26). In what follows, in Acts and in the other New Testament passages examined below, are stories and advice about the significance of what God has done and continues to do through Jesus Christ as well as messages that disclose how the scriptures illumine this divine purpose and how God enables these agents to experience the range of challenges, opportunities, and strategies that they are to encounter and engage in. The lectionary texts represent those preparatory features for the divine purpose as they are set forth in the scriptural narratives, the messages of the prophets, and the liturgical features of the psalms. We want to discern the way in which images and prophetic features of God's purpose for his people through Jesus have found—and continue to find—their fulfillment in what God has launched through Christ and has called us to proclaim and to embody. The outpouring of the Spirit is depicted in Acts 1 as both the instrument and the guarantee of the fulfillment of that purpose.

HOWARD
CLARK KEE

THE DAY OF PENTECOST

JUNE 3, 2001

REVISED COMMON	EPISCOPAL (BCP)	ROMAN CATHOLIC
Acts 2:1-21	Acts 2:1-11	Acts 2:1-11
or Gen. 11:1-9	or Joel 2:28-32	
Ps. 104:24-34, 35b	Ps. 104:25-37	Ps. 104:1, 24, 29-31, 34
	or 104:25-32	
	or 33:12-15, 18-22	
Rom. 8:14-17	1 Cor. 12:4-13	1 Cor. 12:3b-7, 12-13
or Acts 2:1-21	or Acts 2:1-11	or Rom. 8:8-17
John 14:8-17 (25-27)	John 20:19-23	John 20:19-23
	or John 14:8-17	or John 14:15-16, 23b-26

FIRST READING

ACTS 2:1-21; 2:1-11 (BCP/RC)

In the Jewish tradition the Day of Pentecost came to be a celebration of the end of the grain harvest. The fifty days began with the bringing to the altar of the first grain to be gathered and ended with giving thanks at the completion of the harvest (Lev. 23:15-16). This celebration came to be associated with God's gift of the Law at Mount Sinai and the expectation of renewal of the covenant, as promised in Jer 31:31-37 and attested in the Book of Jubilees and other first-century Jewish documents, including some of the Dead Sea Scrolls.[1]

On that day the apostles were gathered in a house when an extraordinary presence among them in the form of wind and fire was matched by the inner experience of their all being filled with the Holy Spirit. That wind and fire can serve as evidence of divine presence and action is documented in Ps. 104:1-4 and in "the flame of fire" in which the LORD appeared to Moses at the burning bush (Exod. 3:1-6). Here the presence is not only outwardly visible but also inwardly experienced, as the Spirit enables them to "speak in other tongues," that is, in other languages. This event is the reverse of the story in Gen. 11:1-9, which describes the act of divine judgment that falls on the human race when they exploit their unity and their construction capabilities with the intention of building a tower that will extend their realm upward to that of God. The name of the tower, Babel, involves a play on words: the literal meaning is "Gate of God," but the kindred verb, *balal*, means "to confuse." It is used here for the Lord's judgment on the people for their ambitious, blasphemous scheme. This evidence of divine disapproval leads to the resultant diversity of human languages. The Acts account symbolizes the God-given capacity of the apostles to reach out across the world with their message in multiple languages and to achieve unity in spite of ethnic and linguistic differences.

The diversity of those who, in the subsequent history of the apostolic mission, will hear the message in their own language is dramatically evident in the experience of the devout Jews in Jerusalem whose places of origin encompass "every nation under heaven" (2:5), but each of whom hears the message "in his own native language." The list of nations of origin of this throng—which includes both Jews and proselytes—reaches from modern Iran and Iraq across the Levant and Asia Minor to Egypt and Africa in the south and Rome in

> THE ACTS ACCOUNT SYMBOLIZES THE GOD-GIVEN CAPACITY OF THE APOSTLES TO REACH OUT ACROSS THE WORLD WITH THEIR MESSAGE IN MULTIPLE LANGUAGES AND TO ACHIEVE UNITY IN SPITE OF ETHNIC AND LINGUISTIC DIFFERENCES.

the west. All of them hear the message of God's "mighty works," but they cannot identify the source of this speech capability, and they assume that the apostles are drunk.

Peter explains that this astonishing communication capability comes from the power of God's Spirit, as foreseen by the prophet Joel, who is quoted in 2:14-21. He predicted that God's Spirit would be poured out on all humanity ("flesh"), including males and females, servants and free. It would manifest itself in their ability to speak as God's messengers ("prophesy") and through accompanying marvels in the heavens and on the earth. These cosmic signs are in anticipation of the climax of fulfillment of God's purpose in "the day of the Lord."

This term "day of the Lord" was variously understood by the prophets of Israel. For some it was seen as the time of God's judgment on the other nations (Isa. 9:4; Jer. 30:31; Ezek. 32:10), for others as judgment on Israel or Judah (Amos 2:13-16; Hos. 1:4-5). But it was also often used for the day of deliverance, when God would restore and renew the people, either directly (Mal. 3:17; Isa. 2:11) or through a chosen agent (Isa. 11:10; Jer. 33:15-16). The result would be health (Isa. 29:18-19), abundance (Isa. 25:6-9), prosperity (Micah 4:4) and peace (Isa. 11:1-10), as God's people experience special favor (Isa. 11:1-12). These benefits will be available to all who "call on the name of the Lord," that is, on the name of Jesus the Lord. They will be enabled to foresee the future as the Spirit is poured out on them (Joel 2:28-32, as quoted in Acts 2:17-21). Joel expects "a great and terrible day of the Lord" before the Lord comes (2:31), but Peter here foresees cosmic disturbances. These include "wonders in the heaven" and "signs on the earth": it is events such as these that are seen in the Gospel of Luke (volume one of Luke–Acts) to have occurred through Jesus and to portend the coming of the new age. For example, Jesus expelling a demon is interpreted in Luke 11:19 as a sign that "the kingdom of God has [already] come to you." That is, the powers of evil are already being overcome through Jesus as visible signs that God's rule is being established in the world.

A clear anticipation of this outreach through the Holy Spirit is evident in Luke's account of Jesus' launching his ministry (Luke 4:14-21). Under the power of the Spirit he goes to his hometown, Nazareth, and addresses those at the synagogue in Nazareth. Quoting Isa. 61:1-2, he claims that the promise of someone to be anointed by the Spirit who will bring God's good news to the poor, the blind, the oppressed is now being fulfilled through him. "Anointed" is the verb akin to *Christos* = Messiah. What is seen here is not merely a title or an office but a role to be carried out, which is here launched through the power of the Spirit. It is this mission to which the apostles are now called and which they now are enabled to carry out by the Holy Spirit. The inclusiveness of Jesus' message and ministry as portrayed in Luke is dramatically extended by the apostles in Acts, whose effective proclamation of the good news begins in Jerusalem, the center for the presence and worship of the God of Israel, and reaches its climax in the encounter of Paul with the center of human authority and purpose symbolized by and located in the city of Rome.

In the final section of Peter's sermon (2:22-31), there are references to the signs and wonders Jesus performed and to God's having raised him from the dead, which is seen to be in fulfillment of the hope expressed in the Psalms. It is through God's having raised Jesus from the dead and the ongoing direction by the Holy Spirit that the apostles are able to carry out this world-encompassing mission for the good news of what God is doing through Jesus. This triumph by God's "Holy One" over the power of death and his consequent ongoing gladness in the presence of God were prophesied by David, as is evident in Peter's quotation of Ps. 15:8-11 in Acts 2:25-28. Thus David is perceived to have foreseen the death and resurrection of Jesus, his exaltation "at the right hand of God," and his role in the outpouring of God's Spirit, whose work is now seen and heard by the new community. Jesus will continue in his place of honor at the "right hand" of God as "Lord and Christ" until the prophecy of the psalmist is fulfilled by the defeat of the powers of evil, when "I make your enemies your footstool" (2:34-35 = Ps. 110:1). Assurance about the accomplishment of God's purpose is provided by the scriptures and—above all—by God's having raised the crucified Jesus from the dead and exalted him at the divine throne "as Lord and Christ" (2:36).

For those who have heard and believed this message, there are to be two major responses: (1) repentance, or changing the mind about what God has done and is doing for his people, and (2) public acknowledgment of this new commitment by acceptance of the rite of baptism "in the name of Jesus Christ" (2:38). The result will be the receiving of the renewing and empowering presence of the Holy Spirit (2:38). This opportunity is available to the adult hearers of the message, to their offspring, as well as to those who by traditional rules for covenant participation were considered to be "far off." All who are called by the Lord have the possibility of responding in faith (2:39). The response is phenomenal—"about three thousand souls"—and these are then united and confirmed in their understanding of the new relationship to God through participation in instruction ("the apostles' teaching"), the common life of the community ("fellowship"), and in the sacraments and worship ("breaking of bread and prayers"; 2:42).

JOEL 2:28–32 (BCP alt.)

This lection is the text quoted in Peter's speech at Pentecost (Acts 2:17-21). Joel 2 warns the people of God's impending judgment on the nation and the seismic disturbances that will accompany it. When they ask for mercy, however, God—who is gracious and merciful (2:23)—will respond by intervening in their behalf and will vindicate them among the nations that belittle them. They will benefit from abundant rain and harvest much grain, which are to be seen as God's gracious presence in their midst. The great visible sign of this divine care will be an outpouring of the Spirit of God, which will manifest itself in dreams, visions, and prophecies, as well as in cosmic signs that will precede the final judgment of God on the evil forces of the world. Those who call on the Lord for deliverance will be gathered in Jerusalem (2:28-32).

GENESIS 11:1–9 (RCL alt.)

Following the long list in Genesis 10 of Noah's descendants and the nations that evolved from them and spread across the world (10:32), the story is told of the proud, audacious plans of humans to rule the world and gain access to the heavens. Seen as having one universal language and having developed skills in building that leads them to suppose that they can build a tower that will have "its top in the heavens" (11:1-4) and will bring them a reputation for achievement and power, they assume that nothing is impossible for them (11:6). Divine judgment falls on them for their pride and for their lack of concern for the divine purpose. This results in their being scattered over the face of the earth and in the diversity of their languages. The city they had built is called Babel, based on the Hebrew word for "confuse"—reminding them of the confusion of languages that results from this divine judgment. Ironically, in Akkadian (the language of the Babylonians), Babel means "gate of God." Thus the prideful motivation of this building project is evident and leads to its destruction. God-given human capa-bilities are often perverted into prideful, self-serving undertakings—with disas-trous results. The intention to construct a symbol of human cosmic achievement results in divine judgment.

RESPONSIVE READING
PSALM 104:24-34, 35b (RCL);
PS. 104:25-37 or 104:25-32 (BCP);
PS. 104:1, 24, 29-31, 34 (RC)

After the call to the soul to "bless the Lord" and the attribution of great-ness to God, Psalm 104 moves to pronouncements of praise for the power and wisdom of God, which are manifest in the creation of the world. The faithful community joins in the praise of God, but the wicked may expect doom and destruction (104:35).

PSALM 33:12-15, 18-22 (BCP alt.)

In Psalm 33 there is celebration by "the nation whose God is the Lord," which thus enjoys a special relationship to the Creator and a central role in the future of the divine purpose. But God's special care is for those (1) who "fear him"; that is, are serious about his demands upon them, and (2) who trust in his enduring love to free them from death and to sustain them in times of grave deprivation (vv. 18-19).

SECOND READING
ROMANS 8:14-17 (RCL);
ROM. 8:8-17 (RC alt.)

Life in the Spirit is to characterize the new people of God, Paul declares. To "set one's mind on the Spirit" (8:6) is to adopt the values and grasp the insights that God provides his new people through the Holy Spirit. It results in authentic "life and peace," not merely continuing existence and calm. Peace is possible because through Christ the powers of evil have been overcome. Direction and power for life are provided by the Spirit. This experience is not merely private or individual: to rely on one's personal capacities—to "live according to the flesh"—will lead to fear, destruction, and death. That is a life of slavery from which God has provided liberation through Jesus. Instead, power and direction come for

God's new people—here identified as "sons of God"—through the guidance and power of the Holy Spirit. The special and intimate relationship of these new people with God is epitomized in the affectionate Semitic name by which they address God: "Abba," which carries the intimate connotations of "Papa" or "Daddy," and which matches well the warm, personal relationship with God that the community members experience. The effective force, which makes possible this relationship, is the Holy Spirit, who attests to the inner being ("our spirit") of the members that they are indeed "children of God." Furthermore, the blessings of this relationship are not only for the present but for the future as well, in which God's purpose for the people will be fulfilled as it is being accomplished through the risen Christ. This involves fidelity in the face of suffering that the community will experience by virtue of their having identified with him. But it looks beyond suffering to divine vindication, triumph over the powers of evil, and eventually being "glorified with him."

1 CORINTHIANS 12:4-13 (BCP); 1 COR. 12:3b-7, 12-13 (RC)

Other facets of this new community relationship through Christ are set forth in 1 Cor. 12:3-13. Here Paul describes both the unity and the diversity of the new community, which he designates as "the body of Christ." It is the Spirit who guides and enables them to make public confession of Jesus as Lord, and who keeps them from pronouncing a curse on him. The one Spirit is manifest in the lives and activities of the members in a variety of ways, though in every case it is God who provides direction and enabling power. And the roles performed through that power are diverse, though all are effected through the Holy Spirit and all are thereby performed for the benefit and enrichment of the community as a whole. The gifts through the Spirit provide a range of services, but in every case ultimate authority rests with Christ as Lord and derives from the outworking of God's purpose (12:4-6). All are operative "for the common good" (12:7).

The functions carried out through the enabling power of the Spirit are not human "gifts" but divinely provided modes of bestowal on the members of the community of insights and capabilities essential for the welfare of the group and the carrying out of its mission. They are designated as *charismata* (12:4) and include the ability to communicate "wisdom" and "knowledge" (12:8)—terms which may be differentiated as broad, comprehensive understanding ("wisdom") in distinction from specific insights and perceptions ("knowledge"). Both are available through the work of the Spirit. "Faith" is also a gift of the Spirit; that is, the capacity to discern and to have full confidence in God's power to fulfill the divine purpose and in the ways by which it is being carried out in the experience of the community. Special manifestations of divine power and purpose are seen to be granted to members of the community who are able to perform extraordinary acts for the benefit of members in need or of the whole group: healing and miracles (12:9-10a).

Essential information of various kinds is made available by the Spirit, including the role of conveying the purpose of God to his people through "prophecy," which involves not only foretelling the future but discernment and divine insights concerning the divine plan (2:10a). It is likewise essential that, when unusual and, humanly speaking, inexplicable events occur in the experience of the community, the capacity may be granted for someone to discern whether the effective force behind what is happening is God or some evil power. Similarly, messages addressed to the community in strange languages ("tongues") must be evaluated and interpreted by those with the gift of "tongues" in order to determine whether they are in fact of divine origin (12:10b). It is the Holy Spirit that is seen to provide these capabilities for members of the community: they do not result from human accomplishments, but occur "as the Spirit chooses" (12:11).

The diversity of roles within the community is comparable to the diversity of origins of "the members of the body" which is the new people of God (12:13). They have been called from radically different backgrounds, religiously and culturally: Jew and Gentile (or "Greek"); and socially and economically: "slave and free." Through Christ they have become "one body." Now they all share in the insights and enabling power, which God provides, in that "we were all made to drink of one Spirit."

The Gospel
JOHN 14:8-17 (25-27) (RCL);
JOHN 14:8-17 (BCP alt.);
JOHN 14:15-16, 23b-26 (RC alt.)

John, after reporting Jesus' claim to being one with the Father, describes how God will be present and active among his people through the Spirit. The Father is not disclosed in some sort of isolated, private revelatory experience such as Philip requested (14:8) but is manifest through the person of Jesus, and especially through what he says and the works which he performs. The authority by which he speaks and acts is not his own but represents specific, discernible manifestations of the unity of Jesus the Son and God the Father. Even if one does not believe this about Jesus on the basis of what he says, the works which he performs in carrying out God's purpose may be persuasive (14:10-11).

Further, those who trust in Jesus as God's unique agent in the world will be able to carry out similar divinely empowered acts. The requests of his followers for such capabilities are to be addressed to God in the name of Jesus, and the result will be to bring glory to God through the manifestation of his power and purpose accomplished on the authority granted to the Son. Any request that is worthy to be made in Jesus' name will be carried out by the power of the exalted Lord (14:12-14).

After Jesus has claimed to be the only true way by which anyone can have access to God (14:7-8), he goes on to declare that if his followers really knew and understood him they would also know God the Father. To see Jesus and to hear the instruction he gives to his followers is to see God the Father. By this time, his disciples should clearly recognize that this is the case, that the instructions he gives them are from God, and that the ability to do good works in his name is the result of God's presence with Jesus, and through him, with his followers. This awareness of God's powerful presence in Jesus is confirmed by "the works"—the good deeds of love, of service, of healing, of reconciliation, of peacemaking—which his followers now are to do through him. Indeed, if they live lives of trust in him, they will be able to perform works of healing and renewal, which are comparable to those that he has done. God has been at work in Jesus, but now is at work in the same way through those who have become followers of Jesus, by whom even greater deeds of love and mercy are being performed. The power for this to happen comes upon God's people in ever greater and more effective ways because Jesus is now with God and intercedes with God in their behalf when they make petitions to God "in Christ's name."

> THIS AWARENESS OF GOD'S POWERFUL PRESENCE IN JESUS IS CONFIRMED BY "THE WORKS"—THE GOOD DEEDS OF LOVE, OF SERVICE, OF HEALING, OF RECONCILIATION, OF PEACEMAKING—WHICH HIS FOLLOWERS NOW ARE TO DO THROUGH HIM.

Their claim to love him must be matched by their obedience to his commandments. His response to such loving faith will be experienced by them through the Holy Spirit, the "counselor, helper, aide, agent" who is at work through Christ's people, now and "forever." Those who live in and by the standards of the world will not receive the divine help and guidance, because they did not recognize God at work through Jesus and do not have the ability to see or experience the Spirit's enabling, transforming power. But the Spirit is present with the members of the faithful community and will be experienced by them through the power and purpose of God, which is at work within and through them to accomplish the renewal of God's people.

In 14:25-27 there are promises of two further spiritual resources for the members of the new community: (1) instruction through the Holy Spirit, which will be comprehensive in its scope ("all things") and will enable them to recall fully what Jesus has taught them, and (2) the Spirit's teaching, which will bring them peace and confidence—free of troubled hearts and minds, free of fear—as they are aware of God's continuing presence with them and God's purpose for them.

The ongoing power and presence of God in the lives of his people will be experienced through God's Spirit, here described in the role of Paraclete. The term literally means "one called alongside" and has been variously translated as "advocate, comforter, helper, counselor"—all of which imply God's continuing support, counsel, enabling power, and abiding presence. This resource is not available to the wider world, which cannot even perceive or understand the role, which God continues to carry out through the Spirit's indwelling presence in the lives of the members of the new community.

The Spirit, which is sent by the Father in the name of Jesus to those who receive and identify with that name, will fulfill a multiple role within the new community. By the Spirit the members will be provided instruction of an encompassing scope—"all things"—and will be enabled to recall and to comprehend everything that Jesus taught his followers. His heritage to them is one of peace—of a sort that nothing else in the world can provide. It is more than absence of conflict, personal or social, but includes assurance about the status and future of God's people, of the triumph over the powers of evil that will come through Christ, and of divine love and justice operative within the life of the new community. Accordingly, the members are to have no anxiety about the present or the future, and their hearts are not to be filled with fear. The ground of this assurance is yet to be disclosed in the Gospel of John: it involves the triumph over sin, over hostile human powers and agencies, represented by the Roman authorities, and over death itself, as evident in the resurrection of Christ.

JOHN 20:19-23 (BCP/RC)

John 20:19-23 reports the appearance of the risen Christ to the disciples on the evening of the day of his resurrection, "the first day of the week." In spite of the call of Jesus for them to be free of fear (14:27), they have gathered in a secret place behind closed doors, out of fear of harassment or harm from the Jewish religious authorities. In spite of the closed door—and hence in triumph over human fear—Jesus appeared among them and called for peace to be with them. Clearly this is not merely for freedom from conflict but for peace of mind, for confidence about their place in the purpose of God. In spite of the conflict and violence and his agonizing death, which they witnessed taking place at the hands of the Roman civil authorities, he tells them that God's purpose assures them of peace. This is not only inward tranquility, but also certainty regarding the ultimate triumph of God's purpose over forces hostile to God and his people, and over the very powers of evil. Their confidence is to rest in the accomplishment, through Jesus, of God's purpose for his people and for the creation.

This assured and powerful relationship with God is already to be experienced through the presence of the Holy Spirit, which Jesus conveys to them as he breathes on them. The continuing presence and work of the Holy Spirit include the role that the disciples are to fulfill in discerning the moral status of members of the new community, as well as the pronouncement or withholding of forgiveness for the members. To demonstrate that this one who has appeared among them is the same as the one who suffered and died in their behalf, he shows them his pierced hand and side. The central significance of his sacrificial death for their entering into the new life of love and forgiveness in the new community is thus dramatically evident.

(On this lection, see also the comments on the Gospel for the Second Sunday of Easter.)

Jesus is here seen as addressing the basic questions that arise from the claim to know God, but they are now given distinctive answers. How is the love of God evident in the world? How can one see God? How can one do God's works? How can one learn the will of God? The call of God to the community to love Christ concerns not merely their inner feelings but is to manifest itself publicly in how they live and act. If they love Christ, they are to keep his commandments (14:15) and obey his "word" (14:23). In this way they can be sure of and personally experience God's love and the ongoing revelation within their hearts of who Christ is and what he has done and continues to do for them.

HOLY TRINITY SUNDAY (FIRST SUNDAY AFTER PENTECOST)

JUNE 10, 2001

REVISED COMMON	EPISCOPAL (BCP)	ROMAN CATHOLIC
Prov. 8:1-4, 22-31	Isa. 6:1-8	Prov. 8:22-31
Ps. 8	Ps. 29 or Cant. 2 or 13	Ps. 8:4-9
Rom. 5:1-5	Rev. 4:1-11	Rom. 5:1-5
John 16: 12-15	John 16:(5-11), 12-15	John 16:12-15

FIRST READING
PROVERBS 8:1-4, 22-31 (RCL); PROV. 8:22-31 (RC)

In the Old Testament, God is perceived as having created Wisdom to serve as the divine agent (1) in the creation of the world, including human beings, and (2) in conveying the divine purpose to them. Wisdom is pictured here as calling humans to share in insights and perceptions about the divine purpose, and to realize how humans are intended to recognize and affirm what God has done. She addresses humans wherever they may be—"on the heights, beside the way, at the crossroads, beside the gates" (8:2-3). All living creatures are summoned to give heed to her message, and thereby to "learn prudence, acquire intelligence," but above all to overcome wickedness by obeying the "righteous" words of wisdom (8:8-9). To gain such insights is far more valuable than to acquire "gold" and "jewels" (8:10-11).

Wisdom is seen to have been present and active in the achievement of the divine purpose at the very beginning of the enterprise of creation, before the heavens, the earth, and the seas were established (8:22-31). Wisdom shared in the creative process "like a master workman" (8:30) and helped to establish the order and structure of the whole of the universe. Wisdom also shared—and continues to share—in the divine joy, which came in response to the creation of the world, but especially to God's establishment of the human race (8:31). Thus wisdom is perceived as the agent and companion of God in the process which began with the creation of the world and which continues in the maintenance of cosmic order, but especially in the guidance of human affairs on the earth. Moreover, wisdom is the divine instrument through which understanding of God and of God's purpose are conveyed to and grasped by humans.

ISAIAH 6:1-8 (BCP)

Isaiah here describes the divine presence in the world and human access to God in terms of imagery very different from that of Wisdom. Here the prophet reports his experience, which is dated to 742 B.C.E., the year of the death of King Uzziah. Isaiah is taken into the presence of Yahweh on his throne, which is depicted as matching God's presence in the Temple, where God was perceived as dwelling in the Holy of Holies and hence inaccessible to everyone but the high priest (1 Kings 6:5; 2 Chron. 4:20; 5:9). Central in this most holy place was the ark of the covenant (1 Kings 6:19), above which God was said to be present as a living flame. Present and active here in the vision are angelic beings, "seraphs" ("fiery ones"), each with six wings: two to shield their faces from the divine presence, two to cover their "feet" (a euphemism for their genitals), and two to fly—thereby fulfilling their mission from God. Their acclaim of God's holiness and their assertion of God's universal sovereignty evoke seismic trembling and a cloud of smoke as evidence of the powerful divine presence. The prophet acknowledges his awareness of the sin that besets him and his people and hence of his unfitness to have seen the glory of God. But one of the seraphs purifies him and his lips with sacred fire from the altar, thereby qualifying and authorizing the prophet to take his mission and message to the people. When the voice of Yahweh asks who should be commissioned and who would offer to carry God's message to his people, Isaiah declares that he is there in God's presence and offers to be the agent to carry out this divine purpose (6:8). Sadly, the message he is to proclaim is that the people will lack understanding of and openness to God's purpose, and that judgment will fall on them until only a "stump remains" of the covenant people (6:15). Yet from this stump will come the "holy seed" that would fulfill God's purpose for them.

RESPONSIVE READING
PSALM 8 (RCL); PS. 8:4-9 (RC)

The special name for God in ancient Israel, YHWH, appears more than 6,000 times in the Hebrew scriptures and was probably pronounced "Yahweh." It meant "I am" or "I cause to be" and was linked with God's role as creator of the universe and as the one who entered into a covenant relationship with the people. This psalm describes God's work in creating and sustaining the world and how God has assigned to humans an honorable and glorious role to foster life and maintain order on land and sea. All forms of life on the earth are to be controlled by humans in accord with this divine assignment of responsibility. The utterance of the sacred name of God should remind the people constantly of God's role as creator and as the one whose purpose in the world is to be carried out by those who were formed at the peak of God's creative process: humans.

PSALM 29 (BCP)

Psalm 29 celebrates God's sovereignty over the whole of the universe and calls on those at the apex of the creation, "heavenly beings" or "sons of God," to join in this worship of Yahweh (29:1-2). There are ascriptions of praise for God's sovereignty over the sea, the trees, and the mountains—including seismic disturbances! The instrument for maintaining this control over the creation is "the voice of the Lord" (29:3, 5, 7, 8), as it was in the account of the creation of the universe in Genesis 1: "God said" (1:3, 6, 9, 11, 14, 20, 24, 26, 28, 29).

SECOND READING
ROMANS 5:1-5 (RCL, RC)

In explicit language, Paul here describes the basis and the essence of the new relationship that God has established with his people through Jesus Christ. The ground of this shared participation in the life of the covenant people—being "justified"—is trust in what God has done and continues to do through Jesus Christ. This is the essence of "faith," and what it produces is "peace," which means the overcoming of the hostility of humans toward God and the new relationship which is established. The life, death, and resurrection of Jesus are the divine actions that have made possible this new shared life which is available as God's gift = "grace" through Christ.

This relationship is significant not merely for the present but for the future, when God's people will "share in the glory of God," which is to attain the intention of God when humans were created in the image of God (Gen. 1:26-27), as Paul affirms in 1 Cor. 11:7. Self-centered and filled with pride, humans have replaced "the glory of the immortal God" with images and agents subject to their own control (Rom. 1:22-23). But the relationship that God makes possible through Jesus leads to the ful-

THE RELATIONSHIP THAT GOD MAKES POSSIBLE THROUGH JESUS LEADS TO THE FULFILLMENT OF THE PROMISE OF HUMAN CONFORMITY TO THE DIVINE IMAGE.

fillment of the promise of human conformity to the divine image. It takes place through the sufferings that the faithful experience, which are analogous to the pangs experienced by mothers in the process of childbirth. What these painful experiences produce is a chain of moral qualities, which Paul describes using the terminology of Stoic philosophy: endurance, by which one is enabled to persevere in spite of pain; character, which is the proof of moral integrity through a time of testing; and hope, by which one remains confident that God's plan for human and cosmic renewal will reach its goal. That confidence is confirmed for the faithful by the presence and power of the Holy Spirit, which God has sent to be at work within the hearts of the faithful who are the new community.

REVELATION 4:1–11 (BCP)

This reading presents a vision of the throne of God and offers assurance of the fulfillment of God's purpose to overcome the powers of evil and to achieve the renewal of the creation. John is called up and transported by the Spirit to heaven, where he sees the throne of God and those of the twenty-four elders, as well as the four living creatures around the divine throne. God's appearance and the radiant light that surrounds it are compared with glistening jewels. The four "living creatures" resemble a lion, an ox, a man, and an eagle, respectively, although each of them has wings like an eagle and is "full of eyes." The multiple eyes symbolize the vast range of perception that these creatures possess.

The twenty-four elders probably represent a combination of the two sets of twelve leaders in the old and new covenant communities: the heads of the twelve tribes of Israel and the twelve apostles. Their purity and their leadership roles are symbolized by their white garments and their golden crowns.

The four living creatures correspond to (1) the four beasts in Daniel 7, who represent the successive pagan empires—down to the time of the Hellenistic successors of Alexander the Great—that are overcome and replaced by the kingdom of God, and (2) those creatures pictured in Isaiah 6 and Ezekiel 10 around the divine throne. In the second century, the animals came to symbolize the four Gospels: John, the lion; Luke, the ox; Matthew, the human; Mark, the eagle. Here multiple eyes and wings represent their vision and power, and their song, "Holy, holy, holy . . . ," echoes the acclaim of God by the seraphs in Isa. 6:1–5, here praising the divine power and purpose to create and sustain the universe. These creatures seem to represent the true powers and agents of God at work in the world, in contrast to the various pagan rulers who seek to thwart the purpose of God and who at the end of the present age will face destruction.

THE GOSPEL

JOHN 16:12–15 (RCL/RC);
JOHN 16:(5–11), 12–15 (BCP)

In vv. 5–11, Jesus informs the disciples that he is going to give them new insights and instructions in preparation for his imminent departure from them, when he will return to the one "who sent me." They have been saddened by learning of his leaving them, but he now tells them that they will receive benefits, which previously were not accessible to them. Only after he leaves them will the Counselor come, who will have been sent to them by Jesus. The role of the Holy Spirit, who is here designated as the advocate or counselor, is then described.

The Greek term thus translated is *paraklētos* (Paraclete), which is occasionally used to denote a lawyer or legal advocate but usually means someone who appears or acts on behalf of another as mediator in a dispute or as intercessor or helper for one in need of support. Sent by the risen Christ (16:7), the Advocate's role will be crucial in enabling the new community to make its case to "the world concerning sin and righteousness and judgment" (16:8). The specifics of each of these factors are then made clear. The primary "sin" of the human race is failure to recognize and acknowledge Jesus as God's agent for renewal of his people and of the world (16:9). "Righteousness" does not mean here primarily superior moral quality of humans, but "setting things right." This consists of the divine plan for renewal of the covenant people and the social and moral transformation, through Jesus, of its members and, through them, of the world. Doubts about this divine mode of human transformation will arise because of the current absence of Jesus, following his return to the presence of "the Father" (16:10). Conviction concerning the divine mode of setting things right should be based on the fact that the "ruler of this world is judged"—whether that title is understood as referring to the cosmic power of evil (Satan, or the Devil) or to the ruler of the Mediterranean world, the Roman emperor. Both are now surely to be deprived of their authority as God's plan of cosmic renewal begins to unfold and to accomplish its purpose (16:11).

The divine method of conveying this understanding of God's plan for human renewal through Jesus is further explained in the next paragraph of John 16 (vv.12–15). Jesus' being taken from the presence of his followers means that his instruction of them in the way of God is not yet complete, but the essential agent for carrying out that task is coming: the Spirit, who "will guide [them] into all the truth" (16:13). His message derives from what he hears in the presence of God

> THE ADVOCATE'S ROLE WILL BE CRUCIAL IN ENABLING THE NEW COMMUNITY TO MAKE ITS CASE TO "THE WORLD CONCERNING SIN AND RIGHTEOUSNESS AND JUDGMENT."

and of the Risen Christ. It is this that he will convey to the new community. They will be instructed about the future features of the divine plan, "the things that are to come" (16:13). In all that the Spirit communicates to them, he will be glorifying Jesus—explaining and broadening the understanding of his divinely intended role for the renewal of the covenant people. These insights and promises are inherent in who Jesus is and in what God is doing through him and will culminate in the divine goal that is thereby in process of fulfillment. It is this vast range of perceptions about what God is doing through Jesus that is to be conveyed to his followers by the Holy Spirit. The risen Christ Jesus has full access to the mind and purpose of God, and it will now be transmitted by the Spirit to the members of the new community.

How is God's continuing, powerful presence in the world to be experienced? Through the Holy Spirit it is evident for God's people, but also for the wider world as well. The world is reminded of human sin and its consequences for people as a whole, but the Spirit also enables God's people to perceive what is right, to recognize and distance themselves from the powers of evil that are at work in the world. To the members of the new community are disclosed what constitutes truth and justice and to discern both what is God's ultimate purpose for the world and to grasp and appropriate for themselves the meaning of Christ for his people in their day-to-day lives.

SECOND SUNDAY AFTER PENTECOST; BODY AND BLOOD OF CHRIST

JUNE 17, 2001 / PROPER 6

REVISED COMMON	EPISCOPAL (BCP)	ROMAN CATHOLIC
2 Sam. 11:26—12:10, 13-15 or 1 Kings 21: 1-10 (11-14), 15-21a	2 Sam. 11:26—12:10, 13-15	Gen. 14:18-20
Ps. 32 or Ps. 5:1-8	Ps. 32 or 32:1-8	Ps. 110:1-4
Gal. 2:15-21	Gal. 2:11-21	1 Cor. 11:23-26
Luke 7:36—8:3	Luke 7:36-50	Luke 9:11b-17

FIRST READING
2 SAMUEL 11:26—12:10, 13-15 (RCL/BCP)

In what is one of the most ironic and sordid narratives in the whole of the Old Testament, David—to whom God promised continuing "steadfast love" and a posterity and kingdom that would be "established forever" (2 Sam. 7:13-16)—commits adultery with the wife of one of his military men, Uriah, and then arranges to have him killed in battle. Having seen the beautiful Bathsheba bathing, he sent for her and had sex with her, and she became pregnant (11:2-5). His subsequent effort to urge Uriah to have sex with her so that he would think the child to be born was his failed. Then David plotted to have him killed, and took Bathsheba as one of his wives (11:26-27).

David was severely rebuked by the prophet Nathan, who predicted that the illegitimate child would die. He did, but David "lay with her" again, and she gave birth to Solomon, whose name is based on the Hebrew word for peace, *shalom*. Nathan, however, gave him another name, Jedidiah, which means "beloved of the Lord" (12:1-25). Thus David's sexual sin is not a secret known to the sinful couple alone. Further, David is warned by Nathan that he will be confronted by sexual promiscuity within his own household. Yet when David confesses his sin to the prophet, he is assured that God will not put him to death for this gross misdeed, but will "put away this sin" (12:14). Thus David is punished for his sin by the death of the child, but he is not himself put to death as punishment for his gross misdeed. In David's old age there is a struggle for succession and, ironically, it is his son by Bathsheba, Solomon, who is confirmed by the prophet Nathan as the proper heir to the throne (1 Kings 1).

1 KINGS 21:1-10 (11-14), 15-21a

First Kings 21:1-21a tells a similar tale of a wicked scheme by which Ahab, the king of Israel, is able to acquire something he craves. In this story, the king wanted to own an ancestral vineyard that belonged to Naboth from Jezreel (a city south of Mount Tabor and the Sea of Galilee) and was adjacent to the royal palace. Ahab offered to exchange this vineyard for another, but Naboth was convinced that he should keep this property within his family's possessions, and refused the king's offer. To assist Ahab in getting this property, his wife, Jezebel, arranged for a false charge to be brought against Naboth: that he had cursed God and the king. This resulted in his being executed by stoning, whereupon she told Ahab to take possession of the vineyard he coveted.

There he was confronted by Elijah, the prophet who had been informed by God of this evil scheme by which the man was killed and his property seized. Elijah predicts that Ahab will suffer the same kind of shameful death—dogs licking up his blood—that was experienced by his victim, Naboth. The prophet says that the king has sold himself "to do what was evil in the sight of the Lord," and that disaster will come upon not only him but also the whole of his posterity and his slaves. Cut off from him will be "every male, bond or free, in Israel" (1 Kings 21:21). He will have no heirs, so his dynasty will come to an end. And his wife, Jezebel, who plotted this scheme, will be devoured by dogs, as will all who are linked with Ahab (21:23-24). Ahab's deep sorrow and contrition on hearing of this destiny results in Elijah telling him that the judgment will not take place during his lifetime, but that "in [your] son's days [God] will bring disaster on this house" (21:29). Thus divine judgment for Ahab is deferred but not set aside. Moral accountability is thus transferred to the subsequent generations.

GENESIS 14:18-20 (RC)

This is a brief account of divine recognition and acclaim of Abraham through a priest named Melchizedek following Abraham's return from successful attacks against a coalition of rulers from Mesopotamia (modern Iraq) who had invaded cities in the valley of the Jordan and the Dead Sea (Gen. 14:1-17). Among those taken captive by the invaders was Lot, the nephew of Abraham (14:12). Therefore, Abraham and more than three hundred trained men from his household pursued and harassed the invaders north to Dan, on the border of

Israel. On returning to his own land with Lot and the loot, which the invaders had taken with them, he was met by King Melchizedek of Salem (= Jerusalem), whose name means "king of righteousness" or "one who rules in accord with justice" (14:18). But he is also a "priest of God Most High" (14:18). This dual role as king/priest is celebrated in Psalm 110, which was written to honor the king as God's agent of justice and power, as well as the one through whom the people have access to God. It is these kindred features of the agent of God—to rule God's people and to overcome the powers of evil—that are assigned to Christ in the letter to the Hebrews (5:5-6). His perfect obedience to God and his faithful endurance of suffering led to his role as "the source of salvation to all who obey him," symbolized in his designation by God as "a high priest after the order of Melchizedek." That role is anticipated in the blessing here pronounced on Abraham, the ancestor of Jesus.

RESPONSIVE READING
PSALM 32 or PS. 5:1-8 (RCL); PS. 32:1-8 (RCL alt.)

The psalmist pronounces the happiness that is experienced by those who turn to God for forgiveness. Those who pursue this way of contrite obedience are preserved from trouble and filled with a sense of divinely provided safety (32:6-7). Above all, they receive instruction from God, are shown the intended way for their lives, and are supported by God's steadfast love. Instead of being overcome with guilt, they are filled with joy "in the Lord" (32:8-11).

PSALM 110:1-4 (RC)

The roles of king and priest are linked in Psalm 110:1-4. This person who is to be the king of Israel is here pictured as seated at God's right hand, which is the place of honor and authority for the one who is to be God's agent. The Lord promises the priest-king that his enemies will be overcome and made subservient to him as his "footstool"—a promise recalled by Jesus in the Gospel tradition (Mark 12:35-37; Luke 20:41-44; Matt. 22:41-46). There, Jesus responds to the question as to why, if the Christ/Messiah is the son of David, David in this psalm refers to him as "my Lord." What is implied here is that the true Messiah is both a human descendant of David—and hence in line for his throne—but also has the unique relationship to God which is shown by his designation as "Lord."

GALATIANS 2:15-21 (RCL);
GAL. 2:11-21 (BCP)

In his letter to the Galatians, Paul gives more autobiographical information than in any of his other preserved letters. His major concern is whether Gentiles who become members of the new covenant people through Christ are obliged to conform to the ritual and moral requirements of the Jewish Law. After describing how he came to understand and affirm the good news in Jesus Christ, he notes how it has transformed his understanding of God's purpose for his people. This insight came to him, not through any human instruction, but "through a revelation of Jesus Christ" (1:12). Previously he had sought to destroy "the church of God," because he saw its insistence on religious and ethnic inclusiveness to be a major challenge to his own understanding and commitment to live up to the Jewish traditions developed from appropriation of the Law of Moses (1:13-14). But God's provision to him of a revelatory vision of the risen Christ was linked with his being called to carry out a mission to Gentiles. He embarked on this role without any human consultation—not even with the apostles who had already been chosen and empowered to carry forth the message of Jesus. Three years later, after a stay in Arabia and Syria (of which Damascus was the chief city), he visited the inner core of the apostles in Jerusalem, who thereafter affirmed to the new community that the former persecutor of the church was now "preaching the faith he once tried to destroy" (1:15-23). Fourteen years later, in order to be certain that he was in fact properly proclaiming the good news about Jesus, he conferred privately with the apostles. Opponents sought to convince the apostles that Paul's message of freedom from the law for those in Christ was wrong, but he did not yield on this central issue. The result was that a distinction was drawn between the two primary agents and the twin targets of the apostolic mission: Peter was the messenger of Christ to the Jews, while Paul was the primary one reaching out to the Gentiles. The divine power and purpose were at work through both of them and the movements they represented and the sharing of the symbolic act of unity—"the right hand of fellowship"—confirmed both these diverse missionary undertakings.

Verses 11-21 recount how Peter (Cephas) was confronted by Paul in Antioch. This was the third largest city in the entire Roman Empire and the capital of the combined regions of Syria and Cilicia (which included Tarsus, designated in Acts [21:39] as Paul's home city). Paul was critical of Peter for his vacillation on the issue as to whether Gentile converts must obey the Jewish dietary laws. On arrival in Antioch, Peter initially shared meals with Gentiles in the new community. But when certain members of the community arrived who were connected with

James, the leader of the Jerusalem church, Peter refused to continue this practice. He was fearful of criticism from the "circumcision party"—members of the community who insisted that Gentile converts conform to the ritual and dietary requirements of the Jewish laws. Peter's separatist position was emulated by Barnabas and other Jewish members. Paul directly challenged Peter's self-contradictory actions, reminding him that, although he was Jewish, he had been living as a Gentile, but now wanted to impose Jewish requirements on Gentile members of the new covenant people (2:13-14). He reminds Peter that it is precisely those reared in the Jewish legal tradition who had now come to recognize that one's coming into right relationship with God—"being justified"—is not the result of conformity to the Jewish legal requirements, but is based solely on trusting in Jesus Christ as God's instrument of covenant renewal. On the other hand, obedience to the Law of Moses does not establish this relationship to God and his people for anyone, Jews or Gentiles (2:15-16).

Even if, in the process of seeking to find right relationship with God, one falls into sin, this does not mean that Christ is "an agent of sin." Yet if Paul or anyone were to try to gain acceptance with God by going back to requiring obedience to the Law, they would be showing only that their moral failures demonstrated they were sinners, rather than their being those who had been able to find the right relationship. The one who trusts Christ as the sole ground of new life in the covenant people is effectively "dead to the law." It has no control and no potential to reshape his life. Specifically, the ground of the true relationship is the death of Christ. But it is he who now lives and gives life to those who trust in him as God's agent of human renewal. His love was manifest in his death for the sake of others, and now continues to be evident and active in the new life, which he provides: "the Christ who lives in me." Paul's refusal to place those in the new community under obligation to conform to the requirements of the Law is based on his insight that he, like all members of the new community, now "lives by faith in the Son of God." If the basis for this relationship were to be conformity to the law, "then Christ died to no purpose" (3:20-21). This is the radically new ground for men and women to find acceptance with God: it rests solely on what God has done through Christ, and is in no way a human achievement.

> COMING INTO RIGHT RELATIONSHIP WITH GOD IS BASED SOLELY ON TRUSTING IN JESUS CHRIST AS GOD'S INSTRUMENT OF COVENANT RENEWAL.

1 CORINTHIANS 11:23-26 (RC)

The liturgical dimensions of the life of the new community are set forth in 1 Cor. 11:23-26. Paul asserts that he is not inventing the details or the wording of this mode of worship, but is transmitting what had been passed on to him by "the Lord." This feature of the letters of Paul is rare, in that it matches what was passed on in the Gospel tradition, where the account is given of Jesus' final meal with his disciples (Matt. 26:26-28; Mark 14:23-24; Luke 22:17-20), although there are some differences in details. Both traditions highlight the bread and the cup, the former linked with the body of Jesus and the contents of the cup as his lifeblood, which is to be "poured out for many." The blood in both traditions is seen as the instrument by which the sacrificial death of Jesus seals God's covenant with the new community.

THE GOSPEL
LUKE 7:36—8:3 (RCL); LUKE 7:36-50 (BCP)

The RCL includes two passages from Luke that highlight the role of women in the community of faith, the first of which is also in BCP. Luke reports what occurred at the home of a Pharisee who had invited Jesus to dinner. When Jesus took his place, "a woman of the city . . . , a sinner"—clearly a prostitute—came and stood by his feet, began wetting them with her tears, wiping them with her hair and kissing them, and then anointing them with ointment. She is overcome with contrition for her sinful mode of life, and turns to Jesus as the agent who can enable her to gain forgiveness and divine acceptance. Jesus' host, however, is concerned only with Jesus' seeming inability to recognize her sinful mode of life and the resulting ritual impurity, which he assumed would have been brought about by her physical contact with Jesus.

Jesus' response to the host's perplexity is to suggest an analogy between the forgiveness he is bestowing on this sinful woman and the creditor who forgives the obligation of both a debtor who owes him a great deal and one who owes a far lesser amount. The one who will be filled with greater gratitude is the one who was forgiven much more. This woman is not only greatly in need of forgiveness, but she has publicly demonstrated her confidence in Jesus and her concern for gaining purification through him by her having kissed his feet and wet them with her tears, as well as her anointing his feet. She is the embodiment of one who is deeply in need of moral cleansing and renewal, and who perceives Jesus to be the one through whom that new status can be achieved. The climax of the relationship comes when Jesus pronounces forgiveness of her sins. The other guests question his identity and hence his right to make such a declaration, since it implies a divine transaction. But Jesus tells the woman that her trust in him as the one through whom cleansing and forgiveness can be gained has brought her into right relationship with God and delivered her from the punitive consequences of her sinful way of life: "Your faith has saved you." Hence she may "go in peace," confident that Jesus has enabled her to be delivered from the impact of her immoral career; thus, she is ready to enter a new mode of life. (The story of Jesus being anointed is told also in a briefer version in Matt. 26:6-13 and Mark 14:3-9, and takes place in the house of "Simon the leper," rather than that of a Pharisee. The woman is not a harlot, but someone of considerable wealth, as evident in the very costly ointment that she pours on the head of Jesus. The complaint of the disciples is the seeming waste of this expensive ointment, the money for which could have been expended for feeding the poor. Jesus commends their concern for the poor but asserts that the anointing is a preparation for his death and burial, which will assure the woman enduring and worldwide commendation.)

The second story in the RCL Gospel for today is in Luke 8:1-3. After a summary of Jesus' itinerant ministry, accompanied by the twelve disciples, there is mention of "some women" who accompanied these itinerant messengers of the good news. These women were especially eager to support Jesus' work because they had themselves directly benefited from the healings and exorcisms that he had performed for their benefit. Two of them—one named

THE WOMAN HAS PUBLICLY DEMONSTRATED HER CONFIDENCE IN JESUS AND HER CONCERN FOR GAINING PURIFICATION THROUGH HIM.

Joanna, the wife of Chuza (a manager for Herod Antipas, the son of Herod the Great and tetrarch of Galilee and Perea) and the other Susanna—provided for the material needs of Jesus and the disciples.

Forgiveness leads not only to pardon for one's sin but to renewal of relationships—with God and with other human beings, both within and outside the community of faith. How does one achieve a new beginning in life? It is not a matter of simply closing the door on what is past, but facing candidly the errors one has made, gaining forgiveness from God through Christ, and entering a new way of life characterized by love—even for one's enemies—and taking the initiative to overcome the powers of evil and to gain reconciliation with those from whom one feels estranged and alienated. This is the thrust of Paul's call to share in "the ministry of reconciliation" (2 Cor. 5:18-19).

LUKE 9:11b-17 (RC)

Luke 9:11b-17 is a somewhat abbreviated version of the story in Mark 6:30-44 of Jesus' feeding the five thousand. Here Jesus is speaking to the crowds that follow him concerning the "kingdom of God"—the new era in which God's purpose will prevail in the world, the powers of evil will be overcome, and the needs of his people will be fully supplied. The coming of this kingdom is foreshadowed by (1) his curing those who are in need of healing (9:11) and (2) his provision of food for them "in a deserted place" (9:12-17), just as God had provided manna for Israel in the desert on their way to the promised land, as described in the Pentateuch (Exod. 16:1-36; Num. 11:4-9). In addition to this link with the story of God's provision for his people in the time of the exodus of Israel from Egypt to the promised land, there is also clearly an intended correspondence between this account and the significance of the Last Supper as it is set forth in the Gospel tradition (Mark 14:22-25; Matt. 26:26-29; Luke 22:15-20) and by Paul (1 Cor. 11:23-26). As in the Markan account of this miraculous provision for God's people, the language of the eucharist is reflected here: "He took, he blessed, he broke, he gave. . . ." The divine provision through Christ for the nurture of his new people is a repeated motif in the Gospel tradition. Symbolized by the Last Supper, it is a part of the ongoing experience of the new covenant people, as it was of the people of Israel as they were led from enslavement in Egypt to the new, divinely provided mode of life that was theirs in the Promised Land. This no longer merely a promise; it is a transforming reality already being experienced by the members of the new community.

THIRD SUNDAY
AFTER PENTECOST

JUNE 24, 2001 / PROPER 7

REVISED COMMON	EPISCOPAL (BCP)	ROMAN CATHOLIC
Isa. 65:1-9	Zech. 12:8-10; 13:1	Zech 12:10-11; 13:1
or 1 Kings 19:1-4		
(5-7), 8-15a		
Ps. 22:19-28	Ps. 63:1-8	Ps. 63:2-6, 8-9
or Psalms 42–43		
Gal. 3:23-29	Gal. 3:23-29	Gal. 3:26-29
Luke 8:26-39	Luke 9:18-24	Luke 9:18-24

FIRST READING
ISAIAH 65:1-9 (RCL)

Isaiah 55–66 probably dates from the period after the Jews' return from their exile in Babylon had begun, but before the governmental reforms of the rebuilt nation were launched by Ezra and Nehemiah in the fifth century B.C.E. Far from existing in a secret realm that is difficult of access for humans, God is reported in 65:1 as eager to be sought out and found by the people, even though they did not inquire about God (65:1). God kept announcing his identity and presence to them, hoping that they would respond. Instead, these "rebellious people" have not called on God's name, but are following their own way of life, dependent on their own schemes and "devices." Their behavior involves not merely indifference: they continually perform in offensive ways, taking part in heathen sacrificial ceremonies, offering incense at sites of idolatrous worship, and engaging in veneration of the dead. They spend nights in seats of pagan worship, eating and drinking items forbidden by the Law of Moses—while claiming to have achieved a kind of holiness that requires them to keep separate from others. Their shameful liturgical tactics are like offensive smoke in the divine nostrils (65:5), yet they insist that their self-styled holy condition requires them to keep aloof from others. Here they are warned that God will speak out in criticism of them, and will act in ways that will repay them for not only their violations of the Law, but also for the misdeeds of their ancestors, who long ago began offering incense at the pagan holy places (65:6-7).

The acts in which they participate and for which they are to be punished include their participation in the worship of other deities, which often was carried out at certain elevated locations often referred to in scripture as "high places." It is alluded to in Isa 65:7 as "offering incense on the mountains." They keep provoking God by the pagan sacrifices they offer, by their devotion to the dead, by spending nights in pagan shrines, and by their eating swine's flesh and other foods prohibited by the Law of Moses (65:1-4). They claim to be holy and insist that other peoples keep their distance from them. But, in fact, though they are the descendants of God's people, they have become a bad odor in the nostrils of God, and should be prepared for the divine judgment that is to fall on them because of their abandonment of the proper covenant relationship to God and the mode of life and worship that should be theirs. God will no longer be silent and inactive on this fundamental matter of the moral and religious misdeeds of those who claim to be his people. They are to be held accountable for not only their own misdeeds, but also for those of their ancestors (65:5-7).

Yet God will preserve the faithful remnant of his people, just as a vine-grower is careful to preserve those portions of his vineyard that are the most fruitful basis for good wine. There will be a faithful remnant that will be preserved through the coming time of judgment. From them will come the heirs who will take over the land of promise and dwell there. They will be descendants of both Jacob (the figure for the northern tribes of Israel) and Judah, representing those who dwell in the southern area around Jerusalem. Together they comprise God's "chosen" people (65:9), as in the era before the split took place between the two sets of tribes.

1 KINGS 19:1-15 (RCL alt.)

During the time of Ahab, king of Israel (from about 869 to 850 B.C.E.), his successful reign was dramatically challenged by the prophet Elijah when fire from the Lord destroyed the altar erected for worship of the god Baal and his priests were killed (1 Kings 18:20-40). Jezebel, the wife of Ahab, vowed to kill Elijah in retaliation (19:1-2). He fled into the desert of Sinai, where he was fed by an angel of God and instructed to go to Mount Horeb (also known as Sinai), which lies between Egypt and the land of Israel. God's powerful presence became evident to him through the powerful wind and fire, which descended on the mountain while the prophet hid in a cave. After telling God of his protests against the Israelites' failure to live according to the covenant, of his having killed the false prophets, and of the Israelites' murderous response and their attacks on the altars and prophets of God, he is instructed to anoint Jehu as king of Israel and Elisha as the prophet to replace him (19:11-16). Thereafter, Elisha became a disciple of Elijah (19:19-21). Thus God's rule of the people is concretely evident in the rulers and messengers that he provides for guiding their common life.

ZECHARIAH 12:8-10; 13:1 (BCP);
ZECH. 12:10-11; 13:1 (RC)

In Zech. 12:8-11 and 13:1, there is a promise of the victory of Judah and Jerusalem over their enemies. Their status and strength will be transformed so that even the weakest among the people will gain strength like that of David, and the Davidic dynasty will attain status and power which is analogous to that of God and his angels. Human weakness will be replaced by divinely granted strength, in order that God's purpose for his people can be achieved. All the enemies of the people of Jerusalem will be destroyed in accord with the plan of God. At the same time, the royal family and the people as a whole will be filled with contrition for their mistreatment of God's prophetic messenger to them, and will mourn his death like that of an only child. The mourners will include those of the royal ("house of David") and priestly ("house of Levi") families, and their wives and families (Zech. 12:10-11). The contrite people's "looking on the one they have pierced" (12:10) is quoted in John 19:37 as having been fulfilled by a witness at the death of Jesus. The subsequent promises include a fountain for the house of David and the people of Jerusalem, which will constitute a divine resource "to cleanse them from sin and impurity" (12:12—3:1). Both the royal dynasty and all who dwell in Jerusalem are to share in this purification and renewal of the covenant people.

RESPONSIVE READING
PSALM 22:19-28 (RCL)

In this lament at God's seeming abandonment of the psalmist, there is an appeal to and a celebration of God's ongoing care of the people—protecting them from various kinds of attacks, both by human and bestial enemies, although the animals (dogs, lions, oxen) are probably symbolic figures representing human enemies (vv. 19-21). Because God has intervened to preserve the psalmist, there is ongoing praise uttered before the assembled community and a call to all the members who claim to trust the Lord to praise, give glory, and "stand in awe of him." When they were undergoing affliction, God was attentive to their needs and to their appeals for help (vv. 22-24).

In the final lines of this psalm (vv. 10-11), it is evident that the speaker is the king, whose trust is in God and whose confidence in God will be confirmed. The longing of the soul for God is compared with the weakness and thirst that one feels when out in the desert. To overcome this longing and need, one may go to the sanctuary where God dwells. Now the radiant presence of God is visible to the high priest on entering the innermost portion of the temple: the Holy of Holies. But this divine accessibility is also experienced inwardly as loving support. This is more highly prized than life itself and leads to ongoing praise to the God by whom it is provided. The proper response to this divine sustenance is lifelong praise and invocation of the name of God (vv. 1-4).

Second Reading
GALATIANS 3:23-29 (RCL/BCP); GAL. 3:26-29 (RC)

Galatians was written by Paul to Christians in Asia Minor (now Turkey) who were of Celtic (Greek: Galatian) origin. It deals with the issue raised by some Christians of Jewish background who were insisting that the Galatian converts must conform to the Law of Moses in addition to their faith in Jesus as the Messiah. Cephas (Peter), on visiting them, sided with those Christians of Jewish background who insisted that members of the new community must be circumcised, as the Jewish converts obviously had been. The other apostles had agreed in principle that this ritual requirement was not to be imposed on Gentile converts (2:1-10). When Peter visited the Galatian Christians, he at first had full fellowship with them, but then separated himself from them out of fear of being attacked by those insisting on the circumcision of all Christians.

Paul reminded the apostles and the Galatian Christians that the sole basis for their being right with God and for their membership in the covenant people was their trust in Jesus Christ as God's agent for setting them in this right relationship. No one attains this membership in God's people by conforming to the requirements set forth in the Jewish Law. Going back to Abraham, the ground of right relationship with God has been trust in the divine promises and God's historic actions for the renewal of his people. The transforming of God's people has now come about through the death and resurrection of Jesus, not through the Law of Moses (Gal. 2:15-21). To rely on one's own moral performance for divine acceptance leads to a curse for failure to conform completely (3:10-13). The blessed participation in the covenant people promised to Abraham has become available through Jesus and is confirmed by the Holy Spirit at work in the lives of the faithful (3:14). The purpose of the Law was to counter the human tendency toward violation of the divine will (3:19-20), but its effect has been to point out how prone to moral failure all humans are apart from Christ (3:21-22).

Paul's major aim in this letter (3:23-29) is to show that even Jews who had the law of God were merely restrained by it—not morally renewed. The law served as a custodian or school teacher who exercised some moral control over those who sought to conform to it. But the result was enslavement to certain moral and ritual principles, rather than enabling men and women to enter fully and effectively the life of the new people of God. Now they are liberated by Christ from this frustrating enterprise and have become in a full sense members of God's new people.

> THE NEW COMMUNITY "IN CHRIST" IS TO ELIMINATE ALL HUMANLY IMPOSED DISTINCTIONS.

Now they become members through faith (trusting in what God has done through Christ), and public testimony to this relationship is given when they accept baptism in his name. This new community, which Paul defines succinctly as "in Christ," has eliminated all humanly imposed distinctions: Jew and Gentile ("Greek"), slave and free, male and female. Until the coming of Christ, all these categories had had profound effect for determining one's status within the Jewish community at that time. Now all these requirements have been put aside by the life, death, and resurrection of Christ, and by the ongoing work of the Spirit, which God has sent into the hearts of his new people. This new, intimate relationship with God is epitomized in their addressing God the Father as "Abba"—the affectionate Aramaic term for father comparable to modern "Papa" or "Daddy" (4:4-6).

THE GOSPEL
LUKE 8:26-39 (RCL)

This lection is Luke's version of the story of the healing of the demoniac at a Graeco-Roman city east of the Sea of Galilee. Some of the Greek manuscripts of Luke name the city as Gadara, and some as Gergesa, but most call it Gerasa, which was one of the largest cities in the region. Gadara (which is found in some manuscripts) is closer to the Sea of Galilee, as is implied in 8:26, and was a center for Greek philosophy and literature. The existence of a huge herd of swine there is a further indication that it was in predominantly Gentile territory, because Jews were forbidden to eat the flesh of pigs (Lev. 11:7; Deut. 14:8). The demon-possessed man's unacceptable condition by Jewish standards is further evident in his naked appearance and his living among tombs, which would have made him ritually impure through contact with the dead (Lev. 21:11). Yet another indicator of his Gentile identity is that he had been given the name *Legio*, which was used for Roman military troops, but seems here to refer to the army of demons to which he had become subject (Luke 8:30; Mark 5:9). The demons (only in Luke's version) ask that they not be sent into "the abyss," which was perceived to be the underworld, the realm of darkness that was the abode of the dead (Rom. 10:7; Rev. 9:1-11; 20:1-3). Instead, they were driven into the herd of nearby swine, which thereupon rushed down the steep bank and drowned in the lake (8:33).

When word spreads concerning what Jesus had done in healing the demoniac, the whole region is filled with fear and "all the people" asked Jesus to leave. There is wide recognition of the divine power at work through Jesus, but it does not fit the standard values and methods of the society, and accordingly evokes fear and anxiety

WHAT JESUS HAD DONE DID NOT FIT THE STANDARD VALUES AND METHODS OF SOCIETY.

rather than respect or gratitude for the divine results accomplished through Jesus (8:37). The healed man is urged by Jesus to report "how much *God* has done for you," but tells throughout the whole area "what *Jesus* had done for him" (8:39). The impact of the healing activities of Jesus among Gentiles is here dramatically evident.

For Jesus, there are no ethnic or ritual qualifications to be insisted upon for those to whom he reaches out with his message and ministry of God's grace. There is no preselection of the audience or the potential beneficiaries of Jesus' words and works—and this is intended to characterize the work of his followers as they proclaim his message of grace and serve as the divinely empowered instruments of God's love. All are invited to share in the transforming benefits of what God has done and continues to do through Jesus Christ.

LUKE 9:18-24 (BCP/RC)

This lection builds on a subsequent passage in Luke 9:18-24, where Jesus requests and receives from the disciples reports as to whom he is perceived to be by the people who hear of him and by the disciples themselves. Their answers are three: John the Baptist, Elijah, and "one of the prophets [who] has risen." Jesus' call of the disciples to follow him was modeled after the call of Elisha by Elijah described in 1 Kings 19:19-21, which involved a break with the family. The call of John the Baptist in Mark 1:2-4 begins with a quotation from an Elijah tradition (Mal. 3:1—4:5), and John's garb resembles that of Elijah (2 Kings 1:8). The central feature in all these traditions is the expectation of an eschatological messenger and agent of God who will prepare for the coming of God's triumphant rule in the world. This matches with the role of the prophetic voice foretold in Isa. 40:4-5, which Luke extends beyond the briefer quote in Mark 1:2-3 to include the promise that "all flesh [= all humanity] will see the salvation of God." The outreach of this prophetic figure is also expanded by Luke in his report that among those who ask how they should respond to this call to repentance are such alien figures from the standpoint of Jewish piety as tax-collectors (who collaborate with the Romans) and soldiers (who maintain Roman rule) who came to John to be baptized (Luke 3:7-8). A clear indication of the continuity of God's purpose as disclosed in the Law and the prophets with what is happening through Jesus is provided at the transfiguration of Jesus when Moses and Elijah appear (Luke 9:28-25).

In contrast to the identification of Jesus with these figures from the past is the testimony of Peter that Jesus is "the Messiah of God." Lest the disciples see in this claim a promise of speedy defeat of the political and cosmic powers of evil, Jesus tells them that they are not to make that claim in his behalf now, since he must first experience rejection by the Jewish leadership. His opponents include (1) elders, who served in the collaborationist council [Greek, the *synedrion*]; (2) the chief priests, whose leader (the high priest) was appointed by the Roman senate; and (3) the scribes, whose task was to transmit the interpretations of the Jewish scriptures to their contemporaries. It is ironic that included in Jesus' role as "Son of Man," is his experience of rejection and death prior to his role in the ultimate triumph, through him, of God's purpose for renewal of his covenant people and of the creation. But the climax will come in his ultimate vindication, because this title derives from the promises in Dan. 7:13-14 that to "one like a human being" [= Son of Man] will be given by God "dominion and glory and kingship," that "all peoples, nations, and languages shall serve him," and that "his dominion is everlasting." This is the coming of the kingdom of God, predicted by the prophets of Israel, now announced by Jesus, and to be prayed for by his followers in the Lord's Prayer. Clear indications of what is happening to prepare for that kingdom, what the qualifications are for sharing in it, and the transformation of his followers and of the world as a whole are given in the Gospel tradition. It involves the renewal of the creation, not merely entering a pious state of mind.

Those who claim to be followers of Jesus as Son of Man must be prepared to experience suffering and rejection, however, including ongoing threats to life itself, here pictured as taking up one's cross daily. But those who are put to death because of their following Jesus will find ultimate renewal of life in the age to come, when God's rule is established in all the world (9:27).

THE NATIVITY OF
ST. JOHN THE BAPTIST

JUNE 24, 2001

REVISED COMMON AND EPISCOPAL (BCP)
Mal. 3:1–4
  or Isa. 40:1–11
Ps. 141
Acts 13:13–26
Luke 1:57–67 (68–80)

ROMAN CATHOLIC
Isa. 49:1–6

Ps. 139:1–3, 13–15
Acts 13:22–26
Luke 1:57–66, 80

FIRST READING
MALACHI 3:1–4 (RCL/BCP)

The role of the expected "messenger of the covenant" is to carry out
God's punitive judgment on the disobedient people. His task is to prepare the way
for the coming of "the Lord," who will suddenly appear in the temple—even
though Jewish tradition held that God was invisibly present in the innermost
shrine of the Temple. The people claim that they are seeking the Lord and that
they will take delight in his coming, but they must be prepared for severe punishment when he comes. Indeed, they may not be able to survive this time of
judgment. The coming one is compared to such agents of cleansing and purifying as the metal-worker who, by fire, removes impurities from the metal, or the
fuller: the worker who cleans, bleaches, or thickens cloth.

Chief among those who will be refined by this agent of God will be the
"descendants of Levi," who were the tribe of Israel linked with priestly duties.
In spite of the earlier traditions that report attacks by the Levites on other tribes
of Israel (as in Genesis 34) and the warning that they would experience divine
judgment (Genesis 49), they eventually became the curators and operators of the
Urim and Thummim, which was a device for determining God's response to
yes/no questions raised by the leadership of the people (Exod. 28:30).

The priestly status and role of the Levites are specified in Deut. 18:1–8, where
rules are given that they are to receive food from the offerings that are presented
in the Temple, but they are to gain no inheritances, although they may continue
to benefit from property already owned by their family. It seems that they were
subsequently demoted as a group to a lower position on the priestly staff (2 Kings

23:8-9) and that some of them became involved in pagan religious practices (Ezek. 44:10-14). After the return from the exile in Babylon, there was a clear division between them and the priests, although in Num. 18:2-6 this is read back into the preexilic time. Thus the process of purifying "the descendants of Levi" is predicted in Mal. 3:3, by which they will be able to "present offerings to the Lord in righteousness." The one chosen and empowered to launch this program of purification of the people and to prepare them for God's ultimate messenger (Mal. 3:1) is identified in Luke 1:17 as John the Baptist.

ISAIAH 49:1-6 (RC)

The servant of the Lord announces his mission, beginning with the claim that he was called by God to this role before he was born, and that he was named by God while he was still in his mother's womb. His work is pictured by comparing his ability to speak with a "sharp sword," and his function as God's agent of renewal is like a "polished arrow." Yet he is the representative of the whole faithful remnant of Israel. Even though his work in calling his people to fulfill their role as covenant people has resulted in disappointment in the past, he is assured that his "cause is with the Lord," and that he will be ultimately rewarded for his efforts. God has shaped him before he was born to carry out a major role as servant of God in restoring Israel to right relationship to Yahweh. He is God's servant, honored in the sight of God and empowered by strength from God to fulfill his task. Those who share in the benefits that come from his redemptive role are not only the tribes of Israel, who will be brought back to God, but also all the nations of the world. Thus this servant is to be "as a light to the nations" and, in this way, the renewal and fulfillment of human destiny that constitutes God's "salvation" will "reach to the end of the earth." It is to be perceived that, through John the Baptist, this program of divine renewal of the covenant and of the creation will be launched.

RESPONSIVE READING
PSALM 141 (RCL)

Here the psalmist calls upon God to enable him to fulfill an inward, spiritual role comparable to that of the priests, who offer up to God incense and sacrifices. At the same time, he needs divine protection lest what he speaks or what enters his mind may lead to evil deeds—by himself, or in association with other evildoers. He does not want to be enticed by the "delicacies" of their evil thoughts and schemes (141:1-4).

PSALM 139:1-3, 13-15 (RC)

All the thoughts and actions of the psalmist are known to God, who perceives both the directions in which he moves and the places where he settles down, as well as all the "ways" in which he plans and follows through his way of life. Even before words are articulated by him, God knows fully what is taking shape in his thoughts. In what follows in the psalm, he declares how God surrounds him with limits and actions in a manner that directly affects the course of his life, and does so in ways that are beyond the power of the psalmist to comprehend or to imitate (139:5-7). This divine perception is possible because it was God who shaped him in his mother's womb.

SECOND READING
ACTS 13:13-26 (RCL);
ACTS 13:22-26 (RC)

Setting sail from Paphos on the eastern end of the island of Cyprus, Paul and his associates reached the city of Perga in the south-central section of Asia Minor then known as Pamphylia, which was founded by the Greeks after the Trojan War (probably in the twelfth century B.C.E.). The Romans took over that area, which had a sizable Jewish community at that time, in the second century B.C.E. Tarsus, Paul's hometown, was along the coast well to the east. Proceeding northward, they came to another city named Antioch, located in Pisidia in the central region of Asia Minor known as Galatia, named for the Celtics (or Gauls) who had migrated there from northern Europe.

Paul attended the Jewish synagogue in Antioch and took up the offer of its leaders to address the group gathered there. In his speech he sketched the history of God's people, Israel, describing their divine deliverance from slavery in Egypt, the land that was given to them and the anointing of David as their king (13:21-22), as described in 1 Sam. 16:1-13, attested as the one whose descendant will carry out God's plan for his people. It is from this man's posterity that Jesus has come to Israel as its Savior, as attested by John the Baptist and now by the apostolic messengers—even though the people of Jerusalem as a whole and their leaders did not recognize him as God's agent of renewal of the covenant people (13:23-26). God's confirmation of Jesus in this role of renewal was given dramatically by his having been raised from the dead (13:30). It is declared by Paul to have been attested by witnesses and to be in accord with the promises reported in scripture (13:31-39). There is also a solemn warning of divine punishment for those who refuse to believe that he has been raised from the dead (13:41a = Hab.

1:5a). For those who do believe in his resurrection, there is assurance of an unprecedented work of God (vv. 41b), as is documented by the testimony of those who have witnessed his having been raised from the dead.

THE GOSPEL
LUKE 1:57-67 (68-80) (RCL);
LUKE 1:57-66, 80 (RC)

The birth of John the Baptist as heir to the priest Zechariah by the previously barren Elizabeth was foretold by an angel (Luke 1:1-23). It is described in 1:57-66, and was foreseen by his father, Zechariah, as preparation for the coming of the Lord (1:67-80). His doubt about this occurring led to his losing the power to speak (1:18-20), which he regained when he gave the name John for his newly born son (1:57-64). It is when the virgin Mary—now pregnant—visited Elizabeth (1:39-45) that both of them uttered praise to God (1:42-45; 46-55) for the divine acts by which the agents were to be born who would bring about renewal of God's people: John and Jesus.

These evidences of divine action and purpose lead to praise but also to astonishment and puzzlement as to what the roles of these two are to be (1:65-66). The Holy Spirit leads Zechariah to utter the prophetic hymn, the "Benedictus" (1:67), in which are announced the respective roles of John as the prophet who prepares the way of the Lord and of Jesus as the Savior from the house of David, through whom the covenant promises to Abraham will be fulfilled and who will bring to God's people knowledge of salvation, light, and peace.

It is in the poetic prophecy of John's father, Zechariah, that the details of the divine preparation and fulfillment for the coming of the Messiah are set forth (1:68-79). He begins with praise to God, who has already begun the announced program of his presence and liberating activity among his people. The agent by which this divine purpose will be accomplished, "the horn of salvation," is already present in the world, having been born as a descendant of David. David's celebration of what God has done through him for the freedom and renewal of his people and the defeat of his enemies (2 Sam. 22:1-51; Ps.7 18) is not merely for what has already

> THE AGENT BY WHICH THE DIVINE PURPOSE WILL BE ACCOMPLISHED IS ALREADY PRESENT IN THE WORLD, HAVING BEEN BORN AS A DESCENDANT OF DAVID.

happened, but looks forward to the "salvation" and "love" of God which will bless "David and his descendants forever" (22:51). This promise of God's renewal and transformation of his people goes back to the time of Abraham (22:73; Gen. 22:15-18) and includes "all the nations of the earth" who will "gain blessing" through the divinely given descendant of Abraham. God's people will experience defeat of their "enemies" and will live "in holiness and righteousness before him all the days of our lives" (1:73-74). The role of John the Baptist, who is here identified as "the prophet of the Most High," is to "go before the Lord to prepare his way," and to make them ready to hear his message of "the forgiveness of their sins through the tender mercy of God" (1:77-78). That day has now dawned "from on high" with the birth of Jesus, through whom the light of the knowledge of God is reaching out to those "who sit in darkness and in the shadow of death, to guide our feet into the way of peace" (1:79). Instead of darkness, light! Instead of conflict, peace! Instead of the present era of evil and ignorance, "the day shall dawn upon us from on high."

It is the role of John to prepare the way for the one whom God has sent to accomplish this cosmic and deeply personal renewal (1:80). From childhood onward, John continued to grow and to gain strength through the Spirit at work within him. He remained withdrawn in the wilderness area of the Jordan Valley, until the time arrived for his public proclamation concerning Jesus and the outpouring of the Spirit, in preparation for the new age that was dawning in accord with the prophetic promise of God.

The message of these stories of God's sending his agents and messengers in ways that would never be expected by ordinary humans matches the words of the familiar hymn, "God moves in a mysterious way his wonders to perform." God's people must be prepared to see that God always has been—and still is!—at work in the lives of people and of world leaders in ways that will accomplish God's purpose. Through the weak, the humble, the scorned, the martyred, God continues to work to show love and forgiveness, to call the self-centered to turn from self-seeking to share in the transforming work of God in and through Christ.

FOURTH SUNDAY
AFTER PENTECOST

JULY 1, 2001
THIRTEENTH SUNDAY IN ORDINARY TIME
PROPER 8

REVISED COMMON	EPISCOPAL (BCP)	ROMAN CATHOLIC
1 Kings 19:15-16, 19-21 or 2 Kings 2:1-2, 6-14	1 Kings 19:15-16, 19-21	1 Kings 19:16b, 19-21
Ps. 16 or Ps. 77:1-2, 11-20	Ps. 16 or 16:5-11	Ps. 16:1-2, 5, 7-11
Gal. 5:1, 13-25	Gal. 5:1, 13-25	Gal. 5:1, 13-18
Luke 9:51-62	Luke 9:51-62	Luke 9:51-62

FIRST READING
1 KINGS 19:15-16, 19-21 (RCL/BCP);
1 KINGS 19:16b, 19-21 (RC)

This reading follows the account of Elijah's victory over the priests of Baal (1 Kings 18:20-46). When Ahab reported to Jezebel Elijah's triumph over, and execution of, the priests of Baal, she announced her intention to destroy him. He fled to Beersheba in the south of Judah and then on into the wilderness, experiencing an encounter with God and with an angel of the LORD on the way. After a journey of forty days and forty nights, he finally reached Mount Horeb, another name for Mount Sinai (1 Kings 19:1-10). Asked by "the word of the LORD" why he had come there, he stated that his zeal for the LORD and his deep regrets that Israel had abandoned its relationship to and obligations with Yahweh, had dismantled the altars, and killed the prophets who were bringing them God's message. He alone is left, and they are seeking to take his life as well. Then he was instructed to go and stand on the mountain: there he is to have an encounter with Yahweh. This takes place, preceded by wind, an earthquake, and fire. When he told the LORD why he had fled—because the people had abandoned the covenant and killed the prophets of Yahweh—he was sent back to anoint a new king (Jehu) and a prophet (Elisha), who would be able to overcome their enemies and to support the faithful remnant of the people who refused to worship Baal (19:11-18).

The lection resumes at vv. 19-21, where Elijah finds Elisha, the son of a farmer in the northern hills of Palestine, in the kingdom of Aram, which often attacked Israel (1 Kings 15; 20) until it was taken over by Israel's King Jeroboam II during his long reign (786–746 B.C.E.). Elijah's placing of his mantle on the shoulders of Elisha as he plowed is clearly symbolic of the transfer of the prophetic role, as the young man realizes. But he must first return to bid farewell to his parents and to serve the needs of his people by preparing food for them to eat. Only then does he feel free to leave them and to become a follower and a servant of Elijah. The call of God to the role of prophet does not remove the sense of love and obligation to his family.

2 KINGS 2:1-2, 6-14 (RCL alt.)

Elijah, whose name means, "My God is Yahweh," is both messenger of God and agent for bringing about God's punishment of the disobedient leaders and people of Israel (2 Kings 1). He has carried out that role and his prophetic mission is complete, so God now has at hand a replacement for him: Elisha, whose name means, "My God is salvation." The two of them go together to Bethel (which means "house of God"). Clearly they are both perceived as living in the presence of and in accord with the purpose of God. Their role as representative of God's people is further indicated by their descending into the valley of the Jordan and to Jericho. It was there that God gathered the people of Israel and then held back the waters of the river so that they could cross over into the promised land (Joshua 1–3). Implicit here is that, as the people move to obedience to God's messengers, they will enter a new relationship with God and a new era in their history as God's people.

RESPONSIVE READING
PSALM 16 or 77:1-2, 11-20 (RCL); 16:5-11 (BCP alt.); 16:1-2, 5, 7-11 (RC)

God is the refuge and protector, the master and guide ("Lord"), and the sole source of good for the psalmist. God's care and direction of the people continue day and night, providing assurance and stability in life. This produces joy in the "heart" and in the "soul," which refers to the whole of human life, as is evident when Adam was created as a "living soul" (Gen. 2:7). For the faithful, there is assurance that God will show them "the path of life" by which they are to live. This will lead to ongoing life in God's "presence" and the joys of continuing at God's right hand "forevermore."

SECOND READING

GALATIANS 5:1, 13-25 (RCL, BCP);
GAL. 5:1, 13-18 (RC)

The power and moral guidelines for life in the new community are presented by Paul in Galatians in a twofold way, by which he emphasizes both freedom and moral qualities that are to characterize the people of God. Following his contrast of the two modes of covenant relationship—(1) conformity to the requirements of the Law, symbolized by the slave child of Abraham and the rules given at Mount Sinai and (2) the freedom from the Law that has been made possible through the death and resurrection of Christ (Gal. 4:21-31)—Paul declares that the freedom that Christ has brought for his people (5:1) must be preserved. To insist on conformity to legal requirements would be to submit oneself to a new form of slavery.

Yet the members of the community have choices to make that are of major importance for their moral life and their relationship with God. They are to be careful not to exploit their freedom in Christ by engaging in "self-indulgence"—for which the Greek word is *sarx*, which means literally "flesh." It does not mean the material aspect of human existence as contrasted with the spiritual. Instead it implies the weakness, frailty, and unwarranted self-confidence that characterize human life. Instead of relying on the self-serving impulses and limited resources of humanity, one is called to depend on the power that God provides for direction and the ability to carry out moral and social purposes.

"Freedom" as Paul perceives it (5:13-14) is far removed from radical individualism and self-gratification. Rather it is the uncoerced decision to commit oneself to the concerns, needs, and welfare of one another within the shared life of the new community. He states this in radical form: "Become slaves to one another." The basis for this charge is the commandment found in the Law of Moses (Lev. 19:18), which Paul perceives to be the epitome of the Law: "You shall love your neighbor as you love yourself." It is by taking on this responsible relationship to one's neighbor that true freedom is achieved! Conversely, to live by attacking one another will result in one's being "consumed" by this evil, misguided self-seeking (5:15).

> "FREEDOM" AS PAUL PERCEIVES IT IS FAR REMOVED FROM RADICAL INDIVIDUALISM AND SELF-GRATIFICATION.

There follows a detailed contrast between a life lived in reliance upon the Spirit and one dependent upon the "flesh," which is self-seeking existence. These two ways of life are directly "opposed to each other." Yet the life in the power of the Spirit is not based on conformity to the requirements of the Law. The self-centered life results in immoral sexual relations, gross self-indulgence, idolatry, hostility, sorcery, conflict, carousing, envy, and anger. In short, the wholly self-centered life leads one into an existence dominated by conflict and debased behavior, with the result that one can have no place in the kingdom of God (5:16-21).

Life in reliance on God's Spirit, however, produces an utterly different manner of life (5:22-26). The virtues highlighted here are not simply human moral actions, but are seen as "the fruit" which the Spirit is said to produce in the lives of God's people. These include virtues, which are essential in the biblical tradition, such as "love, joy, peace," but also those which are important elements in Stoic ethics: "kindness, generosity, faithfulness, gentleness, self-control." Those who have identified themselves as belonging to the crucified and risen Christ experience death to their former way of life—the selfish life seeking only personal gratification and control. This has been replaced by the power of the Spirit, which produces true virtue and guides the life of the faithful, with conceit, competition, and envy overcome (5:22-26) and replaced by the loving concern for spiritual health of the community of God's people.

THE GOSPEL
LUKE 9:51-62

More than half of this passage appears only in the Gospel of Luke (9:51-56, 60-62), while the rest derives from what scholars have called the Sayings Source Q that was drawn upon by Luke and Matthew (8:19-22). There are three major messages in this section of Luke. (1) The rejection of Jesus or his message by any group should not be the occasion for his followers to call down divine judgment ("fire from heaven") to fall upon them. This is the case even with the Samaritans, who claimed to be the true descendants of Israel but who were despised by the Jews as a whole because they had their own sacred mountain (Gerizim), their own temple and priesthood, and their own version of the legal traditions from Moses. All of these they claimed were authentic as contrasted with the Jewish Law and with the Temple and priesthood in Jerusalem. Jesus' effort to speak to those in one of the Samaritan villages as he was on his way to Jerusalem met with rejection from the inhabitants. This moved his disciples to propose calling down divine judgment on them—a suggestion he rejected. There are no human qualifications—religious, ethnic, cultural, or moral—that exclude anyone from being addressed by God's message of forgiveness, reconciliation, and renewal, which are the essence of Jesus, his life, and his teachings.

The other messages deal with the rigorous demands of discipleship. (2) The man who offered to become a follower of Jesus wherever he goes is informed that, unlike even animals and birds who have caves and nests, Jesus has no continuing place of residence: "The Son of Man has nowhere to lay his head" (9:57). There is no assurance of stable setting or status for those who become true followers of Jesus: they must be prepared for uncertainty as they carry out the demanding role of discipleship. Their confidence is not to be placed in any humanly produced structures or resources but solely in the divine purpose at work through Jesus, which they are now called to proclaim. In this role they have no human guarantees: their sole assurance is that God will achieve through Jesus and his people the work of renewal and reconciliation.

(3) The third message is given in response to Jesus' call to become a follower to a man who wants to give priority to his obligations to family and tradition, specifically in arranging for the burial of his father. Jesus points out the urgency of the work to which he and the disciples are called in proclaiming the coming of the kingdom of God. Those who can be characterized as "dead" because they have not heeded Jesus' summons to prepare for the imminent coming of the kingdom and the new life it brings can carry out such ordinary obligations. What is most urgent for his followers, on the other hand, is to engage in announcing the inbreaking of God's rule in the world. It is more important even than performing the routine and ordinarily commendable action of notifying one's family of a major break with the past and tradition—in this case, that one is about to take on the role of messenger of the coming new age of God's rule. But Jesus' radical statement is that, once one is committed to announcing and preparing for the coming of the kingdom of God, there is no place for returning to such traditional matters as bidding farewell to one's family. The urgency of the call and the radical break with tradition and institutions must dominate the agenda of the messengers of the new age that is being launched through Jesus and proclaimed by his followers. Further, there are to be no regrets once one has committed oneself to this divinely initiated role. In spite of the difficulties and obstacles that may be encountered, those who have taken on the role of proclaimers and agents of the coming of the kingdom of God must not have any regrets. Instead, the central role must be proclaiming the coming of the kingdom of God by word and act.

THERE ARE NO HUMAN QUALIFICATIONS— RELIGIOUS, ETHNIC, CULTURAL, OR MORAL— THAT EXCLUDE ANYONE FROM BEING ADDRESSED BY GOD'S MESSAGE OF FORGIVENESS, RECONCILIATION, AND RENEWAL.

FIFTH SUNDAY AFTER PENTECOST

JULY 8, 2001
FOURTEENTH SUNDAY IN ORDINARY TIME
PROPER 9

REVISED COMMON	EPISCOPAL (BCP)	ROMAN CATHOLIC
Isa. 66:10-14	Isa. 66:10-16	Isa. 66:10-14c
or 2 Kings 5:1-14		
Ps. 66:1-9 or Ps. 30	Ps. 66 or 66:1-8	Ps. 66:1-7, 16, 20
Gal. 6:(1-6), 7-16	Gal. 6:(1-10), 14-18	Gal. 6:14-18
Luke 10:1-11, 16-20	Luke 10:1-12, 16-20	Luke 10:1-12, 17-20 or 10:1-9

FIRST READING

ISAIAH 66:10-14 (RCL); ISA. 66:10-16 (BCP); ISA. 66:10-14C (RC)

The promise of God's provision for the people is pictured in a series of images of a woman about to give birth to a child. The prophecy is uttered from the temple, and it is "the voice of the LORD" (66:6). The difficulties that the people of God have been experiencing are compared to birth pangs, and the child is about to be born—that is, the new nation is soon to appear. The present people are called to "rejoice with Jerusalem"—but also to mourn over the difficulties the covenant people have experienced. All this is in anticipation of the new era that is coming, in expectation of which they are to be filled with joy for the divine provision of the "child" that is about to be born.

Those who join in rejoicing over this divine renewal are motivated by love for God's people, and they will be sustained by sharing in the new life that is being made available, which is here compared with the milk from a nursing mother that the newborn child/people "drink deeply with delight from her consoling breast" (66:11). The image of abundant supply from the mother's breast shifts to that of a city, the prosperity of which will be increased by the inflow into it of "the wealth of the nations"—and then to that of a caring mother who provides support and "comfort" for her child (66:12-13). These multiple images are focussed on Jerusalem as the center from which will flow forth God's provision for the renewal and sustaining of the covenant people.

At the same time that the faithful covenant community is benefiting from God's gracious supply of needs, so that their "bodies flourish like the grass" and this divine support is widely known, there will come signs of God's wrath against the enemies of his people (66:14). God will act in forceful ways against those who are hostile toward his purpose and his people (66:14). The outpouring of the divine wrath against these forces is pictured in images of fire and whirlwind. The result will be the punishment of those who oppose the divine process of renewal, and many are to die as a consequence of their opposition to God's acts of transformation. The effects of this judgment will be evident "on all flesh"—that is, on people throughout the whole of the human race. The acts of divine judgment are pictured as "flames of fire" and the "sword" of the LORD. Clearly, God's purpose for the renewal of the creation and of the people is seen to involve not only divine acts of liberation and renewal for the community of the faithful but also punitive effects on those who resist God's plan of renewal and mistreat God's people.

2 KINGS 5:1–14 (RCL alt.)

Naaman was commander of the army in Aram, which was a state or confederation of states in what is now Syria, with its capital in Damascus. Although he achieved victory for his people, he was stricken with leprosy or some kind of serious skin disease. A young Israelite servant maid of his wife told him that he could be cured through a prophet in Israel. This message was passed on to the king of Aram, who sent Naaman to the king of Israel, with a huge gift of money and garments. The king thought he was being asked to cure Naaman, but the prophet Elisha wrote to the king, telling him to send the leper to him so "that he may learn that there is a prophet in Israel" (5:8). When the ailing man came to Elisha's house, the prophet sent out instructions for him to go and wash in the Jordan seven times and he would be cured. He expected a personal, public healing, but followed instructions and was cured. Returning to the prophet he publicly affirmed that "there is no God in all the earth except in Israel" (5:15), and then promised he would offer sacrifices to no God other than the LORD, the God of Israel. Though he would have to go through the motions of honoring the storm-god of the Syrians, it is Yahweh alone whom he worships. The prophet sends Naaman off with the assurance, "Go in peace!"

The story shows not only that God is active and healing those outside the tribes that officially honor him, but that God's grace is available and operates with all who trust him.

PSALM 66:1-9 or PS. 30 (RCL); PS. 66 or 66:1-8 (BCP); 66:1-7, 16, 20 (RC)

"All the earth" is called to join in joyful celebration of God, whose beneficent purpose and power are symbolized by his glorious name, Yahweh. The psalmist praises God, who has put his people to severe tests, like a metal worker refining silver with fire, or a fisherman sorting out good and useless fish or being attacked by cavalry forces (66:10-12). Yet they have remained faithful and obedient and have come through to a time of abundance. In 66:16-20, there is an invitation by the community of faith addressed to all who seek to obey ("fear") God. They are asked to come and hear what God has done for them, and how they have raised their voices to praise him and acknowledge their indebtedness to him.

SECOND READING

GALATIANS 6:(1-6), 7-16 (RCL); GAL. 6:(1-10), 14-18 (BCP); GAL. 6:14-18 (RC)

Paul's letter to the Galatians closes with advice (vv. 1-10) and warnings to the readers (vv. 11-17) before the benediction (v. 18). The counsel concerns how members of the community are to come to the aid of those who have violated the rules by which they are to live. Instead of rejecting or expelling such a transgressor, the leaders of the community should allow the Spirit to restore the deviant "in a spirit of gentleness." They are to avoid temptations similar to the one done by the violator of the community rules, and are to take action to provide support. In so doing, they will carry out "the law of Christ," which Paul describes in Rom 8:2-6 as the guidelines and moral capability provided by the Spirit in the lives of the new community. In contrast to those whose moral failure is the result of their prideful, misguided reliance on what they have perceived as their own moral capacities (Gal. 5:16-21), those who rely on the Spirit are granted "life and peace."

In 5:22-23, Paul enumerates the moral qualities that are produced by the Spirit in the lives of the faithful community. The members must carefully examine their own motivation, to see whether it derives from self-seeking inner values or the moral qualities produced by the Spirit in the lives of those who identify themselves with Christ and are liberated from the selfish urges that have dominated their lives. Yet they dare not become morally "conceited." Instead, as they live in dependence on the Spirit, examining critically their own moral lives, they will be able to restore the erring to the community, to fulfill Christ's law of love, to work for the good of the whole family of God. Paul's sole boast, which is written in his own handwriting (6:11-18), is that by identifying himself with the death of Christ on the cross, he and the world are separated as to mode of life, and a "new creation" has come into being (6:14-15). The physical scars he has from the punishment he received are continuing evidence to him and to all who see them that he is to be fully identified with the Christ who was crucified (6:17)—and is now risen!

THE GOSPEL
LUKE 10:1-11, 16-20 (RCL);
LUKE 10:1-12, 16-20 (BCP);
LUKE 10:1-12, 17-20 or 10:1-9 (RC)

The lectionaries do not include Luke 9:1-6, which depicts Jesus' sending out his twelve disciples, having empowered them with authority over demons and the ability to heal the sick, as they "proclaim the kingdom of God." They are to move through the villages, accepting hospitality where offered, and shaking the dust off their feet where they are not welcomed. The symbolism of the story as a whole is clear: the number of those sent matches the number of the tribes of Israel, which implies that the disciples' initial mission is to be to Jews. But in 10:1-12, the number of those sent out—seventy—matches the number of the non-Israelite nations in ancient Jewish tradition. That tradition was incorporated into an account in the *Letter of Aristeas*, according to which the translation of the Hebrew scriptures into Greek was carried out in the third century B.C.E. by seventy translators, who produced the Septuagint (= 70) version of the Bible to make it accessible to the wider Hellenistic world.

Like the earlier messengers sent by Jesus, the seventy are warned of the danger involved in their mission. They are told to take no financial support, but they may accept hospitality as it is offered to them. They are to heal the sick and to announce the imminence of God's kingdom. Where they encounter rejection, they are to make their mission explicit, while claiming freedom from responsibility for convincing or converting those who reject them and their message. Divine judgment is to fall on such hostile persons and the places where they are. (Some ancient manuscripts read "seventy-two" rather than seventy, but this variant matches the Jewish tradition, in some of which the number of the Gentile nations is seventy-two.) The point remains the same with either reading: the messengers of the good news are to reach out to all the nations of the world. According to Acts, Jews were gathered in Jerusalem from "every nation under heaven" (2:5); yet when the Spirit was poured out "on all flesh" [= all humanity], each of them heard the message "in our own native language" (2:6). Symbolized here is the outreach to all the world of the good news of what God is doing through Jesus. That universal outreach is anticipated in Luke 10:1.

The seventy launch their mission, and offer solemn warnings of this doom that will fall on those who do not recognize the cosmic importance of "the deeds of power" performed by Jesus and his disciples, and who consequently refuse to heed the messengers' call to repentance (10:10-15). The response of the hearers to the message about Jesus matches their response to him—faith or rejection. When the seventy messengers return from their mission, they are filled with joy and attest to the way in which they had been able to overcome the demons—the powers of evil and those forces hostile to God and his

> THE ENABLING POWER OF THE HOLY SPIRIT PROVIDES THE MODELS FOR THE MINISTRIES THAT ARE TO BE CARRIED OUT BY AND THROUGH THE PEOPLE OF GOD.

purpose of human renewal through Jesus. Yet they are told that the essence of their joy is not to be in the control of the evil powers that they were granted, but that their "names are written in heaven." They have an important, divinely ordained and enabled role to fulfill in proclaiming the name of Jesus, in calling people to prepare for the coming kingdom. But they also have a symbolic role in the defeat of the powers of evil, as is evident in their vision of Satan's "fall from heaven" and in the exorcisms they perform, which give promise of the ultimate triumph of God's purpose in the world. Above all, they are to rejoice that their enduring role in God's renewal of his covenant people and of the creation is confirmed by the heavenly records where their names are recorded (10:19-20).

The work to which these messengers are called by Jesus has both positive and negative dimensions. They are to proclaim the love, forgiveness, and reconciliation that God is accomplishing through Jesus. But they are also to identify the forces and agents of evil that are opposed to God and his purpose for the world. And they are to seek to be the agents of God by which those evil powers can be identified and overcome. The enabling power of the Holy Spirit, as demonstrated through the reports in Acts of the work of the apostles, provides the models for the ministries that are to be carried out by and through the people of God— whom Jesus is seen in Luke as summoning to faith and obedience across humanly imposed boundaries of race, religious tradition, occupation, social status, and mode of life. All are to be invited to share in God's new people.

SIXTH SUNDAY
AFTER PENTECOST

JULY 15, 2001
FIFTEENTH SUNDAY IN ORDINARY TIME / PROPER 10

REVISED COMMON	EPISCOPAL (BCP)	ROMAN CATHOLIC
Deut. 30:9-14	Deut. 30:9-14	Deut. 30:10-14
or Amos 7:7-17		
Ps. 25:1-10 or Ps. 82	Ps. 25 or 25:3-9	Ps. 69:14, 17, 30-31,
		33-34, 36-37
		or Ps. 19:8-11
Col. 1:1-14	Col. 1:1-14	Col. 1:15-20
Luke 10:25-37	Luke 10:25-37	Luke 10:25-37

FIRST READING
DEUTERONOMY 30:9-14 (RCL, BCP);
DEUT. 30:10-14 (RC)

God's instruction here follows a promise that, however far the people may be scattered across the world in subsequent years and generations, if they are obedient to his laws, he will gather them once again in their own land. When they are in God's chosen place for them, their crops and their flocks will flourish if they observe his "commandments and decrees that are written in the book of the law." This way of life will prevail among them "because you turn to the LORD your God with all your heart and with all your soul."

This Law of God is not beyond their capacity to grasp, understand, and obey. It is not a body of inaccessible divine truths kept in heaven, so that they would need to ask for some messenger to ascend to heaven, where the Law would be found, and from where it then could be brought back to them on the earth. Neither is it so difficult for them to conform to that they are unable to meet its demands. Nor is it inaccessible, as though it were located far across the sea, so that it is only if someone made a long journey across the earth in order to find it and bring it back to the covenant people might they hear it directly and thus be able to meet its demands on them. Instead, it is very near to them: in their "mouth," which means that it is expressed in words that are familiar to them and that they can readily understand; and in their "heart," which means that it conveys insights and understandings of human behavior that can be achieved by the response of the human will. With this accessible message from God stated in ways that fit the perceptions, needs, values, and longings of the human mind and heart, his people are indeed ready to heed and obey God's will and purpose for them.

RESPONSIVE READING
PSALM 25:1-10 (RCL);
PS. 25 or 25:3-9 (BCP)

This psalm expresses the inner convictions and longing for one who truly seeks to be in right relationship with God. To "lift up the soul" is to reach upward and outward in order to gain and maintain the sense of participation in God's purpose and to share in the support that God provides. This trusting link to God will enable one to avoid embarrassment and shame, and to remain strong and firm even as one experiences attack and subversion from one's enemies. The ground of this relationship is the love and mercy of God, which has been at work among the people from ancient times.

PSALM 69:14, 17, 30-31, 33-34, 36-37 (RC)

Psalm 69 includes impassioned pleas to God to come to the support of the faithful as they experience grave difficulties, both inwardly as well as from their enemies and from hostile forces and situations that threaten to overcome them. Only the steadfast love of God can sustain them in these times of trial.

PSALM 19:8-11 (RC alt.)

In Psalm 19:7-11, the central theme is the perfection of the Law of God and the blessings that come to those who seek its insights and guides for the life of God's people. In this psalm is celebrated the perfection of God's Law in its essence and in its function within the life of the covenant community (34:11; Prov. 1:7). The laws of God are not to be feared, nor are they to be compromised out of misguided self-interest. They are enduringly "true and righteous altogether," so that God's expectation of love and justice, of compassion and fidelity are not to be set aside but are to continue as the norms for the lives of God's people "forever."

SECOND READING

COLOSSIANS 1:1-14 (RCL/BCP)

Timothy is identified here (1:1) as co-author with Paul of this letter to the community of "saints and faithful brothers and sisters in Christ in Colossae," a city in Asia Minor about one hundred miles east of Ephesus on the Aegean Sea. In this letter are emphasized the cosmic role of Christ in the renewal of God's people and of the world and how this is already transforming the members of the faithful community and their lives (2:9-15). They now manifest this faith and love in the way that they live because they are confident of God's ultimate purpose: "the hope laid up for you in heaven" (1:5). They are now to let the good news continue to grow and be fruitful within them, increasing in knowledge of God's will and in understanding of his purpose for them and for the world. These new understandings of what God intends for them will result in greatly enriched perceptions, and these will lead to morally renewed and strengthened lives. Such a way of life will be "fully pleasing" to God and will result in increased "good work"—a life "worthy of the Lord" (1:10). To fulfill this call to a renewed life, they must be reliant on the qualities that God has provided for them—strength, endurance, patience, and joy—as they foresee the accomplishment of God's purpose for the renewal of his people and of the world. They can be confident that this will take place because they have already personally experienced deliverance "from the dominion of darkness" and a transformed life in "the kingdom of [God's] beloved Son" (1:12-13). Their assurance about God's ultimate renewal of his people and of the creation is based not only on the promises made through Christ but also on their present experience of transformation by God's grace. They already share in benefits of God's work of "redemption" through Christ, because they know that they have been granted "the forgiveness of sins." This sharing confirms for them that they have been enabled by God to have access to the blessings and renewal that God has promised to "the saints in light." The faith and hope of the new community are grounded in what God has already done, as evident not only in the divine promises but also in their own experience of transformed life.

> THEY HAVE ALREADY PERSONALLY EXPERIENCED DELIVERANCE "FROM THE DOMINION OF DARKNESS" AND HAVE BEEN TRANSFERRED TO LIFE IN "THE KINGDOM OF [GOD'S] BELOVED SON."

*See the comments on the Second Reading for the Seventh Sunday
after Pentecost.*

THE GOSPEL
LUKE 10:25-37

The Parable of the Good Samaritan, unique to Luke's Gospel, is told by
Jesus in response to an inquiry from a "lawyer"—that is, someone whose life work
was the interpretation of the Law of Moses and its application in the contemporary setting of the people of Israel. The lawyer's question concerns what he must
do in order to be certain of sharing in the life of God's people in the age to come
("to inherit eternal life"). His assumption is that, for anyone to hope to have a
part in the life of God's people now and in the age to come, one must conform
to the moral and ritual requirements laid down in the Law of Moses, but he wants
to know what Jesus considers to be the most important of these.

Jesus responds with a question to him as to what is written in the Law on this
matter, to which he replies with a composite quotation from the Torah: Deut. 6:5
and Lev. 19:18. The first of these calls for one to love "the Lord your God with
all your heart, and with all your soul, and with all your might." In the Jewish
scriptures "heart" occurs 814 times with reference to the human heart. It is seen
to be the center of emotions, ranging from passion, grief, anger, and arrogance,
to courage and joy. But it is also the seat of human understanding (Deut. 8:5; Isa.
42:25) and decision making (2 Sam. 7:21). The soul is the life which empowers
the body, as evident when Adam became "a living soul" (Gen. 2:7). The mind is
the capacity to perceive, to contemplate, and to make decisions. The love within
the individual is to be centered on God, on one's neighbor, and on oneself,
including what we would call self-acceptance and self-respect (Luke 10:27).

The inquirer's question then shifts to, "Who is my neighbor?" which evokes
Jesus' parable of the Good Samaritan (10:29). The story describes a man going
down the road that leads from the hills where Jerusalem is located to Jericho at
the bottom of the Jordan Valley. Jerusalem is on a ridge about 2500 feet above sea
level, and Jericho is about 1200 feet below sea level. Most of this road passes
through barren, uninhabited land, and so it was a convenient place for robbers to
attack travelers. In the parable the injured victim of the robbers' attack was left
unaided by the passing religious officials, priest and Levite, who feared ritual pol-
lution if they touched an injured person or a corpse. But the one who stopped
to help him was a member of a group despised by Jews as those who claimed to

have the true sanctuary of God and the proper version of the Law of Moses: the Samaritans, whose temple and priesthood were located on Mount Gerizim, some thirty miles north of Jerusalem.

The dominant factor in the Samaritan's decision to help the wounded man was "pity"—the opposite attitude from the concern of the other travelers for their own ritual purity and personal safety, both of which they saw as possibly endangered by stopping to help this victim. If he were bloody he would be ritually impure. The Samaritan ignored ritual restrictions when he treated the wounds of the injured man and then provided him with transportation to a safe place and lodging where he could recover. Then he provided the money to pay the innkeeper. Neither this traveler's personal safety, his personal possessions, nor preserving his ritual purity was a factor behind his actions. His only concern was to seek to come to the aid and meet the needs of another human. Clearly, "the one who showed him mercy" in spite of all these potential difficulties was the true neighbor. And Jesus exhorts his questioner to follow the same kind of open, caring response if one is truly to love one's "neighbor."

> LOVE WITHIN THE INDIVIDUAL IS BE CENTERED ON GOD, ON ONE'S NEIGHBOR, AND ON ONESELF, INCLUDING WHAT WE WOULD CALL SELF-ACCEPTANCE AND SELF-RESPECT.

The story tells the hearer that what is central in seeking to live as the people of God is not one's personal safety or religious purity but readiness to reach out in spite of dangers and traditional boundaries to show the love of God in concrete acts of mercy and in works of love toward those in need. Here is a most radical answer to the question, "Who is my neighbor?"

SEVENTH SUNDAY AFTER PENTECOST

JULY 22, 2001

SIXTEENTH SUNDAY IN ORDINARY TIME / PROPER 11

REVISED COMMON	EPISCOPAL (BCP)	ROMAN CATHOLIC
Gen. 18:1-10a	Gen. 18:1-10a	Gen. 18:1-10a
or Amos 8:1-12	(10b-14)	
Psalm 15 or Ps. 52	Ps. 15	Ps. 15:1-5
Col. 1:15-28	Col. 1:21-29	Col. 1:24-28
Luke 10:38-42	Luke 10:38-42	Luke 10:38-42

FIRST READING
GENESIS 18:1-10a (RCL/RC);
GEN. 18:1-10a (10b-14) (BCP)

In Genesis 17, God promises a son to Abraham—at the age of one hundred—and to Sarah—age ninety. The son who is to be theirs, contrary to any normal human expectations for the aged and childless, is to be sent to them by God. The three visitors who come to them at their tent are welcomed by the couple and fed cakes, meat, and milk. These who come are messengers sent by God to convey to the aged Abraham the promise that he and the barren Sarah will have a son. There is no human reason to give credence to such a prediction, but it is to be accomplished through the action of one of the visitors who announces that he will return at the appropriate time—"in due season"—to carry out this promise. The son to be born is God's gift. By ordinary human standards and expectations, this is an incredible promise, as is evident in Sarah's inability to believe it, which is shown by her laughter at hearing it. A lifelong reminder of her initial failure to believe God's promise was the name given to this son: Isaac, which is based on the Hebrew word for laughter (Gen. 18:11-15). Thus the name served as an enduring witness to the wonderful promises of God to his people, of the regrettable reluctance of humans to believe them, and of the grace of God which fulfills them nonetheless. This part of the story is included in BCP, which continues the reading through vv. 10b-14. Here is the note that Sarah was able to hear this promise from her place outside the tent, where she was eavesdropping.

A specific comment is made that both Abraham and Sarah were too old to expect to have children, and that Sarah had ceased to have menstruation, and hence was physically unable to have children. The prediction understandably evoked laughter from Sarah, since it was humanly impossible for her to assume that such a development would take place. The inability of someone her age to have such a sexual experience—ovulation, copulation, impregnation, gestation, and delivery of offspring—seemed so preposterous that she laughed. The rhetorical question is raised for incredulous Sarah, however: "Is anything too wonderful for the Lord?" and she is told once again that she is indeed to have a son. The gracious gifts of God to his people are not based on, or conditioned by, human inability to trust fully the promises of God. God's promises are sure!

RESPONSIVE READING
PSALM 15 (RCL/BCP); PS. 15:1-5 (RC)

This brief psalm offers details of the requirements for those who are qualified to remain in the sanctuary where God dwells on the "holy hill" of Jerusalem. What is required is not merely outward conformity to ritual and moral rules, but living a "blameless" life, doing only "what is right," and "speaking the truth" not merely in a formal, external mode, but based on inward insights, convictions, and commitments—and therefore "from the heart."

SECOND READING
COLOSSIANS 1:15-28 (RCL);
COL. 1:21-29 (BCP); COL. 1:24-28 (RC)

Colossians 1:15-20 consists of a hymn in which the role of Christ as agent of creation and of renewal for God's people is depicted. Jesus Christ is the one through whom the nature and purpose of God for the creation and for his people have been revealed, and they are now being carried out through him. These features of the creation include not only visible items, such as earthly rulers and powers at work in human history, but invisible powers as well, which shape the history of the world. This divine agent came into being before any of the earthly authorities, and he is the divine instrument through which the universe functions and coheres (vv. 15-17).

But he is also the divine instrument for the emergence, growth, and redemptive role of his people, the church. He established the possibility of new life for his new people as "the firstborn from the dead," and his destiny is to attain "first place in everything." Full disclosure of the nature and purpose of God has been taking place through him, and he is the one who is overcoming the hostility of earthly forces and humans toward God. The result is that, through the human act of violence that led religious and political leaders to join in putting Jesus to death on the cross, he is now "making peace" by reconciling hostile humans to God (vv. 19-20).

This perception of God's achieving his purpose through Jesus is presented as not merely a theory of redemption or human renewal but as what has been experienced by the readers of this letter. They were formerly hostile toward and alienated from God by their evil minds and hostile actions. But Jesus' death has effected reconciliation between them and God and continues to work as a force for moral renewal and transformation of the faithful, which will result in their being presented to God by Christ as a pure and flawless sacrifice (1:21-22), if they continue firmly and with commitment in the faithful community and do not shift from basing their hope in the message which they have heard concerning Jesus—and which has been proclaimed "to every creature under heaven" (1:23). Paul has dedicated his life to the service of the gospel, which provides the message concerning the redemptive events as well as the goals for his ministry.

JESUS CHRIST IS THE DIVINE INSTRUMENT FOR THE EMERGENCE, GROWTH, AND REDEMPTIVE ROLE OF HIS PEOPLE, THE CHURCH.

Accordingly, the focus shifts from the cosmic redemption that was launched through Christ to the apostle's assessment of his own role as the messenger and agent of the divine purpose (1:24-29). Instead of complaining or losing faith as a result of the sufferings that he has been experiencing, he considers them to be beneficial for the members of the community. A basic assumption of the apocalyptic outlook within Judaism was that the painful experiences of the faithful community served positive functions: they contributed to the discipline and commitment of the people of God. In the divine scheme of history, these struggles were analogous to the birth pangs that a mother experiences as she brings a new life into the world. What is produced in the apocalyptic perspective is the new age of fulfillment of God's purpose for his people. Just as the sufferings of Jesus were essential for the redemption of the new community, so Paul's painful experiences serve to foster the growth and maturity of the "church" (1:24).

He is the one through whom God's word has been communicated to the new people of God—who has thereby become more "fully known"—and the long-hidden mystery of God's purpose has now been "revealed to his saints" (1:25-26). The most amazing feature of this divine disclosure is that the message of hope is going out not only to the Jews as the traditional people of God but to "Gentiles" as well, who may now share in "the riches of the glory of this mystery." This mystery is not only conveyed by but is embodied in the person of Jesus Christ. He is the ground of this hope for renewal of God's people and of the whole creation, which is not merely known conceptually but is also experienced inwardly by members of the community of faith, who embody "the hope of glory." God's glory is proclaimed by the heavens, and the splendor of the created order shows that it is God's "handiwork" (Ps. 19:1). But the "riches of glory" and the "hope" of fulfillment of the divine purpose are disclosed in Christ. Through preaching of the good news and instruction in divine wisdom, the apostles seek and struggle to develop the community so that it may achieve its divinely intended maturity in Christ (1:28-29).

THE GOSPEL
LUKE 10:38-42

The responses to Jesus by the two sisters, Martha and Mary, represent the alternatives open to members of the new community. Martha was the owner of the home to which Jesus was invited, and was constantly busy with domestic tasks. She complained to Jesus that her sister neglected to take her share of the household responsibilities. Instead, she spent all of her time close to Jesus, listening attentively to his teachings. Jesus responded by telling Martha that her time and energies were taken up with worries and "distraction." Mary, he said, had chosen instead the one really important thing: to give full and ongoing attention to what Jesus was saying and teaching. This is really "the better part," and the results of such concentration on his message and agenda will have an enduring impact on her.

This assessment of the differing roles of the two sisters serves as an appeal and a warning to the members of the ongoing community of faith. Although the practical necessities of the life of community require close and frequent attention, they must not be viewed as the truly important features of the life of God's people. Instead, the primary and enduring feature of the shared life is constant

THE TWO SISTERS SERVE AS AN APPEAL AND A WARNING TO THE MEMBERS OF THE ONGOING COMMUNITY OF FAITH.

eagerness and openness on the part of the members of the community to hear and to comprehend the significance for them as individuals and as a group of Jesus' "teaching." By precept and by example, he conveys to them the purpose of God for his people and the loving, courageous means by which it may be achieved by them. These insights and the relationship to Christ and to his people are indeed "the better part" (10:42).

ST. MARY MAGDALENE

JULY 22

REVISED COMMON, EPISCOPAL (BCP), AND ROMAN CATHOLIC
Ruth 1:6-18 or Exod. 2:1-10 or Judith 9:1,11-14
Ps. 73:23-28
Acts 13:26-33a or 2 Cor. 5:14-18
John 20:1-2, 11-18

FIRST READING
RUTH 1:6-18

Naomi, who had migrated with her husband, Elimelech, from Bethlehem across the Jordan Valley to the land of Moab in a time of famine, was preparing to return to her native place after her sons had married and then died. Her bereaved daughters-in-law, Ruth and Orpah, proposed to accompany her back to her native land, but she advised them to remain in their own land, where they might find a husband and have children. It would be foolish of these women to await the unlikely possibility that—at her age—she would marry, have children, and produce sons who could be husbands for them. In response to this discouraging advice, Orpah bade farewell to her mother-in-law. But Ruth went with her, promising to go with her no matter where she went and lodged. She declared herself to be one with Naomi's people, and with her God. She said that she would remain with her until death and would stay in that land until she died and was buried. She committed herself to the care of the God who had led and cared for Naomi. Accordingly, Naomi no longer sought to dissuade Ruth from accompanying her on her return to her native land.

EXODUS 2:1-10 (alt.)

This lection describes the action of other women in a time of duress that had historic consequences. It speaks of the courage and cunning of a mother, the pity of a princess, and quick thinking on the part of a baby's sister, all of which resulted in the preparation of Moses to be the deliverer of his people. Although stories of threat and deliverance during infancy are frequently told of ancient heroes, the purpose of this story, at least in part, is to explain how Moses learned to move in royal circles in the Egyptian capital while retaining his feeling for his own people, the Hebrews. There is nothing overtly "religious" about this narrative; implicit in it, however, is faith in the meaningfulness of human events and in God's direction of the sweep of history.

RESPONSIVE READING
PSALM 73:23-28

Troubled by the seeming prosperity of the wicked and the wide acclaim that they receive (73:1-12) and by the ongoing difficulties he had experienced, in spite of his efforts to maintain purity and to obey God's way, the psalmist entered the sanctuary of God. From this perspective he was able to see the horrible fate that the wicked would ultimately suffer and the ephemeral nature of their schemes and expectations (vv. 13-17). Although he had become embittered by the seeming welfare of the wicked, he realized the folly of such conclusions (vv. 18-22).

Now he lives in continual consciousness of God's presence and guidance (73:21-26): "You hold my right hand." And he knows that, in the future, he will be taken into the glorious presence of God: received "with honor" or "into glory."

SECOND READING
ACTS 13:26-33a

Antioch in Pisidia in central Asia Minor served in the Roman period as the military and administrative center for the province of Galatia. Its culture and way of life were thoroughly shaped by the Greco-Roman rulers who had dominated the region for centuries, but there was a synagogue of the Jews there as well. In his address to the Jews there, Paul describes how God had cared for his people over the years, and had finally brought to them a descendant of David to be the Savior of his people, who was recognized and acclaimed as Savior by John the Baptist. The leaders of the Jews did not perceive who Jesus was, however, nor did they understand the role that he was to fulfill in accord with the words of the prophets. Their leaders—unable to find a cause for execution by their own laws—asked the Romans to put him to death (vv. 27-29). Crucified and then buried, God raised him from the dead, and he then appeared over a period of "many days" to those who had been his followers from Galilee to Jerusalem. These disciples continue to bear witness to him as the one promised by God in the scriptures, which have now been fulfilled through this Jesus, who is the Son of God (v. 33; Ps. 2:7).

The Gospel
JOHN 20:1-2, 11-18

In this account of the postresurrection appearances of Jesus, Mary Magdalene was the first one to go to the tomb of Jesus after he had been buried on Friday just before the Sabbath began. Since she could not have found her way to the tomb that night after dark, she went before dawn at the earliest possible time: on Sunday morning. Finding the stone that had closed the tomb removed, she reported this to Peter and "the other disciple" (which implies that he is the one whose traditions and perspectives are preserved in this Gospel). This unnamed disciple outran Peter, looked in, saw the linen wrappings that had been around the body, but did not enter. Peter went in first, and was followed by the other disciple, who also "believed"; that is, he confirmed that God had indeed raised Jesus from the dead. Hence, according to this Gospel, the initial witness that Christ was not in the tomb was Mary Magdalene, although she was at first puzzled by the missing body and the presence of

ONLY WHEN HE CALLED HER BY NAME DID SHE RECOGNIZE HIM.

the two angels, and began to weep (v. 11). After asking the angels who were there where the body of Jesus was, she failed to recognize him when he came to her and asked her why she was weeping (vv. 14-15). Only when he called her by name did she recognize him. He then informed her that he was ascending to God the Father, so she went to the disciples to report that she had "seen the Lord" and to convey to them the things that he had said to her. In the subsequent passage (John 20:24-29) Thomas—who was not present at the earlier encounter of the disciples with the risen Christ—shares with them another visit by Christ, who invites him to see his wounded hands and touch his pierced side as evidence that it is the same Jesus who was crucified who is now risen and among them. In response to Jesus' call to him to believe in him, Thomas utters the central affirmation of the church: "My Lord and my God!"

Thus, these experiences by the women of seeing the risen Christ not only confirm the claims of the apostles, but they show that the experience of encounter with the risen Lord on the part of his followers is not limited to his official representatives, but is available to women and men of any time and status who recognize Jesus to be God's agent of human renewal and the victor over sin and death.

These stories are followed in the Gospel of John by accounts of the appearances of the risen Jesus to the disciples as a group, and his confirmation to them that he had indeed been put to death, but was now raised from the dead (20:19-23, 24-30). It is the initially doubting Thomas who acclaims him as "My Lord and my God."

NOTE

1. *Jubilees* 15:1; 44:4-5; Damascus Rule (CD) 6:19; 8:21; 19:34; 20:12; Dead Sea Commentary on Habakkuk (1QpHab 2:3).

EIGHTH SUNDAY
AFTER PENTECOST

JULY 29, 2001
SEVENTEENTH SUNDAY IN ORDINARY TIME
PROPER 12

REVISED COMMON	EPISCOPAL (BCP)	ROMAN CATHOLIC
Gen. 18:20-32	Gen. 18:20-33	Gen. 18:20-32
or Hos. 1:2-10		
Ps. 138 or Ps. 85	Ps. 138	Ps. 138:1-3, 6-8
Col. 2:6-15 (16-19)	Col. 2:6-15	Col. 2:12-14
Luke 11:1-13	Luke 11:1-13	Luke 11:1-13

Love, faithfulness, betrayal, and forgiveness are woven into the texts for today, texts that disclose in different ways the intimate relationship God desires to have with us. Despite God's desire, we often turn from the Creator of the universe to worship enticing gods who promise us salvation, power, and prestige. The problem is as old as these ancient texts and as current as today's news. Despite our inconstancy, God continues calling us to an intimate relationship irradiated by God's steadfast love and faithfulness.

FIRST READING

GENESIS 18:20-32 (RCL/RC);
GEN. 18:20-33 (BCP)

Interpreting the Text

In the verses preceding this pericope, Abraham is depicted as a just man through whom God will bless all the nations of the earth. Abraham is charged with teaching his descendants to "keep the way of the Lord by doing righteousness and justice." It is because Abraham is just that God tells him the plan regarding Sodom (note Amos 3:7). Abraham's standing as a just person emboldens him to question God to assure himself of God's justice.

The outcries against Sodom and Gomorrah provoke God's inquiry, which leads to the appearance before Abraham. It is not clear, however, how God's appearance to Abraham (18:1) is related to the three men whom Abraham welcomes. When the men turn from Abraham, he remains "standing before the

Lord." The three men are described later as two angels whom Lot invites into his home (19:1).

YHWH tells Abraham about the inquiry regarding Sodom (18:21). Tension grows with each of Abraham's questions as he decreases the number of righteous people required to save the city. The use of the "if" clause in Abraham's questions indicates that Sodom's future is open to the results of YHWH's inquiry. Abraham's dialogue with God serves to establish that the "Judge of all the earth [will] do what is just" (18:25).

Abraham recognizes the temerity of his questions: "Let me take it upon myself to speak to the Lord, I who am but dust and ashes. Suppose. . . . Oh do not let the Lord be angry if I speak. Suppose. . . . Oh do not let the Lord be angry if I speak just once more. Suppose . . ." (18:27-28, 30-32). Many commentators describe Abraham as bargaining with God. A different perspective is suggested, however, by focusing on the justification God provides for speaking to Abraham (17-19), who is charged with following the "way of the Lord," which entails "doing righteousness and justice" (18:19). Abraham seems not so much to be bargaining with God as reassuring himself that whatever action YHWH takes will be righteous and just.

Abraham stops after asking if YHWH will save the city for the sake of ten righteous persons. A common interpretation is that ten was probably the smallest number that would be considered as a group. Fewer than ten persons could be saved individually, which is what occurs with Lot and his family.

Responding to the Text

Abraham's dialogue with God turns on the salvific effect a small number of righteous people can have on behalf of a whole community. The text portrays God as destroying a community because there are no righteous people in it. This understanding of God is challenged by other biblical texts that proclaim the radical faithfulness of God's love and mercy, despite our human failures. That being said, the text leads us to ponder the profound effect a few righteous people can have on a community.

People who act courageously in the face of opposition and hostility provoke us to evaluate the justice of our own actions—individually and corporately. In the 1940s, the courage of Christians in Le Chambon, France, demonstrated that a small, committed community could save the lives of thousands of Jews—despite their physical proximity to a Nazi SS division.[1]

THE RIGHTEOUS ACTS OF A FEW CAN GALVANIZE THE GOODNESS AND COURAGE OF A WHOLE COMMUNITY.

Religious-based hatred drives many of the hundreds of violent groups operating in the United States today that dream "of a white Christian homeland, free of the despised 'Zionist Occupation Government.'"[2] Christians must speak out against the heresy of those who promote violence and bigotry in the name of Christ. The evil acts of a few can terrorize a whole community. The righteous acts of a few, however, can galvanize the goodness and courage of a whole community. We are called to walk in "the way of the Lord by doing righteousness and justice" (18:19), even when we are surrounded by those who scorn the way of the Lord.[3]

HOSEA 1:2-10 (RCL alt.)

Interpreting the Text

The long career of the eighth-century prophet Hosea began during a prosperous period in Jeroboam II's reign over Israel and continued through the turbulent years following Jeroboam's death. Hosea was deeply aware of God's passionate love and expressed the pain and anger that sprang from it when the people turned from reliance on YHWH to pursue dangerous political alliances and worship Canaanite deities.

Israel's unfaithfulness to God (1:2b) is offered as the reason that God directs Hosea to marry Gomer, who was unfaithful to him. They have three children, each named symbolically: Jezreel signaled God's intention to put an end to the dynasty of Jehu, of which Jeroboam II was part;[4] Lo-ruhamah means "no pity" for Israel; and Lo-ammi, "you are *not my people* and I am not your God" (1:8).

The naming of the children is interrupted to direct these threats toward Israel, but not Judah. After naming the third child, YHWH's faithfulness to Israel emerges. Echoing promises of old, YHWH affirms that the people of Israel will be as numerous as the grains of sand (compare Gen. 22:17), and "where it was said to them, 'You are not my people,' it shall be said to them, 'Children of the living God.'"

YHWH's bitter response to Israel's unfaithfulness is reinforced by the use of eight verses to detail the rejection. When reading this text in worship, a long pause is needed between vv. 9 and 10, and a clear difference in rate of speech and intonation in reading v. 10 is necessary in order for people to hear the shift from the verses of rejection to the declaration of God's faithfulness.

Did Hosea know Gomer was promiscuous before he married her? Interpreters disagree. Rabbinic interpretations led Abraham Heschel to argue that Hosea loved Gomer, married her, had children, and subsequently discovered her promiscuity. Heschel emphasized that "[t]he primarily given and immediate spiritual datum in the story of the marriage is the prophet's experience."[5] Hosea is deeply affected by Gomer's betrayal, which helps him understand the "divine pathos." Because of his experience, Hosea consistently identifies with God's perspective and never intercedes on behalf of the people.

We cannot know for sure *when* Hosea learned about Gomer's promiscuity. The tension and power of the story are diminished, however, if his marriage is merely an act for public illustration. Nor do we know the nature of Gomer's promiscuity. The phrase *'eshet zenunim*, translated "wife of whoredom," refers to a "habitually promiscuous" woman. *Zonah*, the technical word for prostitute, is never used.[6] A popular interpretation is that Gomer was a cult prostitute for the worship of Baal. Scholars studying the cult, however, find no clear evidence to support the long-held assumption that there were cult prostitutes.[7]

Responding to the Text

Hosea is the first biblical writer to use marriage as a metaphor for God's relationship to Israel. According to Heschel, "Hosea's conception of Israel as the consort of God represents one of the most important ideas in the history of Judaism (cf. Isa. 49:14-15; 62:5) and foreshadows the traditional interpretation of the Song of Songs."[8]

Imagining God as a loving and beloved spouse evokes thoughts of an intimate relationship of mutual responsiveness, respect, and love. Meditating on our relationship with God in such terms can help us internalize more deeply a sense of God's profound and passionate love for us. It can also increase our sensitivity to the pain and suffering God experiences when we are not faithful to God.

The value of the marriage metaphor comes with a price, however, because of the troubling way it is developed in Hosea and other biblical texts. Israel's unfaithfulness provokes God's anger, depicted as a husband publicly humiliating and physically abusing an unfaithful wife. Hosea commands his children to tell Gomer she must stop pursuing her lovers or he will "strip her naked and expose her . . . and make her like a wilderness, and turn her into a parched land, and kill her with thirst" (2:3). He will take away her food and clothing and expose her physically to her lovers (2:10).

The metaphor depicts God as betrayed husband, thus portraying the husband/wife relationship as parallel to the power and authority God has over Israel. The imagery can easily be interpreted as approving the violent treatment of disobedient wives. Although chapter 2 is not included in today's reading, a sermon based on chapter 1 needs to address—if only briefly—the imagery in chapter 2 that many women find terrifying. Silence in regard to such texts may be taken as approval. Some interpreters believe they can "explain away" the problem of such violent imagery. Their awareness of the importance of criticizing such imagery in the context of today's world might be heightened, however, if they would allow themselves to imagine having a beloved daughter who was physically abused and publicly humiliated by her husband. The physical abuse of spouses, particularly women, is a poisonous secret in the lives of far too many people in churches of every economic class in cultures throughout the world, including the United States.[9]

RESPONSIVE READING

PSALM 138 (RCL/BCP); PS. 138:1-3, 6-8 (RC)

In this psalm of thanksgiving, the singer enthusiastically thanks God for God's "steadfast love and faithfulness" (138:2). Old translations found various ways around the unacceptable notion that the psalmist thanks YHWH "before the gods" (138:1). The phrase has been interpreted as a reference to Canaanite "gods," "demoted divine entities of the heavenly world," or gods of the nations (having been influenced by YHWH's "final showdown" with them in Deutero-Isaiah), thus establishing YHWH's universal dominion.[10]

Although the psalm has features associated with individual psalms of praise, events evoking praise from "all the kings of the earth" (138:4) point to salvific acts that would evoke a liturgical psalm of praise sung by the congregation. In good times and bad, God regards each life—no matter how lowly one may be in the eyes the community. Though God's glory is great, the steadfast faithfulness and love of God pour out on each of us, the work of God's hands.

PSALM 85 (RCL alt.)

This communal lament reflects a congregation experiencing trouble and remembering the past salvific acts of God. God has brought the people out of exile, but they are again in need of deliverance. "Restore us again. . . . Will you be angry with us forever?" (85:4, 5).

Israel turned again and again to God, repenting and seeking forgiveness and restoration. We, too, must turn to God repeatedly. It is the assurance of God's steadfast love and forgiveness—revealed to us through Jesus Christ—that emboldens us to join the psalmist in praying for restoration despite our individual and corporate sins.

COLOSSIANS 2:6-15 (16-19) (RCL);
COL. 2:6-15 (BCP); COL. 2:12-14 (RC)

Interpreting the Text

Paul encourages the congregation at Colossae to remain rooted in Christ Jesus whom they have received (*paralambanein*) as Lord.[11] The verb used implies the receiving of a transmitted tradition. The church at Colossae has received the teaching that Christ Jesus is Lord. Paul calls on them to *continue* in what has been received, to "live [their] lives" in Christ, that is, walk—conduct themselves—as would be appropriate for those who believe Christ Jesus is Lord.

The Colossians have been rooted in the teaching, in Christ. They are admonished to continue walking in the teaching so that it might grow and be "built up" (2:7). The letter reinforces the important role of baptism in the process. It is through baptism that one is buried and raised with Christ Jesus "through faith in the power of God, who raised him from the dead" (2:12). A heart overflowing with thanksgiving is characteristic of one in whom the teaching has taken hold (2:7). Continued growth is threatened, however, if they are taken captive by false teaching (2:8). Speculation abounds regarding the identification of the threat. Martin Dibelius related the false teaching to those who worshiped the "elemental spirits" (*stoicheia*), forces believed to govern the universe (2:8). Such worship denied the lordship of Christ in whom "the whole fullness of deity dwells bodily" (2:9), thus eliminating the need for any mediating god, spirit, or angel.

False teaching may have referred to a strand of Judaism. The metaphor of spiritual circumcision (2:1) and the erasing of the record of their trespasses "with its legal demands" (2:13) by "nailing it to the cross" (2:14) suggest Jewish concerns. Practices associated with Greek mystery cults are mentioned (2:16-19); however, such practices were also features of Jewish mystical practices known as *merkabah* (chariot) mysticism. This tradition of Jewish mysticism involved practices that prepared one to ascend to the highest heaven, originally perhaps the third heaven, and receive the vision of the heavenly chariot granted to Ezekiel (Ezek. 1:26-8).[12] Merkabah mysticism combined rigorous observance of sacred law with a regime of self-discipline. Angels served as mediators, which suggests the "worship of angels" (2:18). Those who experienced such visions may have thought of themselves or been thought of as spiritual elites (note Paul's self-reference in 2 Cor. 12:2-7 as one who boasted about ascending to the third heaven).

Whatever the nature of the teaching Paul feared would take the Colossians captive, the threat to their faith in the sufficiency of Christ Jesus is mirrored in a dizzying array of teachings available in our culture today. Christ's call can be drowned out amidst the cacophony of voices and visual imagery that constantly vie for our attention.

One of the great threats to faith in late modern cultures such as the United States is the pervasiveness of a worldview that denies the existence of any reality beyond that which we experience through our five senses. Such a world is devoid of the sacred, truth, and meaning. One set of values is considered just as good as any other. The world is awash with the ideas and experiences of "virtual reality" and "virtual ethics." It is easy to lose our way.

We are rooted in Christ, but if we are immersed in a life that pulls our attention and energy away from God and the ways of God, we are not living and growing in Christ, walking in accordance with his teaching. No matter how many years we have claimed the identity of being Christian, Paul's letter challenges us to evaluate whether or not we have been taken captive by false teaching. We must search the depths of our own hearts. Do the actions of our daily life involve walking in accordance with Christ's teaching, or is someone or something else lord of our lives? Are our hearts overflowing with thankfulness?

THE GOSPEL
LUKE 11:1-13

Interpreting the Text

Our very familiarity with the Lord's Prayer challenges us to be open to gaining deeper insight and wisdom from this text. The Lukan version of the prayer is introduced by depicting Jesus at prayer. When he had finished, one of his disciples asked him to teach them to pray. It was not uncommon for rabbis to teach followers a particular form of prayer, as John the Baptist apparently had done (11:1).

Jesus responded with a prayer, which in this Lukan version involves two petitions of praise for God and three petitions for human beings. Some commentators emphasize the eschatological qualities of the prayer, noting features such as the brief phrasing, "Your kingdom come." The authors of many New Testament texts believed that the *parousia* would occur within their lifetime, and the theological perspectives they embrace reflect that assumption. Luke, however, was written at a later period when confidence in the imminence of the *parousia* was waning. The pressing issue to which Luke dedicates himself is the recognition of the ongoing work of the Holy Spirit in the world and in the church as a necessary preparation for the return of Jesus Christ and the establishment of God's reign on earth. Given the perspective of the author of Luke and even more the perspective we have 2,000 years later as we continue to await the coming of God's kingdom on earth, much of the power of the Lord's Prayer is diminished if we emphasize only an eschatological interpretation.

Jesus directs his disciples to claim their identity as sons and daughters of God by referring to God as *Abba*, an informal, intimate form of address a child might use for a father, much like "Daddy." As we are sons and daughters of one God, so too are we sisters and brothers of all humanity. The first petition of the prayer acknowledges the holiness of God's name. One of the ways the sacredness of God's name is signaled is by not speaking it aloud, thus Jesus' reference to YHWH as Abba. The sacredness of God's name is a recurring motif in the Old Testament.

It is important theologically that of all the needs humans have, Jesus focuses on three concerns: daily food, forgiveness, and protection from the time of trial (temptation). Although Christian theology has focused heavily on sin, forgiveness, and the treachery of temptation, no place has been made in theology for a doctrine of food. Given the number of children in the world who die every day due to starvation and illness caused by malnutrition, what difference might it have made if Christian theology had also focused on the first petition of the prayer— God's concern for humans to have bread for our stomachs? Spiritualizing the passage to focus only on the spiritual food we receive through Jesus Christ does not eliminate the reality that, without physical food to sustain life, there will be no need for attention to sin, temptation, and forgiveness.[13] The communal rather than individual perspective of the prayer is emphasized by the use of plural pronouns. This should lead us to think deeply about what it means to pray for "*our daily bread*" in a world in which all people could be fed and yet an estimated 1.2 billion people are chronically hungry.[14]

The prayer is followed by the parable of a person knocking on a friend's door at midnight to get bread for an unexpected visitor. The parable is often interpreted as emphasizing the importance of persistence in prayer because it is the neighbor's insistence that finally leads the friend to get up and provide whatever is needed.

An alternative translation describes the action of the friend not as "persistent" but as "shameless" or "importunate." A friend helps another, even if the request is shameless. God loves us with a depth and faithfulness that exceeds that of a friend. The next admonition reveals that prayers will be answered in accordance with the nature of the prayer; note the relationship of the verbs: ask/receive; search/find; knock/open (11:10). The questions in the next unit make the same point: would anyone respond with a snake if a child asked for fish, or a scorpion if the child asked for an egg? It is worth noting that the friend's and child's requests involve *food*.

Responding to the Text

More than any other Gospel, the author of Luke emphasizes prayer. Many of the major events in Jesus' ministry include Jesus praying: after his baptism he is praying when "the Holy Spirit descended upon him in bodily form like a dove" (3:21); before choosing the twelve disciples, he spends "the night in prayer to God" (6:12); we are told that Jesus was praying near his disciples before Peter proclaims him "the Messiah of God," after which Jesus first predicts his death and resurrection (9:18-22); the transfiguration occurs "while he was praying" in the presence of Peter, James, and John (9:28-32).

The importance of prayer in Jesus' life surely underscores the importance of prayer in our own lives. Although Christians know the Lord's Prayer, there is still need for us to talk about what it means to have a prayer life. Some Christians say they do not pray because they believe there is "proper" language for prayer, and their own vocabulary is inadequate. Within the life of

THE IMPORTANCE OF PRAYER IN JESUS' LIFE SURELY UNDERSCORES THE IMPORTANCE OF PRAYER IN OUR OWN LIVES.

the congregation, how often are lay persons encouraged to pray? If prayers are done only by clergy, it reinforces the perception that clergy are the ones who know how to pray. In working with seminarians over the years, I have learned that many are embarrassed by the fact that they do not pray, and they are not even sure how to get a life of prayer going. In private, seminarians, long-time members of congregations, and even clergy have confided that they do not follow a discipline of daily prayer. A sermon that not only focuses on the value of prayer but focuses on helping people know how to pray will be of great value to many Christians—and not only those who are new Christians or unchurched.

A valuable spiritual practice is meditating on the Lord's Prayer, repeating it slowly, allowing the familiar words to sink into our minds and hearts. In planning a sermon on this text, consider carving out twenty minutes each day to meditate on the prayer. Find a quiet, comfortable place to sit. Take a few deep breaths and let your body relax. Close your eyes and say the prayer very slowly. Continue repeating the prayer slowly, using the phrases of the prayer to bring your mind back when it wanders. Meditating on the prayer Christ has given us may lead you to experience a deep, still peace during the long pauses. If that happens, abide in the peace. The peace may expand into a feeling of joy and thanksgiving, or an experience of much-needed comfort. After meditating on the prayer for at least fifteen minutes, sit quietly, staying focused on God. You may find yourself moving naturally into other forms of prayer. It is also helpful to move from meditation on Scripture to reflecting on the texts for this week in relation to your own life and the lives of those for whom you are preparing a sermon. You may find that meditating on the Lord's Prayer leads to valuable questions and insights regarding the texts.

Through God's grace, may our lives become prayers dedicated to the loving will of the steadfast, faithful One.

NINTH SUNDAY AFTER PENTECOST

AUGUST 5, 2001
EIGHTEENTH SUNDAY IN ORDINARY TIME
PROPER 13

REVISED COMMON	EPISCOPAL (BCP)	ROMAN CATHOLIC
Eccl. 1:2, 12-14, 2:18-23 or Hos. 11:1-11	Eccl. 1:12-14; 2:(1-7, 11), 18-23	Eccl. 1:2; 2:21-23
Ps. 49:1-11 or Ps. 107:1-9, 43	Ps. 49 or 49:1-11	Ps. 90:3-6, 12-13
Col. 3:1-11	Col. 3:(5-11), 12-17	Col. 3:1-5, 9-11
Luke 12:13-21	Luke 12:13-21	Luke 12:13-21

What do we really think is important in life? We are bombarded continuously with messages that celebrate wealth and power as the keys to a fulfilling and secure life. Today's readings challenge such a perspective, reminding us of the fragility of life and the counsel of wisdom to walk in the way of God, relying on God's steadfast faithfulness and love.

FIRST READING

ECCLESIASTES 1:2, 12-14, 2:18-23 (RCL); ECCL. 1:12-14; 2:(1-7, 11), 18-23 (BCP); ECCL. 1:2; 2:21-23 (RC)

"Vanity of vanities, says the Teacher, vanity of vanities! All is vanity" (Eccl. 1:2). This thematic statement frames the book, appearing at the beginning and again near the end of the text (12:8). The Teacher who proclaims all is vanity has been interpreted in diverse ways—as a pessimist who claims life is meaningless, an optimist who believes life is to be enjoyed, or one whose philosophy is Buddhist in tone.

The meaning of *hebel*, translated traditionally as "vanity," is crucial in interpreting the text. The literal meaning is something like "vapor," "breath," or "steam."[15] The figurative use of "breath" for human life is found in the Psalms:

"surely everyone stands as a mere breath (*hebel*). Surely everyone goes about like a shadow. Surely for nothing they are in turmoil; they heap up, and do not know who will gather" (Ps. 39:5b).

The thrust of the text is that human life and accomplishment is ephemeral, insubstantial, something on which we cannot rely. Joy, success, and youth are described as *hebel* (2:1, 11; 4:4; 11:10), as are intellectual endeavors. The Teacher, King Solomon, used his mind "to seek and search out by wisdom all that is done under heaven." He concluded that what we strive for with all our busyness is *hebel*. Our efforts are as futile as trying to chase the wind (1:13–14).

Human life is insubstantial because of death. Despite his being king, Solomon knew that whatever he accomplished would be left to others (2:18). The king cannot know whether those who receive the fruit of his toil will be wise or foolish (2:19). Yet they will be master of all for which the king toiled—his ideas, as well as his material wealth (2:19). The inability to determine what others will do with that for which we toil reveals that our sense of accomplishment and control is nothing but air.

The Teacher notes that sometimes one "who has toiled with wisdom and knowledge and skill must leave all to be enjoyed by another who did not toil for it" (2:21). In the KJV, RSV, and NRSV, this is described as not only vanity but *rasa*, "a great evil" (2:21). The NIV reads "a great misfortune." C. L. Seow chooses "a great tragedy."[16]

Responding to the Text

Translating a text necessarily involves interpreting a text, as the difference between "evil" and "tragedy" suggests. Under what conditions might it be a great evil to leave the fruit of one's life efforts to others to enjoy? Under what conditions would it be a great misfortune, tragedy, or sadness (another meaning of the same term)?

The diverse interpretations of Ecclesiastes make it a provocative text to preach and teach. The mind-numbing pace at which so many of us lead our lives speaks to the need for us to take seriously the reminder that no matter how hard we work, how big our bank account, or how long our resume, we will die. What do we get "for all the toil and strain with which [we] toil under the sun" (2:22)? One compelling interpretation is that the Teacher insists we recognize the unpredictability and insubstantiality of life, and yet claims, "There is nothing better for mortals than to eat and drink, and find enjoyment in their toil" (Eccl. 2:24). Resisting the interpretation that the Teacher is cynical, Rolf Knierim argues that these passages point to our human entitlement "to eat and drink, and to enjoy them as long as one lives. . . . [T]he affirmation of eating and drinking . . . reflects the affirmation of the legitimacy of life itself. . . . [L]ack of food denies a person's right to life. It is a fundamental attack against the legitimacy of life itself, against the meaning and goal of the cosmic creation, and ultimately against the existence of God in this world."[17]

HOSEA 11:1-11 (RCL alt.)

In last week's reading, Hosea used the metaphor of God as the husband of Israel to express the passion of God's love and the intimate relationship into which God calls us. This week, we find Hosea using a quite different, but also intimate metaphor: God as mother to her son Israel.

As a mother seeks the welfare of her children, God called the people out of Egypt. However, reacting as willful children often do, the more the divine mother called, the more they ran in other directions—"sacrificing to the Baals, and offering incense to idols" (11:1-2). Despite their waywardness, God taught them to walk, "took them up in [her] arms . . . healed them . . . led them with cords of human kindness, with bands of love," treating them "like those who lift infants to their cheeks. I bent down to them and fed them" (11:3-4).

In this passage, God judges Israel. Unlike last week's text on Abraham's dialogue with God about Sodom (Gen. 18:22-33; see Proper 12), there is no mention in Hosea of a distinction between the sinners and the righteous. The people are "bent on turning away from" God. The tension between the justice of punishment and the justice of pardon is radicalized in Hosea in a way that reflects on God's own identity. As Knierim argues, "Who but the one who says, 'I am God and no human' [author's translation of v. 9], can replace punishment with pardon without controlling or removing the ongoing destructiveness of evil?"[18] Yet this is what God does. With the incomprehensible love of a divine mother whose heart breaks for the waywardness of her children, God asks, "How can I give you up, Ephraim [a favorite name for Israel]? How can I hand you over, O Israel? . . . My heart recoils within me; my compassion grows warm and tender" (11:7-8).

Responding to the Text

When others betray and hurt us, we humans sometimes find it impossible to forgive them and take them back into an intimate relationship. Rather than growing warm and tender, our hearts may become stone. Yet, following the tradition in which "the lion's roar of YHWH" signaled hope,[19] God roars like a lion, calling God's children from exile (11:10-11). YHWH, the Holy One in their midst, will be their God and lead them back home (11:9-11). As God yearned for a loving, faithful response from the Hebrews, so God yearns for a loving, faithful response from us.

Hosea's message of God's passionate, steadfast, and faithful love is a message of great hope. His metaphor of God as a divine mother who lovingly tends, teaches, and heals her children is a much-needed contribution to the overwhelming dominance of male imagery for God in both ancient texts and contemporary liturgy.

RESPONSIVE READING

PSALM 49:1-11 (RCL);
PS. 49 or PS. 49:1-11 (BCP)

This wisdom psalm incorporates many of the themes addressed in the text from Ecclesiastes: "When we look at the wise, they die; fool and dolt perish together and leave their wealth to others" (49:10). All will die, even if they had the power "to name lands their own" (49:11). Although the lectionary ends with v. 12 or v. 11, one may wish to include v. 15, a confident statement of hope. Although we can never accumulate enough wealth to ransom our own soul and avoid death, the psalmist has faith that "God will ransom my soul from the power of Sheol, for he will receive me."

PSALM 107:1-9, 43 (RCL alt.)

This psalm of thanksgiving acknowledges God's redeeming action on behalf of the community. They have been gathered from many lands, "from the east and from the west, from the north and from the south" (cf. above, on Hosea 11:10-11). The people were lost, hungry, and thirsty. They cried to the Lord and in response were delivered. God led them in the right direction, gave them drink because they were "parched with thirst" and "filled the hungry with good things" (note the previous discussion of food in regard to the Lord's Prayer in Proper 12, as well as the comments regarding food in Ecclesiastes, above). Those who are wise will remember that God is the one who redeemed the people (107:43).

PSALM 90:3-4, 5-6, 12-13 (RC)

The psalmist recognizes the fragility and brevity of human existence. The community prays to become cognizant of this human reality that they might have "a wise heart" (90:12). They recognize that their iniquities are before God. After long suffering, they pray for God to have compassion upon them, satisfying them in the morning with God's "steadfast love" that they "may rejoice and be glad all [their] days" (90:14).

COLOSSIANS 3:1-11 (RCL);
COL. 3:(5-11), 12-17 (BCP);
COL. 3:1-5, 9-11 (RC)

Interpreting the Text

In last week's reading, the writer warned the Colossians to reject false teaching and have faith in the sufficiency of Christ. We pick up the Pauline letter this week with a transition setting forth theological claims that warrant the letter's imperatives regarding proper conduct of a Christian life.

Having been "raised with Christ" (3:1) through baptism, believers participate in the "already" of salvation. Therefore, they are enjoined to "seek the things that are above, where Christ is, seated at the right hand of God" (3:1). The spatial metaphor reflects the three-story world imagined by ancients in which God is above (note the reference to the *upward* [in the Greek] call of God in Christ Jesus, Phil. 3:14). Christ "seated at the right hand of God" reflects a messianic interpretation of Ps. 110:1.

Because the Colossians *have died* with Christ (the aorist verb form indicates something that happened in the past) it is possible for them to set their minds on that which is above, which involves both the mind and the will. That the believer's life "is hidden with Christ in God" (3:3) echoes the psalmist's prayers to be hidden in the shadow of God's wings (Ps. 17:8). God's wings provide refuge from enemies and the storms of life that threaten us like the unrelenting desert sun (see Pss. 36:7; 17:8; 91:4). In the protective darkness of God's shadow, the psalmist is able to "sing for joy" (Ps. 63:7). Through intimate union with Christ, believers are hidden with him in God. This "already" is held in tension with the "not yet" of salvation "when Christ who is your life is revealed . . . in glory" (3:4)—an apocalyptic theme indicating that what is already true has yet to be revealed.

The new life of the believer should reflect the qualities of God's "chosen people . . . a compassionate heart, kindness, humility, gentleness, patience, bearing with one another, forgiving" any complaint, and "above all" expressing "love" (3:12-14). Having been reconciled to God, the peace of Christ in the heart of the believer should lead to relations in the community that are permeated with peace. Aware of living out of God's grace, believers should do all that they do "in the name of the Lord Jesus, giving thanks to God the Father through him" (3:17).

Responding to the Text

The theological claims provide the grounding for the imperatives that follow. Because the Colossians have died with Christ, their life should reflect this reality. The sins that are enumerated should be "put to death," which requires transforming the will and the mind. In the Greek, the conjunction, definite article, and relative clause serve to emphasize the last sin "greed (which is idolatry)" (3:5). The linking of greed with idolatry underlines the severity of the threat it poses. Greed leads us away from God, and yet it can present itself in so many respectable guises.

The second list identifies characteristics of their old selves. The list is followed by the imperative, "Do not lie to one another" (3:9). Not lying is emphasized in recognition of the damage done to individuals and communities of faith when Christians lie to one another and violate the promises they have made. The individual and corporate destruction created by greed and lying is at least as great a problem today as it was 2,000 years ago.

What are we to do? According to the text, our old self is already dead, whereas putting on the "new self" (3:10) involves an ongoing process in which the self is "being renewed in knowledge according to the image of its creator" (3:10). Our part involves setting our minds on Christ. Most people find that to be a challenging assignment. Stop periodically throughout the day and spend five minutes watching your mind. To what thoughts, feelings, experiences are you habitually drawn? Do these thoughts and feelings lead toward or away from God? Saints through the ages have described the mind as a team of powerful horses that can race off in directions we did not really plan or want to go. Sound familiar? Gaining the ability to use our own mind as we would like to is difficult. Daily practices that involve intentionally focusing our mind on God can help: meditating on Scripture, repeating the Jesus Prayer during the day, sustaining an appreciative gaze on a beautiful aspect of God's creation, listening deeply to sacred music help.[20]

In the new, developing life in Christ, the unjust divisions humans establish to rank people must be recognized and addressed. The ancient Greeks habitually thought in terms of Greeks, barbarians, and the particularly despised barbarian Scythians (3:11). What assumptions have we internalized from our families and culture—regarding race, gender, age, ethnicity, economic class, sexual orientation—that lead us to pre-judge individuals whom we encounter? How does the unreflective, habitual use of such categories to evaluate others lead us away from God? In the new life in Christ into which we are called, all humanly constructed hierarchies of status and value are eliminated. All are one in Christ.

IN THE NEW, DEVELOPING LIFE IN CHRIST, THE UNJUST DIVISIONS HUMANS ESTABLISH TO RANK PEOPLE MUST BE RECOGNIZED AND ADDRESSED.

LUKE 12:13-21

Interpreting the Text

We are told at the beginning of the chapter that a crowd of thousands had gathered. Jesus is talking with his disciples when someone from the crowd asks him to adjudicate a dispute with his brother regarding the family inheritance. Although this would have been an accepted role for a rabbi to play, Jesus refuses to get involved in the dispute. Instead, he cautions the questioner to be on guard "against all kinds of greed for one's life does not consist in the abundance of possessions" (12:15).

After responding to the person's question, Jesus relates a parable about a rich man who had extensive land holdings that produced a particularly abundant harvest. Through the literary technique of a soliloquy, we are granted access to the farmer's inner musings. The unexpected abundance creates a problem: his barns are not big enough to hold all that he will be able to gather. In considering the problem, the farmer consults only with himself and thinks only in terms of his own future. He asks himself, "What should I do?" and comes up with a satisfying answer: he will build larger barns and store everything for himself so he can relax and enjoy years of leisure.

The farmer's self-references in the soliloquy are noteworthy. In just two verses, he repeats the phrase "I will" four times: "I will do this: I will pull down . . . and build. . . . I will store. . . . I will say to my soul, 'You have ample goods laid up for many years; relax, eat, drink, be merry'" (12:18-19). The farmer seems confident in his understanding of life and his solution to the happy "problem" of unexpected abundance.

Once the barns are built and the bountiful harvest stored, the farmer plans to direct his soul to follow the Epicurean philosophy: "relax, eat, drink, be merry!" Ironically, it is the inevitability of death that evokes an Epicurean attitude toward life. Isaiah warns that when the people should have been weeping and mourning, they chose instead to prepare a festive celebration saying, "Let us eat and drink, for tomorrow we die" (Isa. 22:12-13). Paul uses a common form of the saying in 1 Cor. 15:32: "If the dead are not raised, 'let us eat and drink, for tomorrow we die.'" The farmer's plans fail to consider the reality of death and the possibility that it might be imminent.

Responding to the Text

To learn from this parable, it is important for us not to caricature the farmer. There is no indication that he earned his wealth in any dishonorable or unjust way. The problem is the farmer's lack of concern for the relational dynamics that inevitably connect him, his abundance, and the community in which he lives. He does not talk with anyone else or think about family or friends when considering what to do with the abundant harvest. He does not consider giving the unexpected excess of his harvest to those who are poor and hungry. Rather he resolves to tear down his current barns and build much bigger ones so he can store all of the harvest for himself and secure his future years of leisure.

The farmer's approach to life violated the wisdom of the ancient world, which taught that wealth must be shared because the goods in the world are limited. If goods are limited, one person's hoarding sets into motion a relational dynamic that takes away from others. Bruce Malina's study of first-century society leads him to argue that a person who accumulated capital was perceived as "necessarily dishonorable. . . . A person could not accumulate wealth except through the loss and injury suffered by another."[21] The point of this parable is not that wealth is wrong per se,

> THE FARMER'S APPROACH TO LIFE VIOLATED THE WISDOM OF THE ANCIENT WORLD, WHICH TAUGHT THAT WEALTH MUST BE SHARED BECAUSE THE GOODS IN THE WORLD ARE LIMITED.

although such a warning recurs in Luke and in the wisdom literature. This parable warns against the misuse of wealth, the failure to use it for the common good.

A second problem with the farmer's perspective is even more serious. Believing that accumulation of wealth is the source of his security, his way of life constitutes a form of idolatry. The connection between greed and idolatry is reinforced in Pauline theology (e.g., Eph. 5:5, Col. 3:5). In 1 Timothy, we find the warning that "the love of money is a root of all kinds of evil, and in their eagerness to be rich some have wandered away from the faith" (1Tim. 6:10). The farmer's eagerness to accumulate greater wealth leads him to violate the two great commandments: to love the Lord with all his heart, mind, and strength and his neighbor as himself.

Since the man is not interacting with other people, it is God who intervenes to name his folly. Thus, in the only parable in which God plays a direct role, God—who knows our secret thoughts—responds to the farmer's plans to eat, drink, and be merry by addressing him with a revealing epithet, "You fool!" The way of the fool is noted in Psalm 14: "The fool says in his heart, 'There is no God'" (14:1). The presence of a miraculously bountiful harvest—a sure sign of God's blessing—evokes no thoughts of God in the farmer's heart, only thoughts of his own security and pleasure. The reality of death that stands behind the Epicurean surrender to food, drink, and merriment is not a distant phenomenon. It is a reality the farmer will experience that very night. And those abundant crops he had assumed would secure his future—"whose will they be" (12:20)? The farmer's sin of idolatry is reinforced in the concluding comment of the text: as it was with the farmer, so it will be with those who take care to "store up treasures for themselves but are not rich toward God" (12:21).

Responding to the Text

The miraculously bountiful harvest suggests imagery associated with the kingdom of God. In keeping with parables that describe the kingdom directly, the implicit references to the kingdom in this parable do not meet our expectations. There is no apocalyptic destruction of evil. Rather a man delights in his bountiful harvest, plans to build great barns to store it, imagines the good life ahead, and before he has a chance to enact the first step of his plan, he dies. His neighbors probably have no idea what was in his heart. They may celebrate the man and all the bounty that is now left to others because of his death. The kingdom that is close at hand in the bountiful harvest goes unrecognized.

Bernard Brandon Scott connects this parable to the sayings about the man who should leave his gift at the altar to reconcile first with his brother or sister (Matt. 5:23-24), and the widow in the temple whom Jesus describes as giving more than the rich people gave because she gave her offering out of her need, not her abundance (Mark 12:41-44). Scott sees in these two sayings and the parable of the rich farmer a "radical identification of God's kingdom with community and the demand to provide for the needs of others."[22] The point is spelled out in James: "If a brother or sister is ill-clad and in lack of daily food, and one of you says to them, 'Go in peace, be warmed and filled,' without giving them the things needed for the body, what does it profit?" (James 2:15-16). Caring for one's neighbor is an obedient response to the First Commandment. Failure to consider the good of the community is idolatry.

TENTH SUNDAY AFTER PENTECOST

August 12, 2001
Nineteenth Sunday in Ordinary Time
Proper 14

Revised Common	Episcopal (BCP)	Roman Catholic
Gen. 15:1-6	Gen. 15:1-6	Wis. 18:6-9
or Isa. 1:1, 10-20		
Ps. 33:12-22	Ps. 33 or 33:12-15,	Ps. 33:1, 12, 18-22
or Ps. 50:1-8, 22-23	18-22	
Heb. 11:1-3, 8-16	Heb. 11:1-3 (4-7),	Heb. 11:1-2, 8-19
	8-16	or 11:1-2, 8-12
Luke 12:32-40	Luke 12:32-40	Luke 12:32-48 or 12:35-40

Faith, a recurring theme in today's texts, requires more than proper worship. These texts challenge us to examine the faithfulness embodied in our daily lives. In addition to discussing the great exemplars of the faith, it is valuable to learn about faithful lives in the history of a local congregation and community.

FIRST READING
GENESIS 15:1-6 (RCL/BCP)

Interpreting the Text

This encounter, which occurs before God gives Abram and Sarai the new names by which we know them, begins with God saying to Abram, "Do not be afraid" (15:1). This word of comfort commonly accompanies what humans often experience as the overwhelming and terrifying experience of God's presence. Abram has just returned from a battle that may yet have threatening consequences for him. YHWH assures Abram that he can depend on God as his protection and deliverer because God is his "shield" (15:1). Although Abram takes no rewards for himself from his recent victory, God assures him that his reward will be great. Abram questions this because he is an old man with no children, thus no heir. God's failure to deliver on this promise is uppermost in Abram's mind. YHWH rejects Abram's claim that a slave born in his home will be his heir.

YHWH takes him outside, shows him the night sky, and promises Abram that his descendants will be as numerous as the stars. Abram accepts God's promise, believing that God will do as God has said. Abram's faith in God, despite his old age, is "reckoned . . . to him as righteousness" (15:6).

RESPONDING TO THE TEXT

Faith is a dominant theme in today's texts. Whereas the text from Isaiah points to the dire consequences of leading unfaithful lives, this text tells part of the story of Abraham, who is held up throughout Scripture, as in today's text from Hebrews, as an exemplar of faithfulness. Abraham responds obediently to God's call for him to set out on a journey without knowing where he is going. He trusts God's promise to provide him with descendants, despite his and Sarah's advanced age. We, too, are called to be faithful to God and have faith in God, even when the circumstances of life appear to be desolate or threatening. We are unlikely to have visions in which God addresses us with the clarity that God addressed Abraham. However, through study of the Bible, a life of prayer, and discernment within the community of faith, we can come to hear God's call in our lives. The question is whether we will follow Abraham and Sarah and respond with faithful obedience, even when the call involves a journey that has no clear destination.

WISDOM OF SOLOMON 18:6-9 (RC)

This reading points to the providence of God to explain the actions that occur during the Exodus. The abandoned child (18:5) is Moses, whose mother left him to be found by Pharaoh's daughter after Pharaoh commanded the death of all male Hebrew newborns. In contrast to the story in Exodus, the Pharaoh's command is tied to the later deaths of first-born Egyptian males at the time of the Exodus. The Egyptian deaths are attributed to the unrighteous treatment of the Hebrews. Unlike Egyptians, Hebrews offered sacrifices in secret, "agreed to the divine law," and sang praises to the ancestors—probably the patriarchs (18:9).

ISAIAH 1:1, 10-20 (RCL alt.)

Interpreting the Text

Following identification of the prophet Isaiah, the reading for today depicts the community as the rulers and people of the legendary cities of Sodom and Gomorrah, thus indicating the seriousness of their sin. To fully appreciate the severity of their situation, it is important theologically to consider the analysis of vv. 10-20 in light of v. 2, which is not included in the lection. YHWH calls on the heavens and earth to hear the accusation against the people, for they have "rebelled" against God (Isa. 1:2).

Pesa is translated as "rebelled," which implies an intentional, willful disobedience. Careful textual studies, however, suggest that *pesa* is more adequately translated as "having broken with."[23] The difference is critical. If the people rebel against God, they are still in relationship with God. There is still hope. If, however, the people have broken with God, perhaps without even realizing it, their situation is far more grave. It is because the people have broken with God that their worship is so intolerable. Isaiah is not arguing against the legitimacy of the cultic traditions of worship. Rather, he is proclaiming YHWH's rejection of worship that is performed by those whose lives leave them with "hands that are full of blood" (Isa. 1:15). What YHWH demands is clearly specified by verbs that require action: "*cease* to do evil, *learn* to do good; *seek* justice, *rescue* the oppressed, *defend* the orphan, *plead* for the widow" (Isa. 1:17).

Using the metaphor of a legal suit, YHWH makes an accusation against the people. If they change the ways in which they live, their sins will be forgiven— "though your sins are like scarlet, they shall be like snow" (Isa. 1: 18). Failure to change will lead to dire and inevitable consequences. The reading ends with the relatively rare phrase, "for the mouth of the Lord has spoken," which reinforces the divine authority behind the prophetic message.

Responding to the Text

Although we do not participate in the kinds of sacrifices and forms of worship identified in this passage, it would be a serious error for us to hear the prophet's warning as if it has nothing to say to us. We must ask ourselves if we participate in worship with bloody hands. Are we complicit in the growing gap between the rich and the poor in today's world? In what ways have we broken with God in the reality of our daily lives while deceiving ourselves by participating in "proper" worship?

RESPONSIVE READING
PSALM 33:12-22 (RCL); PS. 33
or PS. 33:12-15, 18-22 (BCP);
PS. 33:1, 12, 18-22 (RC)

In this psalm of praise, those who both fear God and place their hope in God's "steadfast love" (Ps. 33:18) realize that God is the true source of deliverance and salvation. Recognizing that God knows the secrets of every heart, and the deeds of every person (Ps. 33:15), the faithful turn to God as their "help and shield" (Ps. 33:20). Their hearts are glad because they trust in God's "holy name" (Ps. 33:21). The psalm ends with a prayer that captures the dynamic interplay between God's steadfast love for us and our hope in God (Ps. 33:22).

PSALM 50:1-8, 22-23 (RCL alt.)

The psalm begins with a vision of God's appearance accompanied by "a devouring fire" and a "mighty tempest" (50:3). God, the righteous judge, gathers the people for judgment. The psalm then turns to a prophetic judgment: while the sacrifices of the people are continually offered, they fail to live faithful lives. They are exhorted to honor God with the sacrifice of thankful lives in which people go "the right way," that is, live according to the covenant (50:23).

SECOND READING
HEBREWS 11:1-3, 8-16 (RCL);
HEB. 11:1-3 (4-7), 8-16 (BCP);
HEB. 11:1-2, 8-19 or
HEB. 11:1-2, 8-12 (RC)

Interpreting the Text

We are not sure who wrote the letter to the Hebrews or to whom. The text is more closely related to the genre of sermon than letter. The author refers to the text as "a word of exhortation" (13:22), a term also used to refer to a synagogue address (Acts 13:15). There are many allusions to the Old Testament in Hebrews, as well as twenty-nine direct quotations taken from the Pentateuch, Psalms, prophets, writings, and historical books. The author uses scriptural references to create and justify exhortations to an audience in a different setting and time period in a way some commentators describe as an example of homiletic midrash—a sermon or essay that expounds on a particular text or theme of the Old Testament.[24]

The thesis of Hebrews is that Jesus, as the Son of God, is our high priest who, unlike the ongoing human priesthood, has access to the heavenly sanctuary (8:5) in which he has made a sacrifice on our behalf that does not require repetition, a sacrifice of his own blood that secures eternal redemption (9:11-12). Christ is the link between the shadowy life of earth and the reality of the heavenly life.

The audience knows about Christ. The preacher—identifying with the audience—exhorts all to "pay greater attention to what we have heard, so that we do not drift away from it" (2:1). To drift away, to become sluggish (6:12) places the listeners at risk of having "an evil, unbelieving heart that turns away from the living God" (3:12).[25]

This text from Hebrews is part of an exposition on Habakkuk and Isaiah that speaks of the arrival of one who is to come—a righteous one who "will live by faith" and not "shrink back" (10:37-38). Maintaining one's faith, not turning away from God or becoming sluggish, is critical.

In these passages, *pistis* (faith) is described as the *hypostasis* (assurance) of things hoped for, the *elengchos* (conviction) of things not seen (11:1). Scholars disagree about the meaning of both *hypostasis* and *elengchos* in this context. *Hypostasis* may refer to reality with *elengchos* as the objective demonstration of that reality. That is, *hypostasis* may refer objectively to the substance or essence of God and *elengchos* may refer subjectively to one's conviction about that objective reality. Faith would then be a combination of the reality of God and one's conviction about that reality.

In Hebrews 11, there is a highly unusual eighteen-fold list linked rhetorically by the repetition of *pistis*, which occurs eight times in this lection. The repetition emphasizes faith as the tie that binds people in the present audience with their ancestors: Abraham, Sarah, Isaac, and Jacob.

The preacher attributes Abraham's self-description as "a stranger and alien" (Gen. 23:4) to all the ancestors of faith in the list. They died in faith seeking not a homeland on earth, but "a better country . . . a heavenly one" (Heb. 11:16).

THE GOSPEL
LUKE 12:32-40 (RCL/BCP);
LUKE 12:32-48 or 12:35-40 (RC)

Interpreting the Text

Jesus' admonition to his disciples not to worry about what they are to eat, drink, or wear precedes today's reading, which begins, "Do not be afraid, little flock, for it is your Father's good pleasure to give you the kingdom" (12:32). The word *eudokeō,* translated as "good pleasure," also carries the meaning of "choosing" or "making a decision." The followers of Jesus are not to be anxious or afraid because God has *decided* to give them the kingdom.

With faith in God's care and provision, they are encouraged to sell their possessions—not build bigger barns for them as the rich farmer in last week's reading planned to do—and give alms. Sharing one's wealth with those in need creates a different kind of purse, one that will not wear out. This metaphorical purse will hold treasure far more substantial than the material treasures thieves can steal and moths can destroy.

Being honest with ourselves about what it is we treasure is critically important to our spiritual health. Where our treasure is, there will our heart be also. If we treasure God and the ways of God, we can be anywhere in the world and our thoughts and feelings will naturally flow to God. If our real treasure is gold, we can be sitting in worship with our thoughts absorbed elsewhere—perhaps in a review of our stock portfolio in light of the past week on Wall Street.

Using images that evoke the urgency of eschatology, Jesus admonishes the disciples to be "dressed for action"; literally, let their loins be girded with their "lamps lit" (12:35). Being dressed for action echoes the directions given for the Passover meal, which was to be eaten hurriedly with "loins girded . . . sandals on, and a staff in your hand," to commemorate the hasty exit of the Hebrews from Egypt (Exod. 12:11).

The theme of preparedness is reinforced by the parable of the master who returns from the wedding banquet (banquet imagery is associated with the kingdom) to find his slaves watching, opening the door immediately upon his arrival. In response to their preparedness, a remarkable reversal takes place. The master who has just been served as a guest will "fasten his belt"—girding up his loins to get unwieldy clothing out of the way so he can work. The master unexpectedly asks the slaves to sit at the table and serves them.

> BEING HONEST WITH OURSELVES ABOUT WHAT IT IS WE TREASURE IS CRITICALLY IMPORTANT TO OUR SPIRITUAL HEALTH.

The hospitality of meals and the provision of food are a frequent theme in Luke. It would be unheard of within the context of the Roman household master/slave relations, however, for the master to serve the slave. To the social outcasts in the crowd, the gracious provision of food would be good news, the kind of news Jesus repeatedly associates with the kingdom of God. It is the preparedness of the slaves, who have no idea the hour that the master might return, that leads to their being twice-blessed (12:37-38) and exalted far above their social station.

Responding to the Text

Today's Gospel stresses the certainty that Jesus Christ will come for us along with the uncertainty about when that may occur. While the author and perhaps many of the early readers of this text thought of the return of the "Son of Man" in terms of an imminent eschatology, it seems more helpful for us reflect on this text in light of the reality of our own death—an event that may come when we least expect it, as indeed was the case for the rich farmer in last week's text. Our preparedness involves setting our mind and heart on the ways of God and living a life that reflects the values Christ taught. Reflecting honestly about where our personal and communal treasure is, is a critical first step.

This story also gives us a chance to reflect on the radical role reversal initiated by the person of power and status in relation to his slaves. In seeking to more adequately and clearly communicate such equality, where there is no longer Jew or Gentile, slave or free, male or female, it is helpful to reflect with our congregations about the implications of always using "kingdom" language.

The metaphorical field of "kingdom" invokes a powerful hierarchy—one God, one king, one father—that has structured and reinforced patriarchal hierarchies through the centuries. Although we may not think about it consciously, the use of "kingdom" immediately invokes this hierarchy with all its implications for assigning value to people in terms of gender and socioeconomic class. An alternative to "kingdom" would be "commonwealth."

In reality it may be impossible to avoid some form of hierarchy in any community, in the sense that some people have more credibility and greater influence than others. Any institution or congregation that seeks to embody the teachings of Christ, however, must review periodically whether or not the hierarchy it embodies functions in just or unjust ways.

ELEVENTH SUNDAY AFTER PENTECOST

Augustus 19, 2001
Twentieth Sunday in Ordinary Time
Proper 15

Revised Common	Episcopal (bcp)	Roman Catholic
Jer. 23:23-29	Jer. 23:23-29	Jer. 38:4-6, 8-10
or Isa. 5:1-7		
Ps. 82	Ps. 82	Ps. 40:2-4, 18
or Ps. 80:1-2, 8-19		
Heb. 11:29—12:2	Heb. 12:1-7,	Heb. 12:1-4
	(8-10), 11-14	
Luke 12:49-56	Luke 12:49-56	Luke 12:49-53

These texts admonish us to remember others when our own lives are going well. As long as there are people in the world who are oppressed and suffering from lack of food, shelter, and basic medical care, we have a responsibility as Christians to address such issues. Our faith in and commitment to Christ should be observable in the fruit of our daily lives.

FIRST READING
JEREMIAH 23:23-29 (RCL/BCP)

Jeremiah was called to be a prophet when he was young—perhaps a teenager. Having been raised in a family that honored God's covenant and its demands, he was well aware of the tremendous distance between the ways people were conducting their political and religious lives and the ways YHWH commanded them to live.

During Jeremiah's career, Josiah ascended the throne, and the covenant scroll was found (probably a scroll of Deuteronomy) that detailed the requirements for living in faithful covenant with YHWH. Josiah instituted many reforms in an effort to fulfill the requirements. Following Josiah's death in an ill-advised military adventure, one son was put on the throne only to be replaced by his older brother Johoiakim, who was a vassal of the Babylonian Empire that had defeated Assyria and was now extending its territory.

Throughout these years Jeremiah warned that doom was coming. However, other prophets claimed all would be well. Both claimed to speak for YHWH. Who was to be believed? We find this conflict reflected in today's text. The passage begins with three rhetorical questions that reflect on the identity of YHWH: Is God not nearby as well as far off? Is there anyone who can hide in a place that YHWH cannot see? Does YHWH not fill heaven and earth (Jer. 23:23-24)? The imagery found in these questions evokes Psalm 139 as well as the threat in Amos 9:2-4).

YHWH tells Jeremiah that he knows that people are prophesying lies in the name of YHWH. How can a God who knows the secret of every heart and every human deed *not* know! It is not that the prophets claim to have been spoken to in dreams that is the problem—dreams are a legitimate medium through which God communicates with people in the Bible. The problem is the content of their message: the assurance that all is well when great disaster looms.

YHWH's lament, "How long?" (23:26) is remarkable. These are the very words spoken in laments by those who await God's deliverance. The resonance of those well-known words reveals the pathos of divine suffering spoken of so clearly in Hosea, an eighth-century prophet who influenced Jeremiah (see Propers 12 and 13). YHWH suffers over the deceitful hearts of the prophets (Jer. 23:26). Will they ever repent?

Accusations against the false prophets follow. They plan to make the people forget the name of YHWH, just as their ancestors who became Baal worshipers did. YHWH challenges them to a public trial. Let the false prophets tell their dreams, and let the one who truly has been given God's word speak it faithfully. The notion of a public trial suggests the story of Elijah's challenge to four hundred prophets of Baal who were supported and encouraged during the reign of King Ahab and his wife Jezebel (1 Kings 18:20-40). The influence of Canaanite religion on the early Israelite religion and the differences between them were a source of conflict for many generations.

The passage ends with a proverb noting that the false prophets have nothing in common with true prophets, just as straw has nothing in common with wheat. In contrast to a false word, God's word is "like fire" and "like a hammer that breaks a rock in pieces" (23:28-29). In criticizing the rich and powerful who have forsaken those in need, Jeremiah claims that YHWH has "struck" the people, "but they felt no anguish; you have consumed them, but they refused to take correction. They have made their faces harder than rock; they have refused to turn back" (5:3). Many hardships have befallen Judah and Israel before the prophecy of Jeremiah, but it has not been enough to lead the people to true repentance. Intricate cultic worship is offered, but the people have refused to wash their hearts "clean of wickedness" (4:14). "From the least to the greatest of them, everyone is greedy for unjust gain; from prophet to priest everyone deals falsely" (6:13). Though the people believe they will be spared because of their worship, Jeremiah correctly predicts the downfall of Judah that occurs in 587, when Babylon finally takes control of Judah and destroys most of the cities, including the temple and the walls of Jerusalem.

JEREMIAH 38:4-6, 8-10 (RC)

Jeremiah's career as a prophet was a long and difficult one. This text relates only one of the times in which his life was threatened. Jeremiah advised King Zedekiah to surrender to Nebuchadrezzar of Babylon because the destruction of Israel was imminent. Jeremiah's enemies, pro-Egyptian court officials who opposed surrender, gained the king's permission to take custody of Jeremiah. They threw him into a cistern that had no water in it. Ironically, in another oracle YHWH's complaint against Israel involves "two evils: they have forsaken me, the fountain of living water, and dug out cisterns for themselves, cracked cisterns that can hold no water" (2:13). Metaphorically, leaky cisterns refer to Israel's apostasy in turning to other gods and political powers for deliverance and protection. In reality, a muddy cistern was used to try to kill YHWH's prophet. In the final verses of today's lection, a foreigner in the king's court, an Ethiopian, convinces the king to let him pull Jeremiah out of the cistern.

ISAIAH 5:1-7 (RCL alt.)

Interpreting the Text

The parable of the vineyard builds on the intimate imagery of the people as God's beloved that was found in the text of Hosea (see Proper 12). In this case, the reference to Israel as male rather than female suggests the imagery of God as the mother/father and Israel as the son of God, imagery also found in Hosea, among other texts. Use of such personal imagery reinforces the suffering God experiences when humans violate and break their relationship with YHWH.

By presenting a parable, Isaiah draws in his audience. A farmer clears fertile land, plants it with "choice vines," builds a watchtower to be sure it is protected, and prepares a "wine vat" in full expectation of plentiful, delicious grapes (5:1-2). After all the hard work, the farmer discovers that the grapes are not merely "wild," they are rotten and stink, meanings of *be'asîm* that vividly portray the disgusting quality of the grapes (5:2). If they are rotten and stink, one does not even have to eat them to be negatively affected by their existence.

Isaiah asks the people to judge the vineyard. What more could the farmer have done? In disgust, the farmer removes the protective hedge so that wild animals will devour and trample the vineyard. It will no longer be "pruned" or "hoed" but will become "overgrown with briers and thorns" (5:5-6). The next line—that the clouds will be commanded not to rain on the vineyard—may alarm the listeners. Human beings do not command the clouds. What is Isaiah really saying? He leaves no doubt: the vineyard is "the house of Israel," and the "pleasant planting" are the "people of Judah" (5:7). The farmer is YHWH, who expected "justice, but saw bloodshed; righteousness, but heard a cry!" (5:7).

> THE OPPRESSED AND DOWNTRODDEN ARE BEING IGNORED BY THOSE WITH THE POLITICAL AND ECONOMIC POSITION IN THE COMMUNITY TO MAKE THINGS DIFFERENT.

The cry is the cry of the oppressed and downtrodden who are being ignored by those with the political and economic position in the community to make things different. This failure echoes last week's passage in which God rails against their endless sacrifices and festivals, which are intolerable for God because they are conducted with hands that "are full of blood" (1:15; see Proper 14).

Responding to the Text

The metaphor of fruit is important in both Testaments. In Matthew, Jesus warns people to discriminate between false and true prophets by judging their fruits (Matt.7:15-16). We are reminded that bad trees cannot bear good fruit (Matt.7:17-18; Luke 6:43), cautioned to pay attention to the fruits of the Spirit (Gal.5:22); and told that "wisdom . . . is . . . full of mercy and good fruit" (James 3:17). If our individual and corporate lives were compared to fruit, would we be delicious or rotten and stinky?

RESPONSIVE READING
PSALM 82 (RCL/BCP)

This unusual psalm describes God (Elohim) taking God's place at the mythological council of the gods. God judges the other gods and accuses them of injustice. They support the wicked and overlook the rights and needs of the weak, the orphan, the lowly, and the destitute. The gods, having "neither knowledge [nor] understanding" (82:5), are blind. The very foundations of the earth are shaken by their wickedness and injustice. As a result of their activity, the gods are stripped of their divine status and condemned to die as humans do. Having displaced the rest of the heavenly council, the one God now inherits all nations and is called on to rise up and judge them.

PSALM 40:2-4, 18 (NRSV: 40:1-3, 16) (RC)

God is praised for deliverance. Think of Joseph and later Jeremiah being thrown into a well. The experience of being thrown into a pit, a "miry bog" (40:2), functions as a metaphor for many kinds of threat. God has placed the singer on a secure rock. Deliverance leads to praise, which in turn encourages others to put their trust in YHWH. The final verse in the lection describes the singer's current state of need, confidence in God's saving help, and a petition for God to bring deliverance swiftly.

PSALM 80:1-2, 8-19 (RCL alt.)

Naming YHWH's role as the "Shepherd of Israel" (80:1), the community prays for God to hear their petition and deliver them from their current devastation. YHWH brought the people as a vine out of Egypt, cleared the land, and planted the vine. It took deep root and spread over great distances. Then YHWH's face shined on the people, but no more. The protective walls have been destroyed. The once strong and fruitful vine is ravaged by wild animals. The fruit is taken by anyone. The vine has been burned and cut down. It is only YHWH who can restore it. The community calls on YHWH to deliver them with the promise that "they will never turn back" from YHWH if they are saved.

SECOND READING
HEBREWS 11:29—12:2 (RCL);
HEB. 12:1-7, (8-10), 11-14 (BCP);
HEB. 12:1-4 (RC)

This passage continues the list of faithful ancestors, prophets, and martyrs that was begun in last week's reading from Hebrews (see Proper 14). Despite their faith, however, they did not receive immediately the fulfillment of what was promised to them. The delay in the fulfillment of the promise allows those in the present audience to be included.

The preacher repeats the admonition that the listeners not turn away from God or be sluggish. They are encouraged to set aside "every weight and the sin that clings so closely" (12:1), running the race with perseverance. The athletic metaphor invokes a stadium filled with a great cloud of faithful witnesses who have successfully run the first part of the race, and support those who are called to persevere in the last leg of the race. Setting aside "every weight" suggests taking off excess clothing that encumbers a runner. To succeed in the race, they are admonished to keep their eye on Jesus who is named the "pioneer and perfecter of our faith" (12:2). The use of the name Jesus calls attention to the humanity of the historical person who maintained his faith in the face of suffering and an ignominious death. Although perfection is a recurring theme in Hebrews, the noun "perfecter" (*teleiōtēs*) occurs only in this biblical text. Based on the root *telos*, it points to Jesus as the goal, destination, or fulfillment of "our faith" (Heb. 12:2). Those who hear the words are encouraged to look beyond everything else, keeping their eyes on Jesus "who for the sake of the joy that was set before him endured the cross, disregarding its shame" (12:2). Jesus' faithfulness is the exemplar for all others.

The eighteen-fold list of people that ends in today's passage presents a wide range of figures who are among the cloud of faithful witnesses. The speaker hopes to support and encourage faithfulness in the present community by reflecting on those who have been faithful despite suffering and death. The challenges to faithfulness faced by the original audience resonate with contemporary challenges.

God's promise of redemption has been revealed to us through Jesus Christ. Despite this promise, we, too, must guard against turning from God, becoming sluggish in our faith, and failing to persevere while keeping our eyes on Jesus Christ as we run the race that is set before us. The witnesses named in chapter 11 did not live perfect lives. Many of their sins are documented in Scripture.

> THE HEROES ARE HONORED NOT BECAUSE THEY WERE PERFECT BUT BECAUSE THEY PERSEVERED AND WERE FAITHFUL.

They are honored not because they were perfect but because they persevered and were faithful. The admonishment to keep our eyes on the real purpose of life comes within references to community—a reminder of the importance of the congregational dimension of our faith lives. Running alone, we may lose sight of the point and give up when exhaustion, suffering, and disappointment overwhelm us. Mutual support and encouragement helps us run the race God calls us to run.

Members of the congregation are battling against sin and facing trials, although no one has been physically harmed to the point of shedding blood. In responding to their suffering, the author encourages them to realize that their suffering is a sign of God's claim on them as God's children. Quoting from Prov. 3:12, they are encouraged to think of their suffering as the discipline of a loving parent that will yield for them "the peaceful fruit of righteousness" at a later time.

They are admonished to think about the great suffering Jesus endured that they might be strengthened and healed. They should follow straight paths—the way of the Lord—that their current state of lameness will not become even worse, and seek peace and purity.

LUKE 12:49-56 (RCL/BCP);
LUKE 12:49-53 (RC)

Interpreting the Text

In this difficult passage, Jesus, the one we call the Prince of Peace, is presented with his prophetic mantle on, announcing that he came to "bring fire to the earth," to be baptized (perhaps here, as in Mark 10:38, baptism is used to symbolize death), to bring "division" and not "peace" (12:49-51). The divisiveness is intensified through repetition: "three against two and two against three" (12:52). Provocatively, Jesus sharpens the focus for a close-up: "father against son and son against father, mother against daughter and daughter against mother . . ." (12:53). What can it mean that Jesus' *intention* was to bring fire and division?

The image of family members set against one another echoes the lament of a woman, perhaps a personification of Jerusalem, in Micah. She laments that there are no *hasid*, none who live lives characterized by *ḥesed*—faithfulness and loyalty to YHWH. She wanders through the land hungry, but finds nothing to eat (Micah 7:1). "All the faithful have disappeared from the land" (Micah 7:2). Thus, one who is faithful can trust no one—not even one's own family, "for the son treats the father with contempt, the daughter rises up against her mother . . . your enemies are members of your own household" (Micah 7:6). The woman recognizes that she cannot look to her family or friends but to God: "I will wait for the God of my salvation; my God will hear me" (Micah 7:7).

Jesus calls his followers to a life of faithfulness to God. His description of the division that will ensue in families is not a prescription of what *should* occur. Rather, he is saying that if individuals commit their lives to God, which is what following Jesus entails, their commitment will create conflict for them in their relations with others, including their own families. Jesus was not trying to establish a new religion. He was calling people to what he believed was a faithful embodiment of Judaism. His perspective threatened the Jewish leaders of the temple who were negotiating their own power and authority in relation to the oppressive political power of the Roman Empire.

Throughout the Gospel of Luke, Jesus' sharp words regarding those who focus on accumulating wealth and do not share it, his commitment to heal the sick on any day—including the Sabbath—and to eat with the outcasts of society, pushed back the boundaries of community identity and made room for those with little or no economic, political, or religious standing. Jesus' perspective threatened the power and authority of the chief priests in their relationships with others inside the Jewish community as well as in their complex relationship with the imperial Roman government. In addition to challenging the religious leaders and the wealthy within the Jewish community, Jesus' words and activities could also be perceived by the Roman authorities as a threat.

Crowds gathered when Jesus walked through the countryside. Time and again we are told of "thousands" gathering. The Romans were leery of large groups gathering, especially around Passover, when commemoration of being freed from Pharaoh's oppressive hand might incite people to strike out against their Roman oppressors. Hundreds—if not thousands—of Jews had been crucified over the years as a show of Roman power and authority.[26] In such a volatile environment, family members would almost certainly be divided in their reactions to Jesus. Much was at stake in following Jesus. Followers should expect fear and anger from family and friends who thought Jesus' perspective was both wrong and dangerous.

Jesus points out that people in the crowd can read climatic changes that signal impending rain or scorching heat. It does not follow that the ability to read weather signs makes them a "hypocrite" as we normally use that word. Joel Green argues that the Greek word translated "hypocrite" carries the meaning of "godless" in the Septuagint. Given the echo of the prophet Micah heard in announcing the division within families, it makes sense to hear Jesus deploring the lack of faithfulness to God in people's lives. In not leading lives determined by faithfulness to God, they are linked to the Pharisees whom Jesus castigates as "hypocrites." Because so few Christians know much about the early history of Christianity as a sect within Judaism, it is important to discuss the fact that the Pharisees, who sought to renew the religious commitments of Israel that were being corrupted by religious leaders beholden to Roman authorities, were caricatured by New Testament writers.[27] They opposed Jesus' interpretation of faithfulness to God and rejected the ways in which he violated the normative boundaries that defined the identity of the Jewish community.

> WHEN INDIVIDUALS COMMIT THEIR LIVES TO GOD, THEIR COMMITMENT WILL SOMETIMES CREATE CONFLICT FOR THEM IN THEIR RELATIONS WITH OTHERS.

Responding to the Text

We need to step back from our tendency to discuss the family in sentimental and idealized ways. If we are honest, every family has stories of divisive conflicts and troubling "secrets"—families in the Bible are no different. While many family conflicts are fueled by lies and betrayal, serious conflicts are also fueled by faith commitments that are not shared. Jesus chastises the crowd for not being able to read the signs of the time, *kairos*. Are we reading the signs of the times in which we live? Are we willing to accept the conflicts that come if we place faithfulness to God as our highest priority?

TWELFTH SUNDAY AFTER PENTECOST

AUGUST 26, 2001
TWENTY-FIRST SUNDAY IN ORDINARY TIME
PROPER 16

REVISED COMMON	EPISCOPAL (BCP)	ROMAN CATHOLIC
Isa. 58:9b–14	Isa. 28:14–22	Isa. 66:18–21
or Jer. 1:4–10		
Ps. 103:1–8	Ps. 46	Ps. 117:1–2
or Ps. 71:1–6		
Heb. 12:18–29	Heb. 12:18–19, 22–29	Heb. 12:5–7, 11–13
Luke 13:10–17	Luke 13:22–30	Luke 13:22–30

God's steadfast love and faithfulness to all is expressed in many forms. In Jeremiah, God calls a youth to begin a long career of prophecy in an effort to awaken the wealthy and powerful to the disaster that is bearing down on them. In their self-delusion they fail to be faithful to God, as do those who follow the legalities of proper worship but fail to respond to human illness, oppression, and poverty.

FIRST READING
ISAIAH 58:9b-14 (RCL)

In chapter 58, the prophet (identified by scholars as trito-Isaiah) is told to tell the people of their "rebellion" (58:1). The Hebrew word is *pesa*, which carries the connotation of having broken with YHWH more than rebellion against YHWH (see Proper 13). This passage reveals the important distinction. The people have broken with YHWH but are not aware of it, which is not the same as an intentional rebellion. "Day after day they seek [YHWH] and delight to know [YHWH's] ways, as if they were a nation that practiced righteousness and did not forsake the ordinance of their God" (58:2). The people participate in fasts and do not understand why YHWH does not respond to them.

It is within this context that the promise of salvation selected for today's reading is spoken. YHWH notes that the people claim to delight in seeking God's ways; however, they are clearly not following God's ways when they fail to understand the necessary interdependence of faithful worship and living just and righteous lives. They participate in ritual fasting and Sabbath observance, yet they fail to "share . . . bread with the hungry and bring the homeless poor into [their] house" (58:7). As for those originally addressed by this oracle, so for us: faithful worship issues from living just, righteous lives. Concern for embodying justice and righteousness in our individual and corporate lives deepens our knowledge of God, and our awareness of God's love and faithfulness, which leads to faithful and joyful worship.

ISAIAH 28:14-22 (BCP)

This text proclaims YHWH's judgment on the civil leaders who rule the people in Jerusalem. The leaders scoff at God and place their trust in foreign military assistance to help them stave off Assyria. They think they can protect themselves and avoid death. However, YHWH will place a tested "foundation stone" in Zion, and will build on that stone by using "justice [as] the line and righteousness the plummet" (28:16-17). That which is built on such a sure foundation will stand, but the buildings built on lies will not offer refuge, for they will be destroyed by hail and water" (28:17). Thus, the efforts to make a covenant that will protect them from Sheol will be futile. Devastation will overwhelm them. A proverb speaks to the inadequacy of their attempts to save themselves while scoffing at God: "For the bed is too short to stretch oneself on it, and the covering too narrow to wrap oneself in it" (28:20).

ISAIAH 66:18-21 (RC)

The universal dominion of YHWH is underscored in these last verses of trito-Isaiah. At some as yet unspecified time in the future, YHWH, having judged and purified Jerusalem, calls people of "all nations and tongues" to come to Jerusalem (66:18). People will be sent out to the far lands to declare the glory of God to the nations. All the people who have been exiled will be brought back as an offering to God. At a time when Ezekiel, Haggai, and Zechariah were placing increased restrictions on the priesthood, trito-Isaiah proclaims that some of the returning exiles will be made priests. In the all-encompassing vision of holy Jerusalem, "all flesh"—all humanity—will come to worship God (66:23).

JEREMIAH 1:4-10 (RCL alt.)

Interpreting the Text

In the call narrative of Jeremiah, YHWH announces the claim he placed on Jeremiah before he was born. The three verbs "I *formed* (made) you," "I *knew* you," and "I *consecrated* (designated) you" should be considered as a group so the interplay of their meanings is encouraged. There was never a time when YHWH was not calling Jeremiah. Before he was made, he was known and consecrated. The verb "to know" carries the intimate meaning of knowing between a husband and wife. Jeremiah reveals an analogous intimacy that characterizes his relationship with YHWH (15:16; 20:7). "To be known" also points to YHWH's acknowledgment of the covenantal relationship that exists between YHWH and Jeremiah. Similarly, the verb "to consecrate" points to one that is set aside for God's purposes.

Jeremiah responds to YHWH's call by protesting that he is too young and does not know how to speak. Although the exact age of Jeremiah is uncertain, many commentators suggest that he may well have been a teenager when he began his vocation as a prophet. In a culture that values the wisdom of elders, his age would count against him. YHWH does not consider his objection, but gently chides him not to say, "I am only a boy" (1:6). The tone of "Do not say," a phrase that occurs predominantly in the wisdom literature, is similar to the injunction, "Do not be afraid" (1:8). Jeremiah is assured that YHWH will be with him and deliver him.

In an image reminiscent of Isaiah's call, when a seraph places a live coal against Isaiah's lips to purify them (Isa. 6:6-7), YHWH touches Jeremiah's mouth and says, "Now I have put my words in your mouth" (1:9). Jeremiah's lack of speaking experience is now irrelevant. It is YHWH's words that he is to speak. YHWH calls Jeremiah and "appoints" him over nations and kingdoms—an overwhelming assignment for one of any age and experience. Jeremiah's task will be both destructive and constructive, as the verbs at the end of his call make clear: "to pluck up and to pull down, to destroy and to overthrow, to build and to plant" (1:10).

Responding to the Text

The story of Jeremiah reminds us to pay attention to the youth in our congregations. Often they see through facades and speak with a prophetic wisdom we would rather not hear. The challenges youth face today are tremendous. We would be wise to help them and ourselves by developing strong intergenerational relationships in our congregations, giving youth support, respect, and responsibilities as they mature in their Christian lives. Including stories of faithful young people in sermons on a regular basis is one way to engage and encourage youth.

RESPONSIVE READING
PSALM 103:1-8 (RCL)

The imperative clauses in the first two verses present a resounding call to praise God. The individual who sings the words of praise notes the all-encompassing nature of God's mercy and goodness: one is forgiven, healed, redeemed, crowned with love and mercy, satisfied with what is good, and renewed in youthful strength. YHWH works to vindicate and bring justice for all who are oppressed. God gave Moses knowledge of God's ways and acted on behalf of the people of Israel. Although God's anger is evoked by injustice and refusal to live faithful lives, God's steadfast love dominates.

PSALM 46 (BCP)

This psalm reflects a deep, unassailable trust in God. Even if the primeval waters of chaos erupt, and the "mountains shake" (46:2), the people will not fear—knowing that YHWH is their "refuge" (46:1, 11), a "very present help in trouble" (46:1). The prophetic oracles of YHWH's ultimate salvation of Israel echo in this postexilic psalm, which moves toward an eschatological vision of YHWH present in Jerusalem, defending it and finally stopping all war by destroying the instruments of violence. The universality of YHWH's dominion is acknowledged as YHWH is "exalted among the nations [and] . . . in the earth" (46:30).

PSALM 117:1-2 (RC)

Psalm 117, the shortest psalm in the Psalter, is an imperative hymn of praise. The singer calls on all nations and peoples to "extol [YHWH]" (117:1). The justification for such universal praise is YHWH's steadfast love and faithfulness, which "endures forever" (117:2). For a discussion of the universal dominion of YHWH see the comments on Psalm 46 above.

PSALM 71:1-6 (RCL alt.)

This psalm of praise emerges from an aging person who has complete confidence in YHWH's faithfulness, despite a current time of suffering. The person may also be suffering from accusations of those who believe suffering indicates the person is not righteous. The psalmist turns to God for deliverance, for God has always been "a rock of refuge, a strong fortress," the worshiper's "hope" and "trust" (71:3, 5).

HEBREWS 12:18-29 (RCL);
HEB. 12:18-19, 22-29 (BCP);
HEB. 12:5-7, 11-13 (RC)

For Heb. 12:5-7 and 11-13, see the comments for Proper 15. Verses 18-29 bring together many of the themes in the epistle through a contrast between the terrifying experience of God on Mount Sinai and the "festal gathering" of angels that welcome the faithful to Mount Zion. Compare the imagery in Exod. 19:16-22; 20:18-21, and Deut. 4:11-12; 5:22-27; 9:19. The intensity of the experience is magnified by bringing the imagery of these several accounts into one sentence in the Greek text. Through Jesus it is now possible for people to approach God. The verb *proserchomai* (come; 12:18, 22)—a cultic term for approaching God in worship—is in the perfect tense, which implies an action that has begun and continues.

The vision of Mount Zion is an eschatological vision of the heavenly Jerusalem filled with angels. As part of the assembly of the firstborn, the people have the right of inheritance, an important theme in the letter. The reference also links them to Jesus, the firstborn of God. Their names have been written in heaven, a common biblical image (see Exod. 32:32; Dan. 12:1; Luke 10:20; Rev. 13:18; 17:8). In coming to Zion they come to the righteous God, who judges all fairly, and to Jesus, who mediates the new covenant.

God called to the ancestors of old from earth. Now God calls them from the heavenly city. The people are given a stern warning: they dare not refuse God—"the one who is speaking" (12:25). The contrast between heaven and earth includes a quotation from Hag. 2:6 in which God speaks of shaking all the nations of the earth. As used in Hebrews, the image is expanded to encompass the shaking of the entire universe—that which is temporal and transient—leaving only what is unshakable: (1) Christ, who is the high priest of the order of Melchizedek, thus one who never dies, (2) the everlasting treasure of the faithful that cannot be lost or stolen, (3) the heavenly city, and (4) the ongoing benefits of Christ's priesthood. That which is unshakable endures because it is rooted in the unchanging nature and purpose of God. Despite the inviting, festive celebration on Mount Zion, acceptable worship is still characterized by "reverence and awe," for God remains "a consuming fire" (12:29).

THE GOSPEL
LUKE 13:10-17 (RCL)

Interpreting the Text

The setting for the encounter narrated in this text is the synagogue—the heart of Judaism—on the Sabbath. Jesus was teaching when a bent, crippled woman appeared. She did not approach Jesus or ask for help. He called her over, proclaimed her "free from [her] ailment," laid his hands on her, and "immediately she stood up straight and began praising God" (13:12-13).

The leader of the synagogue is "indignant" because Jesus cured the woman on the Sabbath. Rather than criticizing Jesus directly, however, he chastises the crippled woman by saying to the crowd that they should come to be healed on days other than the Sabbath. Jesus intervenes, accusing the leader of being a hypocrite because he would untie an animal to give it water on the Sabbath. Surely this woman, "a daughter of Abraham," deserves to be set free from bondage to Satan on the Sabbath (13:16). The leaders of the synagogue were publicly shamed by Jesus words. The crowd rejoiced at the wonderful things Jesus was doing.

Responding to the Text

By calling to the crippled woman and healing her, Jesus affirms the importance of the physical body, and the importance of health. Morton Kelsey, who writes about the changes in the attitude of the church toward spiritual healing through the centuries, notes that of the 3,779 verses in the four Gospels of the New Testament, 727 relate specifically to healing and another 31 verses refer to miracles that include healings.[28] Contemporary attitudes toward spiritual healings are complicated by the questionable practices of some healers and televangelists who prey on the vulnerable. At the same time, spiritual healing and healing services that invoke the presence of the Holy Spirit on behalf of those who are suffering are part of a long tradition within Christianity. In churches in which healing services are not common, this text may offer an opportunity to explore the theological grounding for such services.

> OF THE 3,779 VERSES IN THE FOUR GOSPELS OF THE NEW TESTAMENT, 727 RELATE SPECIFICALLY TO HEALING AND ANOTHER 31 VERSES REFER TO MIRACLES THAT INCLUDE HEALINGS.

Within the Jewish community at the time of Jesus, healing was not only a physical gift but also served in many cases to allow people with physical or mental illness to be reintegrated into the community. In healing the crippled woman and treating her with dignity, Jesus challenges those who insist on following religious rules, even if it means ignoring profound human needs.

The seriousness of this material is heightened by reminding us that Jesus is making his way toward Jerusalem. As often happens in Luke, a person in the crowd asks a question. Given the picture of discipleship Jesus has been painting in the previous chapters, it is not surprising that someone asks if only a few will be saved (13:23). Jesus responds that one must seek access to salvation through a narrow door. The difficulty of many trying to go through a narrow door is intensified because at some unspecified time the owner will shut the door, making any further access impossible.

When those who have not been disciplined enough to enter through the narrow door stand outside and knock, claiming that Jesus once walked through their town or even ate and drank with them, they will be told that they are not known. They did not *know* Jesus or they would have turned from their evil ways. The suffering of those who cannot get through the door will be increased when they realize how many people have been called from every direction to join Abraham, Issac, Jacob, and the prophets to "eat in the kingdom" (13:29).

THIRTEENTH SUNDAY AFTER PENTECOST

SEPTEMBER 2, 2001
TWENTY-SECOND SUNDAY IN ORDINARY TIME
PROPER 17

REVISED COMMON	EPISCOPAL (BCP)	ROMAN CATHOLIC
Prov. 25:6-7	Sir. 10:(7-11), 12-18	Sir. 3:17-18, 20, 28-29
or Sir. 10:12-18		
or Jer. 2:4-13		
Ps. 112	Ps. 112	Ps. 68:4-7, 10-11
or Ps. 81:1, 10-16		
Heb. 13:1-8, 15-16	Heb. 13:1-8	Heb. 12:18-19, 22-24a
Luke 14:1, 7-14	Luke 14:1, 7-14	Luke 14:1, 7-14

When we bask in self-serving pride and lack humility, we harm others as well as ourselves and violate our relationship with Christ. Following Jesus involves helping and serving others, even though that sometimes requires putting ourselves at risk.

FIRST READING
PROVERBS 25:6-7 (RCL)

Acting in accordance with one's status is advised. It is better not to promote oneself by taking a place of honor, for one might be embarrassed if asked to move to a less prestigious position. If one takes a place that signifies lack of importance, one may be asked to move up to a place of greater honor. The influence of the wisdom literature on Jesus is clearly seen in the way in which this proverb is taken up in the parable of the wedding banquet in today's reading from Luke.

SIRACH 10:(7-11), 12-18 (BCP); 10:12-18 (RCL alt.)

The writings of Jesus ben Sira (also called Ecclesiasticus) resemble the book of Proverbs. Sirach was dedicated to the Israelite religion and concerned that Jews were being drawn into Greek thought, forgetting their heritage. Sirach exhorts readers to study the ancient traditions. Blending traditional wisdom material in an unusual way with Israel's history, legal, and cultic traditions, Sirach provides a guidebook for life.

This section warns of the danger of pride. Arrogance is hated by both other people and God. There is no reason for pride, even among those who are most powerful. During Sirach's lifetime, he witnessed the military conquest of Antiochus III over the Ptolemaic empire. Despite Antiochus III's immense power, Sirach gives a graphic reminder: Antiochus, too, will die and his body will become a home for "maggots . . . vermin and worms" (10:11).

Pride lures people away from God. In their sin they invite "unheard-of calamities" and are destroyed completely (10:13). God calls the arrogant to account and lifts up the lowly to a place of honor.

SIRACH 3:17-18, 20, 28-29 (RC)

Sirach counsels that those who are humble are loved by humans and God. The greater one actually is, the more important it is to humble oneself. In such humility God is glorified. Those who are intelligent will value contemplating proverbs. Attentive listening will characterize the wise.

JEREMIAH 2:4-13 (RCL alt.)

Interpreting the Text

In this oracle, Jeremiah brings YHWH's accusation against the people. YHWH appeals to history to document the ways in which YHWH delivered the people from slavery in Egypt, guided them through long years in the wilderness, and provided food and water for them in a land of "drought and deep darkness . . . a land that no one passes through, where no one lives" (2:6). The people were brought into the promised land, a "plentiful land" (4:7). But when they entered this fruitful land they were unfaithful to YHWH; they relied instead on other gods and pursued those things that "do not profit" (4:8).

The people are admonished that in no other land has a nation changed its gods, even though they are not gods. Yet YHWH's people have forsaken "their glory for something that does not profit" (4:11). Even the heavens are called on to be "appalled . . . shocked . . . and utterly desolate" for the dreadful apostasy of the people (4:12). YHWH accuses the people of committing two evils: "they have forsaken me, the fountain of living water, and dug out cisterns for themselves, cracked cisterns that can hold no water" (4:13). In their delusion, they have forsaken that which is truly life sustaining for nonexistent gods that cannot sustain their life.

Responding to the Text

The challenges faced by the church in North America have little to do with people desiring to follow other religious traditions. Of greater danger is the idolatry of worshiping our own creation. In what ways have we tried to dig our own wells rather than relying on God as the fountain of living water?

RESPONSIVE READING

PSALM 112 (RCL and BCP)

This is a highly complex acrostic psalm in which each half verse begins with a new letter of the Hebrew alphabet. The pattern is created by the incorporation of phrases reflective of psalms of praise, psalms of thanksgiving, and didactic maxims. The psalmist promises that those who "fear the Lord"—who live reverent, obedient lives and "delight in [God's] commandments"—will have a life filled with blessings. Those who are faithful and righteous are generous, just, and merciful to others, sharing their material blessings.

Such people need not be afraid of evil tidings, for their "hearts are firm" (112:7). They have lived righteous lives following the commandments. They are assured that "their righteousness endures forever" (112:9). Their horn will be raised—a sign that they are stronger than their adversaries (112:9). Writhing with intense anger and fury, the godless will know that they are defeated as they witness the salvation of the righteous.

PSALM 68:4-7,10-11 (NRSV 68:3-6, 9-10) (RC)

The righteous are called to praise God, who protects the forsaken and frees the imprisoned. It is YHWH who gives rain to the land and restores the people. Those who rebel against YHWH remain in a "parched land" (68:6).

PSALM 81:1, 10-16 (RCL alt.)

The communal hymn of praise becomes a prophetic warning reminding the people of YHWH's faithfulness and the ways in which God's people failed to honor their covenant with God. Even now, if the people in their current time of trouble would listen and repent—walk in God's ways—God would quickly "subdue their enemies . . . and feed [them] with the finest of the wheat, and with honey from the rock" they would be satisfied (81:16).

HEBREWS 13:1-8,15-16 (RCL);
HEB. 13:1-8 (BCP)

The series of exhortations that begin this reading highlight important aspects of Christian life and community. The congregation is reminded to show mutual love for one another and remember hospitality to strangers, including itinerant Christians dependent on the hospitality of others. The reference to entertaining angels without realizing it echoes Abraham and Sarah's experience (see Proper 12) among others.

Remembering Christians who were imprisoned and tortured because of their faith was critical because prisoners depended on others to bring them food and clothing. Living in solidarity with those who were being persecuted was an important though dangerous aspect of Christian life and witness.

After a brief admonition to honor marriage, the preacher warns against the love of money, an important theme in Jesus' teaching. The exhortation to "be content" with what one has echoes a common theme in Greek thought. Such a mindset is possible when one's full faith and confidence is in God, "who will never leave or forsake you" and will be your helper, so one need not be afraid. The first scriptural quotation (13:5) reflects Deut. 31:6, as well as Gen. 28:15; Deut. 31:8; Josh. 1:5, and 1 Chron. 28:20. The second quotation from Ps. 118:6 (13:6) is offered as the response of the believer to God's promise, which is made in the preceding verse. The believer's response of living fearlessly, with full trust in God, pertains to avoiding the love of money and living with faith in a time of conflict, persecution, and threat of imprisonment.

The motif of discipleship so important in Hebrews continues with the admonition to remember those "who spoke the word of God to you" (13:7). It is unclear what the intended reference is regarding "the outcome of their way of life" (13:7). It may refer to martyrdom or the fruits of their work. The key point is that they remained faithful and should be exemplars whom others imitate. In contrast to human leaders who taught them of God and eventually did or would die, the community is admonished to remember that the one about whom they preached and taught is Jesus Christ who "is the same yesterday and today and forever" (13:8)—the foundation of that which is unshakable.

The final verses in the lection employ expressions associated with genuine worship in Judaism: "sacrifice" and "fruit of lips" (13:15; cf. Hos. 14:3; Ps. 50:14, 23; 107:22; Ps. 34:1; 71:8; 145:2). For this community, the sacrifice required is continual praise confessing Jesus Christ as the one whose life and suffering has given them access to God. This life of continual worship extends into daily life when people do what is good (*eupoiia*) and share what they have with one another (*koinōnia*). Such is the life of faithful discipleship.

HEBREWS 12:18-19, 22-24a (RC)

See Proper 16.

THE GOSPEL
LUKE 14:1, 7-14

Interpreting the Text

In the Gospel of Luke, Jesus is frequently found at table sharing, celebrating, inviting, teaching, and embodying new and more open community boundaries. In this reading, Jesus has been invited to eat at the home of a leader of the Pharisees.

The narrator notes that Jesus is going to the home of a leader of the Pharisees for a Sabbath meal. He is being watched closely by the others present (14:1). In the verses not included in today's Gospel, Jesus sees a man who has dropsy, what we would call edema, a disease that involves swelling due to the retention of fluids, a condition exacerbated by the person's insatiable thirst. Jesus asks if it is lawful to heal on the Sabbath. The religious leaders he is with say nothing. This is not the first time Jesus has confronted the leaders by healing someone on the Sabbath (see Proper 16). Without further comment, Jesus heals the man and sends him away. He then notes that if they had a child or a farm animal that fell into a well on the Sabbath, they would certainly act to pull it out. Again they say nothing. The silence is tense and edgy.

Within ancient culture, the social elite would invite one another to their homes for meals, a practice that helped establish and reinforce status. Status was further conferred by the location of the couch on which each guest reclined relative to the head of the table at a meal. As Jesus gathers with the others to eat, he notices how they choose places of honor for themselves. He does not comment on their behavior directly, but they surely are aware of the parallel when he tells them a parable about a wedding feast. Jesus admonishes them not to take seats of honor at such a feast or the host may come in and ask them to move because someone who is more important has arrived. Placing themselves in seats of honor may lead to humiliation in front of others. If they choose a seat at the "low" end of the table, however, the host may invite them to move up, and everyone present will see that they are being honored.

The text refers to the story as a parable, which suggests that we should look beyond the surface meaning of the story. The choice of a wedding banquet signals a reference to the kingdom of God. God does not grant places of honor based on one's wealth and social status. The unexpected reversal that characterizes many of the parables occurs here, too.

Jesus reinforces the point by telling the host not to invite friends and relatives for a feast—a reciprocal arrangement in which the host would be assured of a return invitation. Rather invite "the poor, the crippled, the lame, and the blind" (Luke 14:13). Jesus tells the Pharisee that if he extends the boundaries of table fellowship to include people who cannot return the favor, he will be blessed at "the resurrection of the righteous" (14:14).

Responding to the Text

It is easy for us to point fingers at the Pharisees who are presented as behaving with such self-importance or at the very wealthy in today's world whose excesses and foibles are eagerly covered by the mass media. We can see their greed and obsession with wealth and power. The Gospel reading becomes less comfortable when we start asking how Jesus' parable might relate to our lives. It is good to consider with whom we eat and share table. It is also helpful to treat the sharing of a meal as a metaphor and ask ourselves in what other ways we may assume the right to status and power and fail to consider those who are politically and socially marginalized, hungry, and ill. How do we do as a church family? To whom do we extend hospitality? Are we placing boundaries that exclude some of God's children from our care and concern?

ARE WE PLACING BOUNDARIES THAT EXCLUDE SOME OF GOD'S CHILDREN FROM OUR CARE AND CONCERN?

FOURTEENTH SUNDAY AFTER PENTECOST

REVISED COMMON	EPISCOPAL (BCP)	ROMAN CATHOLIC
Deut. 30:15-20	Deut. 30:15-20	Wis. 9:13-18b
or Jer. 18:1-11		
Ps. 1 or	Ps. 1	Ps. 90:3-6, 12-17
Ps. 139:1-6, 13-18		
Philemon 1-21	Philemon 1-20	Philemon 9b-10, 12-17
Luke 14:25-33	Luke 14:25-33	Luke 14:25-33

A pot turned by the potter's hand is fragile and easily damaged. So, too, are our lives fragile and easily damaged. The choices we make in life lead us toward God or away from God—toward life or death. Acknowledging that God knows the secrets of our hearts, we are called to a faithful relationship with Christ that qualifies all our other commitments and all the aspects of our life. Christ's loving, healing hands can remake a damaged world.

FIRST READING
DEUTERONOMY 30:15-20 (RCL/BCP)

Interpreting the Text

Scholars recognize Deuteronomy as a later text that reinterprets ancient tradition in light of later historical realities. Quite likely, Deuteronomy is the scroll referred to as the "book of law" that prompted Josiah's extensive religious reform in 621 B.C.E. (2 Kings 22:11, 22-23). The powerful image set forth in today's reading captures the essence of Deuteronomy. In the second of three addresses, Moses presents the heart of covenant theology: "I have set before you life and death, blessings and curses. Choose life so that you and your descendants may live" (30:19).

There are two choices: "life and prosperity" or "death and adversity" (31:15). To honor the covenant relationship the people must obey YHWH's commandments. This requires "loving the Lord your God, walking in his ways, and observing his commandments, decrees, and ordinances" (30:16). The fundamental assumption of Deuteronomic theology is clearly spelled out: the people's fate will be determined by the choices they make.

Responding to the Text

The influence of Deuteronomic theology can be found in many books of the Bible (see the discussion of Psalm 1 for this week as an example). An important doctrine of this theology is that, if people are faithful, their lives will be long and prosperous. Adversity and want provide material evidence of one's failure to be faithful to God. Interpreted without qualification by other theological traditions in the Bible, this doctrine is harsh. Those with good health and prosperity may lack compassion and concern for those who suffer adverse conditions in their lives. It can also stimulate an unhealthy and undeserved sense of guilt and self-recrimination in one who is suffering. It is important to guard against destructive interpretations and uses of this theology by bringing it into conversation with differing biblical traditions. With thoughtful qualification, however, it is helpful to reflect on what we have done and are doing in our individual and corporate lives relative to the choices God sets before us. If we reflect deeply on the secrets of our heart—secrets God knows—what are we really choosing—life or death?

WISDOM OF SOLOMON 9:13-18b (RC)

This selection from Solomon's prayer emphasizes his awareness that, in order to be a worthy king, one who can make wise and just decisions, he must have the wisdom that God bestows. Solomon recognizes that, whereas those who have no power may be "pardoned in mercy," "severe judgment falls on those in high places" (6:5-6). Wisdom knows the ways of God and what is pleasing to God, having been with God even before the world was created (9:9). Without her, one cannot learn "the counsel of God . . . or . . . discern what the Lord wills" (9:13). Solomon prays for God to send Wisdom, who is identified with God's holy spirit, that she might set right his paths and teach him what pleases God (9:18).

JEREMIAH 18:1-11 (RCL alt.)

Interpreting the Text

Jeremiah is told to arise and go to the potter's house. He watches the potter making a pot, probably using a fast wheel. The potter would turn the bottom stone wheel with his feet. That wheel would then turn a platform—perhaps of wood—on which the clay would spin as the potter worked to shape it.

As Jeremiah watched the potter, something about the vessel being made was "spoiled" (18:4). Perhaps it had become misshapen or one side was too thin. In any case, the potter was dissatisfied, squashed the partially formed vessel back into a lump of clay and began again until the result "seemed good to him" (18:4). Watching the process, Jeremiah received a word from YHWH. Cannot YHWH do with Israel as the potter has done with the spoiled vessel? The image is expanded beyond Israel to signal YHWH's universal dominion in history. The verbs used in Jeremiah's call narrative are repeated: YHWH can uproot, demolish, build, or plant. Jeremiah is called to prophecy both the destructive and constructive acts (1:10; 18:7, 9).

The perspective of this text reflects a dynamic ontology in which one's actions have consequences. The underlying assumption is that YHWH's actions will be influenced by what people do. The Hebrew adverb used in vv. 7 and 9 suggests that YHWH may change plans *quickly*. If the plan was to destroy a nation or kingdom, but the people repent, then YHWH will not bring about the disaster. On the other hand, if YHWH's plan was to benefit a nation or kingdom, and the people engage in evil and refuse to repent, YHWH may suddenly change plans, and disaster may follow. Having affirmed that YHWH will respond to the choices people make, the people of Judah are admonished to turn from their evil ways so that disaster will yet be averted.

Responding to the Text

Commentators disagree on the overall tone of this text. Some read it as very hopeful. Just as the potter does not give up on the clay because a vessel is spoiled, but keeps working until a satisfactory vessel is prepared, so, too, YHWH will not give up, nor will YHWH be defeated in bringing about good. Other commentators disagree and read the text as a verdict of doom.

The clay the potter works with is not passive. As the potter's wheel turns, centrifugal forces come into play, pushing the clay out from the center. The potter works the clay, but the clay is an active agent that can get away from the potter and result in a spoiled creation.

To gain more insight into this text, watch a potter work. Better yet, try it yourself and experience what it feels like to place your hands on a mound of wet clay as the wheel spins. Note how the clay responds to even slight changes of pressure, rising into the air with thin or thick walls depending on the placement of your fingers. Encourage the imaginative insights of a class—of older children through the active elderly—by arranging for them to spend some time at potters' wheels, followed by a discussion of the rich metaphor of God as a potter (see also Isa. 45:9; 64:8; Rom. 9:19-26).

RESPONSIVE READING

185

FOURTEENTH
SUNDAY
AFTER PENTECOST

SEPTEMBER 9

PSALM 1 (RCL/BCP)

The covenant theology discussed in relation to the reading from Deuteronomy is reflected in this psalm. Those who are faithful to God and delight in obedience to God's law are like trees that are planted near life-sustaining streams. The psalmist claims that such people prosper in contrast with those who take the "path that sinners tread" (1:1). Not being rooted in God and planted near water, the wicked blow away like chaff.

PSALM 90:3-4, 5-6, 12-13, 14-17 (RC)

The psalmist recognizes the fragility and brevity of human existence. The community prays to become cognizant of this human reality that they might have "a wise heart" (90:12). They recognize that their iniquities are before God. After long suffering, they pray for God to have compassion on them, satisfying them in the morning with God's "steadfast love" that they "may rejoice and be glad all [their] days" (90:14).

PSALM 139:1-6, 13-18 (RCL alt.)

This profoundly moving psalm reckons with the omnipresence of God, who searches us and knows us. God is acquainted with all our ways, knowing our words before they are on our tongue (139:3-4). Our lives are written in the book of God (139:16). In the unfathomable mystery of God, we are known before our birth and when we "come to the end" (139:18).

SECOND READING

PHILEMON 1-21 (RCL);
PHILEMON 1-20 (BCP);
PHILEMON 9b-10, 12-17 (RC)

Paul's note to Philemon has a fascinating history of interpretation that is itself a worthy object of teaching and discussion within the local congregation. Up until the fourth century, there was a strong inclination to reject Philemon as part of the biblical canon. The brief, personal note from Paul (the entire letter is less than one page in length) was considered to have insufficient depth to warrant its inclusion in the Bible. John Chrysostom stemmed the tide against Philemon with an argument designed to establish the substantive import of the letter. In making his case, he laid out what he considered to be the argument of the letter itself, which is the source of the now traditional interpretation of the context in which the letter was written.

Chrysostom was concerned about the issue of slavery in his own day. Some Christians were apparently arguing against slavery and physically extricating slaves from their masters. Chrysostom opposed such action. He used the occasion of writing about the letter to Philemon to address the issue, advocating strongly for adherence to laws regarding slavery. Chrysostom was the first exegete to identify Onesimus as a fugitive slave who was being returned to his owner by Paul.[29] Biblical scholar Allen Dwight Callahan points out that working from the text of Philemon, "Chrysostom told a story about slavery. There is little evidence, however, that his very original reading was *the* original reading. The epistle's earliest audiences, by Chrysostom's admission, were dismissive. Chrysostom's reading, strong and serious, highlighted one urgent matter, leaving other matters suggested in the text to be eclipsed by slavocratic interests."[30] More than a thousand years after Chrysostom's analysis, Bible scholars who were abolitionists began to note that, while it was commonplace to consider Onesimus not only a slave, but a slave who had stolen something from his master, this interpretation is not established in the Greek text.

Callahan notes that the majority of scholars, despite the exegetical work done by scholars who read with eyes sensitized by their abolitionist commitments, repeated Chrysostom's telling of a story about slavery. Most recent commentaries continue in that tradition, which makes Callahan's historical and exegetical work all the more important for congregations to consider. This briefest of all books in the Bible provides a fascinating case for considering in depth how our personal and cultural assumptions and biases inevitably influence the ways in which we read and interpret a text.

> PHILEMON PROVIDES A FASCINATING CASE FOR CONSIDERING HOW OUR PERSONAL AND CULTURAL ASSUMPTIONS AND BIASES INEVITABLY INFLUENCE THE WAYS IN WHICH WE READ AND INTERPRET A TEXT.

Callahan argues that Onesimus is more likely Philemon's brother. Paul notes that Onesimus is a brother to him—Paul—"but how much more to you, both *in the flesh* and in the Lord" (1:16). Conflict between brothers is a frequent theme in the Bible—consider Cain and Abel, Jacob and Esau, and Joseph and his brothers. It was common in ancient culture that a third party would intercede to help reconcile brothers.

Because of the conflict between Philemon and Onesimus, Paul speaks glowingly of what he has heard of Philemon's love for the saints and his faith in Jesus Christ (1:5). It is on the basis of such love, rather than Paul's legitimate authority, that Paul wishes to press his case. He reminds Philemon that he presses the case as a prisoner—literally at this time—of Christ Jesus (1:9). Having said much to establish Philemon's goodwill, Paul finally indicates what he wants and names Onesimus for the first time. Paul identifies Onesimus as his child even before naming him—an effective rhetorical move to stave off Philemon's immediate negative reaction. Callahan suggests that Paul may be indicating that he wants to use Onesimus to help spread the gospel, not that he wants Onesimus to stay physically with Paul to help him while he is in prison.

Paul wants Philemon to receive Onesimus as he would receive Paul. Although Paul emphasizes his desire for Philemon to accept this request as something voluntary and not forced (1:14), he nevertheless uses very strong rhetorical appeals to accomplish his goal. Imagine Philemon receiving a letter from Paul, a noted apostle, in which he says "*If* you consider me your partner, welcome him as you would welcome me" (1:17). If Philemon refuses, he will, in effect, be rejecting his close link with Paul. Following a known cultural practice of third persons paying any debt incurred by one of the parties as part of the process of reconciliation, Paul offers to pay if any wrong has been done or any debt has been incurred.

Again utilizing a not-so-subtle rhetorical strategy, Paul tells Philemon that in asking for this favor, he will "say nothing about your owing me even your own self" (1:19)—an ironic comment, since in saying what it is he will *not* say as part of his argument to gain Philemon's cooperation, he has, of course, just said it—and right at the very end of the letter, which brings heightened attention to it. Does Philemon really feel he has much choice when Paul signs off by noting that he is "confident" of Philemon's "obedience" and believes, in fact, that he will "do even more than [Paul] says" (1:21). Oh, and "one thing more," Paul writes in the following verse, please get a room ready for me. I plan to be there in person soon. Does Philemon really want to have Paul arrive in person and find that he has refused to be reconciled with Onesimus, granting him the status of both a "beloved brother . . . in the flesh and in the Lord" (1:16).[31]

THE GOSPEL
LUKE 14:25-33

Interpreting the Text

Last week's Gospel told of a Sabbath meal in the home of one of the leaders of the Pharisees. Today's lection involves a change of scene. Jesus has resumed his journey to Jerusalem and is once again surrounded by large crowds. He addresses those who would consider themselves his followers, stipulating the demands of discipleship.

The Lukan Jesus challenges the primacy of loyalty to one's family on several occasions (cf. 9:59-62; 12:51-52; 18:29). The call for followers to "hate" families is a translation of *misein*, which may not refer to the strong negative emotion associated with "hate." Rather, calling on people to "hate father and mother, wife and children, brothers and sisters" if they want to be disciples of Jesus carries the meaning of a willingness to dishonor or shame one's family—which is very likely to happen if one follows a controversial leader opposed by religious and political authorities. The emphasis placed on bringing honor and not shame to one's family in the ancient culture of Jesus' time was so great that the harsh word "hate" in English may help us better understand the severity of what was at stake in bringing dishonor to one's family by following Jesus. To subordinate one's loyalty to one's family—and to one's own physical safety, hating "even life itself"—to one's loyalty to Jesus was a requirement for any in the crowd who would become disciples.

The gravity of Jesus' words is clear when we remember that he is headed to Jerusalem knowing what awaits him there. Jesus then includes two brief parables to demonstrate the point: in one a person plans to build a tower, in the other a king evaluates a military encounter. Both begin by sizing up what the task demands. It would be foolhardy to begin a project without recognition of the cost involved. Jesus warns the crowd that any who consider themselves his disciples need to recognize that the commitment comes with a huge price tag. He encapsulates the requirement for discipleship: "None of you can become my disciple if you do not give up all your possessions" (14:33).

Responding to the Text

There are contexts throughout the world in which proclaiming oneself to be a Christian and striving to live a Christian life places one at great personal risk. It is worthwhile to think about such situations—particularly for those of us who have never faced imminent danger simply by affirming that we are Christian.

THE PEOPLE WHOM JESUS ADDRESSED IN THIS STORY WERE PLACING THEIR LIVES AND THEIR CONNECTIONS WITH FAMILIES AT GREAT RISK BY FOLLOWING JESUS.

The people whom Jesus addressed in this story were placing their lives and their connections with families at great risk by following Jesus, whether they realized it at this point or not. By the time the Gospel of Luke was written, people knew of the intense conflicts that erupted as some Jews accepted Jesus as the Messiah and others did not. The conflicts did split families apart and led to death for some who proclaimed Jesus as the Messiah.

We need to place texts such as this within their historical context. At the same time, it is important not to ignore the fact that these texts address us in our contemporary culture as well. The point Jesus made repeatedly was that following him involved the commitment of one's life. Everything else had to be qualified by that commitment. Do we give our Christian faith first priority in our lives? Are we willing to risk judgment and ridicule for living faithful, honest, just lives, even if it places us at odds with our families, friends, or employers? What would it cost us individually—and corporately—if we actually believed that this text was addressed to us?

FIFTEENTH SUNDAY AFTER PENTECOST

SEPTEMBER 16, 2001
TWENTY-FOURTH SUNDAY IN ORDINARY TIME
PROPER 19

REVISED COMMON	EPISCOPAL (BCP)	ROMAN CATHOLIC
Exod. 32:7-14	Exod. 32:1, 7-14	Exod. 32:7-11, 13-14
or Jer. 4:11-12, 22-28		
Ps. 51:1-10 or Psalm 14	Ps. 51:1-8 or 51:1-11	Ps. 51:3-4, 12, 13, 17-19
1 Tim. 1:12-17	1 Tim. 1:12-17	1 Tim. 1:12-17
Luke 15:1-10	Luke 15:1-32 or 15:1-10	

Life can change quickly. Hot desert winds arise unexpectedly. Thoughtless acts can lead us from the ways of God to the way of idolatry or the way of fools. False teaching can capture our imagination, and we become lost. Our hope lies in the promise that God knows when we are lost and searches for us until we are found. The sins that consume us cannot separate us from God—who will run to embrace us if we will but return home.

FIRST READING
EXODUS 32:7-14 (RCL);
EXOD. 32:1, 7-14 (BCP);
EXOD. 32:7-11, 13-14 (RC)

Interpreting the Text

Moses has been away from the people for forty days receiving instructions from YHWH for building the temple. He also has the stone tablets on which God wrote the commandments. The people have given up on Moses ever returning. They ask Aaron to build a golden calf, which he does after collecting gold from the people. Aaron then builds an altar in front of the calf and prepares to have a festival to YHWH.

It is at this point that YHWH sends Moses back to the people. They have violated YHWH's command that they are to make no idols (20:4). The reference to multiple gods when only one calf was built may signal that this is a later text (not earlier than eighth century) and reflects the conflict over the two gold calves at

Dan and Bethel in the northern kingdom. King Jeroboam dedicated the calves using the words found in the quotation (1 Kings 12:28). If this is true, setting the text in the Mosaic era would give added weight to the religious reforms instituted by King Josiah.

According to the text, YHWH is ready to give up on the people and consume them. However, Moses intercedes, imploring YHWH not to do something that will lead the Egyptians to think that YHWH had an evil intent in delivering the people from Egypt. Further, YHWH made a promise to Abraham, Isaac, and Israel—swearing on God's own self—that their descendants would become a great nation. YHWH relents and disaster is averted.

Responding to the Text

Surely we can identify with the restlessness of the Hebrew people. They've been waiting for forty days for Moses to return and there has been no sign of him. In their anxiety they yearn for a visible presence in which they can have confidence. Perhaps they thought of their golden calf as a god, or perhaps they thought of YHWH—the invisible One—seated on the calf. Whatever their concept, their impatience and lack of faith led them to take matters into their own hands in a way that nearly proved their undoing.

It is difficult to discern whether a delay is merely our impatience in the face of God's timing or an indication that something has gone wrong. Because human beings can and do act in ways that affect many other people, God's vision for our lives can be disrupted. God takes disrupted plans into account and continually influences all aspects of existence toward God's vision for the world. The challenge to us—as to the Hebrews of old—is to have faith in God when life is difficult and avoid the recurring temptation to idolatry in any of its many guises.

JEREMIAH 4:11-12, 22-28 (RCL alt.)

Interpreting the Text

Jeremiah's prophecy of the destruction that is advancing on Judah relies on the image of the sirocco, a strong, dry wind from the east that is in marked contrast to the more typical humid wind that blows from the northwest across the country. When the sirocco begins, the humidity drops as much as 40 percent, and the temperature climbs precipitously and quickly—as much as 20 degrees Fahrenheit.[32]

What is predicted is a gale-force wind that cannot be put to constructive use for agriculture. In the midst of the destructive imagery, a note of sadness is struck with the phrase "my poor people" (literally, "my daughter people," 4:11). Although some translations read the "daughter of my people," scholars have challenged the phrasing as unsupported by the original texts. "My daughter people" suggests "my people whom I love as a daughter."

This lection skips vv. 13-21, which reveal Jeremiah's deep mental and spiritual pain. Knowing of the devastation that looms over his people, Jeremiah suffers alone in anticipation of the military invasion and the havoc Babylon will wreak on the people and the land. He will suffer the actual events when the invasion begins.

Today's lection picks up again at YHWH's explanation that the devastation is coming because the people are foolish, stupid, and have no understanding. It is not that they lack intelligence. They are skilled and clever. However, because they do not *know* YHWH, they do not *know* good, and their cleverness is used in "doing evil" (4:22). It is not only the people who will suffer when the disaster begins. The earth itself will be wasted. There will be no sun or moon in the heavens—no way to separate the day from the night, to mark time—a necessity if one is to identify and honor the Sabbath as YHWH requires. The mountains and hills—symbols of stability—"were quaking" and moving "to and fro" (4:24). Jeremiah looks and finds that there are no people or even any birds left. The land that was fertile and fruitful but a moment ago has suddenly become arable desert. The cities are gone (4:25-26). The earth itself "shall mourn" and the heavens will be dark (4:28). There was an opportunity for YHWH to change plans, but the people did not repent (see the discussion of Jer. 18:7-10, Proper 18), so the devastation at the hands of the Babylonians will occur. Despite the severity of the devastation, however, YHWH will still not "make a full end" (4:27). The possibility of a different future is not completely eliminated.

Responding to the Text

The devastating imagery Jeremiah uses to communicate the pending disaster signals a collapse of cosmic order and domination by the forces of chaos. Despite the extremity of the damage to land and people, the passage need not be read as apocalyptic. When one considers the human capacity for inflicting pain and suffering on one another through torture, murder, enforced slavery, separation of spouses and families, destruction of personal effects, homes, temples, and crops, Jeremiah's imagery does not seem unreasonably hyperbolic. Even today we human beings torture one another, destroy communities, families, and any hope individuals might have for a simple, decent life in ways that sometimes suggest the forces of chaos and evil have indeed erupted out of control.

The theological thrust of Jeremiah points to the direct connection between human evil and the experience of suffering and military defeat. YHWH responds to what people do, but it is also clear that YHWH has dominion and causes disasters to occur or stops them. This understanding of God requires critical reflection. Many theologians argue that we have misunderstood and misrepresented the nature of God's power.[33] Because the doctrine of God's omnipotence is frequently claimed, it is easy for us to deceive ourselves by applying this theology to others but not to ourselves. Unless we are suffering ourselves, we may believe that others somehow deserve the suffering and evil that befalls them. Such a view can harden our hearts and block the flow of our compassion for others. Do *we* know God? Do we have wisdom to discern good, or do we cleverly participate in doing evil as if we were following the way of God?

RESPONSIVE READING
PSALM 51:1-10 (RCL); PS. 51:1-8 or 51:1-11 (BCP); PS. 51:3-4, 13, 17-19 (NRSV: 51:2-3, 11, 12, 16-18) (RC)

Out of distress and anguish, the psalmist petitions God for forgiveness—not because it is deserved but because of God's "steadfast love" and "abundant mercy" (51:1). Only God can wash and cleanse us from sin. We cannot do it for ourselves.

In recognition that sins toward others are sins toward God, the singer acknowledges that his or her sins are against God alone; therefore, it is right that God should pass judgment. The claim of having been "born guilty" points to the toxicity that permeates human existence. Yet the psalmist points to a place—one's secret heart—that can receive God's wisdom.

May we join the singer in praying for absolution and pardon. May God "create a clean heart" in us, cleansing our thoughts, emotions, and will and giving us a "new and right spirit" (51:10).

PSALM 14 (RCL alt.)

This prophetic psalm denounces those who have no faith in God's activity in the world. Such fools engage in practical atheism, for lack of faith leads to a lack of good deeds. The prophet laments that all lack wisdom—no one is seeking after God or doing good.

The lament of the prophetic speaker turns to threat. God does exist and is present with the righteous and the poor who are "eaten up . . . as they eat bread" by those who are in positions to make a difference in small or large ways (14:5-6).

SECOND READING
1 TIMOTHY 1:12-17

Because of significant differences in both linguistic choices and content, most scholars concur that the Pauline letters commonly referred to as the Pastoral Epistles, 1 and 2 Timothy and Titus, were written by a disciple of Paul several years after Paul's death.[34] If this hypothesis is correct, they provide insight into a later period in the early history of Christianity and the church.

Although Paul refers to himself in the authentic letters as a sinner and persecutor of the church, he does not refer to himself as "a blasphemer . . . and a man of violence" (1:13). The term *hybristēs* translated here as "man of violence" refers to "violent, insolent, or reckless behavior."[35] The addition of these words to Paul's typical self-description multiples his sinfulness, thus magnifying the degree of God's mercy and grace in not only forgiving him but calling him to be an apostle.

It is not insignificant that "blasphemer" (*blasphēmos* and *hybristēs)* is used to refer to the teachers whom the Pastoral Epistles are opposing. They are "blasphemers" (1:20) and have "a morbid craving for controversy and for disputes about words," which leads to "envy, dissension, slander, base suspicions, and wrangling among those who are depraved in mind and bereft of truth, imagining that godliness is a means of gain" (6:4-5).

By drawing Paul's preconversion sinful behavior more fully into the realm of behavior exhibited by teachers whom the letter opposes, a stronger identification is established between them and Paul. This identification heightens the sharp difference between them: Paul's behavior emerged from ignorance and "unbelief" (6:13). The teachers who oppose Paul's teaching have no such excuse.

The emphasis on Paul's sin magnifies God's grace (1:14). This leads to the first of five sayings that are *pistos* ("faithful" or "trustworthy," translated in NRSV as "sure"; 1:21; see also 3:1; 4:9; 2 Tim 2:11a; Titus 3:8a). The first of these trustworthy claims is that "Christ Jesus came into the world to save sinners" (1:15).

The reading ends with what may be a liturgical fragment. It reflects terms for God found in Jewish and Christian writings.

THE GOSPEL
LUKE 15:1-10 (RCL; BCP; RC alt.)

Interpreting the Text

The parables included in today's Gospel are told by the Lukan Jesus to crowds of people, among whom are many tax collectors and sinners. The grumbling of the Pharisees and scribes heard earlier in the Gospel continue: "This fellow welcomes sinners and eats with them" (Luke 15:2). In the face of compromises by temple priests who were under the thumb of Roman authorities, the Pharisees were concerned about careful adherence to purity laws that played an important role in defining the boundaries of the Jewish community. Jesus was continually engaging in acts of befriending and eating with outcasts—acts that violated the boundaries and threatened the identity of the community, from the Pharisees' point of view.

In responding to the murmurings and grumblings, Jesus tells the parable of a shepherd who has one hundred sheep and loses one. He leaves the ninety-nine in order to go looking for the one that is lost until he finds it. Having found it, he "lays it on his shoulders and rejoices," goes home, calls friends and neighbors together, and invites them to come and rejoice with him (15:4-6). The implication of the opening phrase of the parable is that any good shepherd, including a Pharisee or scribe with such a flock, would do the same thing.

The parable of the lost sheep is paired with the parable of a woman who loses one of her ten silver coins. The conjunction "or" joins the two parables, indicating their interchangeability. The woman is probably poor, living in a very small house with no windows. In order to find the lost coin, she lights a candle, sweeps the floor, and searches until she finds it. Having found it, she, too, calls together friends and neighbors, inviting them to rejoice with her.

Following each parable, an allegorical reading of it is offered to the crowd. Just as the shepherd and the woman rejoice over the lost sheep and coin, so, too God rejoices over each sinner who repents. What are we to make of these parables? What might they have meant to the crowd?

Given the culture of first-century Palestine, it is worth noting that shepherds were no longer held in high esteem as they had been in the periods when the Hebrews were nomadic people. The shepherd was an established image for God in scripture. Psalm 23 is an obvious example. Read also Ezek. 34:11-16. However, during the first century, shepherds were marginalized, included among the forbidden occupations, and excluded, along with tax collectors, from eligibility to serve as a witness.[36] Although there was a long tradition of valuing shepherds in Hebrew scripture, how would the crowds have heard Jesus' description of God as a shepherd?

HOW IS IT THAT GOD IS LIKE A SHEPHERD AND A WOMAN?

The possibility that hearing God referred to as a shepherd might create dissonance is reinforced by the second parable in which God is compared to a woman. Women in first century Palestine were also marginalized. They had little legal protection and were not able to participate fully in all aspects of the religious life of the community. How is it, then, that God is like a shepherd and a woman? The one sheep and coin have little intrinsic value, and yet the person who represents God seeks persistently until that which is lost is found.

Placing unexpected characters in a role that is allegorized as a representation of God reinforces the Lukan Jesus' emphasis on the value of outcasts. The parables also suggest something very important about the nature of God. Neither the sheep nor the coin do anything to warrant attention. Each is considered of great value to the one who has lost it, but has, in fact, little intrinsic value in and of itself. Both the sheep and the coin are passive. They do not do anything to overcome being lost. It is the woman and the shepherd who expend all the effort seeking that which is lost.

Responding to the Text

To gain deeper insight into these very familiar parables, it is important to pay close attention to their role in the larger literary unit in which we find them in Luke. A comparison of the ways in which the parables are told and the contexts within which they are told in Mark and Matthew will reveal differences, although the application of the parables is the same.

By using characters who have no social or religious status in the community to represent God, Jesus may be encouraging people to think about God and the kingdom of God in relation to common, ordinary life events, and in relation to all people, not merely those who have position and power. If we follow this line of thought, what might it mean to us today? Most of us are completely unfamiliar with the daily realities of life as a shepherd. By spending some time learning and thinking about the hour-to-hour realities of the life of a shepherd, we may gain insights into what the parable suggests about the nature of God—and about God's attitude toward sinners who are lost.

LUKE 15:1-32 (RC)

The final parable in this section of Luke, the famous story of the prodigal son, is included in the Roman Catholic lection for today. The first parable begins, "Which one of you . . . ?" thus leading the audience to identify with the shepherd. Similarly, the second parable begins, "What woman . . . ?" (15:8). The questions invite audience response ("none of us," "no woman"). In both cases the implication is that the audience should rejoice with the shepherd and the woman. Since the parables are introduced by pointing out that the Pharisees were grumbling against Jesus' involvement with the sinners and tax collectors that gathered around him, Luke makes clear that the intended audience for the first two parables is the Pharisees.

After this connection has been established in the mind of the reader, it is natural to assume that the third parable will follow the same dynamic. There are, however, some critical differences.[37] The listener is not invited to identify with the father. Instead, a third-person narrator—Jesus—announces that "There was a man who had two sons" (15:11). By the end of the parable, readers of Luke's Gospel tend to identify the elder son with the Pharisees who are grumbling and refusing to rejoice over the inclusion of tax collectors and sinners into the community. The conclusion then seems to be that those who follow Jesus—specifically the sinners and tax collectors—will be welcomed by God, but the angry elder brother will be rejected.

This common interpretation turns on the assumption that the Pharisees identify themselves with the elder brother who is rejected while the audience within the early Christian community of Luke—and the contemporary reader of today—identifies with the younger son. There are two problems with this interpretation. If we stay with the parable itself, it is clear that the elder son is not rejected. In fact, the father goes out to him and, despite the son's anger, the father assures him that all he has belongs to the elder son. If the point of the parable was for the Pharisees to identify with the elder brother, then in the end they are not rejected. The story ends with the younger brother inside at the festivities. The father, however, is outside with the elder son. The second problem is the unquestioned assumption that the Pharisees would have identified with the elder brother. To look at this issue, it is necessary to examine the structure of the larger literary unit.

Luke skillfully weaves three stories together in such a way that important distinctions between the parables are blurred. One story is the parable Jesus tells. At a second level there is the story of Jesus telling parables, including this one, in the presence of tax collectors, sinners, and Pharisees. At a third level there is the story Luke tells when we consider the Gospel as a whole. Our interpretation of the third parable is influenced by the interplay of two audiences, the Pharisees on the one hand and the first-century community of Christians on the other.

Within the first level of the story—the parable itself—the elder son is not rejected. Within the third level of the story—the Gospel of Luke taken as a whole—the characterization of the Pharisees is influenced by the audience's assumption that the Pharisees themselves identify with the elder son, who was also angry about the gracious treatment of a sinner. Certainly Luke pushes this identification. However, it is worth noting that in Hebrew scripture Israel's fate is almost always linked to the favored youngest son. Jacob, Joseph, Benjamin, Saul, and David are prime examples. Why are commentators so sure that we identify with the prodigal son while the Pharisees identified with the elder son? It is also valuable in teaching this parable to ask with whom contemporary listeners identify. In Bible study groups, I have found that many first-born children identify with the elder son, which opens up the question of divisive family dynamics that are generated when parents favor one child more than others. Jacob favors Joseph in such an obvious way that his brothers are seething with anger and finally plan to kill him when they see their chance. They end up sparing his life only to sell him into slavery—despite the pain it will cause their father.

Once again our familiarity with a text demands that we step back and look at it very closely to see what assumptions we are making and how those assumptions influence our interpretation. Bernard Scott argues that the real concern of the father is for the unity of the brothers, just as the kingdom of God is not something that divides, but rather unifies. The younger son behaves disgracefully and gets a feast. The elder son is angry and churlish, rejecting the father, yet he is given everything. The stories of brothers in the traditions of Israel tell of the chosen and the rejected. This parable is different. It tells a story in which both are chosen. The father signals the action of the kingdom by leaving the house to go out to his younger son. He repeats the action by leaving the house to go out to the elder son. The image of the kingdom is the welcoming of both children.

> THIS PARABLE TELLS A STORY IN WHICH BOTH SONS ARE CHOSEN.

SIXTEENTH SUNDAY
AFTER PENTECOST

SEPTEMBER 23, 2001
TWENTY-FIFTH SUNDAY IN ORDINARY TIME
PROPER 20

REVISED COMMON	EPISCOPAL (BCP)	ROMAN CATHOLIC
Amos 8:4-7	Amos 8:4-7 (8-12)	Amos 8:4-7
or Jer. 8:18—9:1		
Ps. 113	Ps. 138	Ps. 113:1-2, 4-8
or Ps. 79:1-9		
1 Tim. 2:1-7	1 Tim. 2:1-8	1 Tim. 2:1-8
Luke 16:1-13	Luke 16:1-13	Luke 16:1-13 or 16:10-13

The prophet Amos was well aware of God's pain and lament for the people. It is sobering to consider the possibility that God really does know all that we think and do and suffers when we make choices that are destructive for ourselves and others. We claim faith in salvation through Christ; however, this does not relieve us from the responsibility to live conscious, self-reflective Christian lives that contribute to the healing rather than suffering of the world.

FIRST READING
AMOS 8:4-12 (RCL/RC);
AMOS 8:4-7 (8-12) (BCP)

Interpreting the Text

During the reign of Jeroboam II (eighth century), the northern kingdom of Israel experienced political expansion and economic strength. Amos, a shepherd from Judah, was called to prophesy against the ruling class in Israel, who enjoyed a lavish lifestyle while ignoring the needs and rights of the poor. The depth of their sin and greed is captured in their desire that Sabbath will end quickly so they can return to their unjust business practices. YHWH swears never to forget the injustice of their acts.

Even creation will be affected by their wickedness (8:7-8). In response God will send a famine "not of . . . bread . . . but of hearing the words of YHWH" (8:11). Although the prophecy of Amos ends with YHWH promising to "restore the fortunes of my people Israel," eventually all those who are living evil lives and covering their acts with a facade of pietistic worship will be destroyed.

Responding to the Text

Amos's words to those who were rich and powerful in Israel fell on deaf ears. Many of us who will read or listen to Amos's prophecy in worship are benefiting from a period of unparalleled economic prosperity the United States. While few of us fall into the category of the rich and powerful, we nevertheless have the responsibility as Christians to know what is happening to the poorest people in this country—a growing population who find it impossible to earn a living wage. What actions need to be taken in our own local community, as well as nationally, to assure that it cannot be said of us, they "trample on the needy and bring to ruin the poor of the land" (8:4)?

JEREMIAH 8:18—9:1 (RCL alt.)

Interpreting the Text

Last week's text from Jeremiah (see Proper 19) laid out the extremity of the disaster that awaited Judah at the hand of Babylonian King Nebuchadrezzar. Today's passage presents a dissonant blending of voices: Jeremiah's grief and anguish, YHWH's anguish, YHWH's anger, and the self-destructive complacency of people who cannot read the signs of the times.

Jeremiah experiences the heartsickness that overtakes a betrayed lover or a grieving parent (8:18). The poor people (literally "the daughter people," see comment in Proper 19) follow the traditional liturgical pattern of asking: "Is YHWH not in Zion?" (8:19a). The question regarding God's presence presupposes the answer that YHWH is present; therefore, the people will be delivered, despite Jeremiah's dire prophecies.

The voice of YHWH then interjects: "Why have they provoked me to anger with their images, with their foreign idols?" (8:19c). The question reflects the repeated accusation that the people have been unfaithful, turning instead to "nothings"—gods that are not actually gods at all. Again the people speak—asking yet another question unrelated to YHWH's accusation (8:20). This liturgical question presses the issue of God's timing. The people are repeating old formulas with unwarranted assurance, refusing to hear what the living God is saying to them in the present through the warnings of the prophet.

Jeremiah's lament follows the unanswered question. The prophet's anguish is multiplied by the prophet's sensitivity to YHWH's love for the people and the subsequent divine suffering their unfaithfulness evokes. The multiplication of phrases signals the intensity of Jeremiah's suffering: "I am hurt, I mourn, and dismay has taken hold of me" (8:21).

It is unclear what the exact reference of "balm in Gilead" may be. The point is that, just as there is no medicine that can save the people locally, there is also no medicine or physician in Gilead that would suffice (8:22). Commentators disagree as to whether this verse is spoken by YHWH or Jeremiah.

The reading concludes with Jeremiah's lament that all the tears he can shed are not enough to express the depth of his pain and grief over the countless deaths. His head would have to be "a spring of water, and [his] eyes a fountain of tears" for the immensity of his grief is more than a human body can express.

Responding to the Text

The poignancy of this lament is heightened because of the interplay of voices. The text lends itself to a reading by multiple speakers: YHWH, Jeremiah, and several voices representing the questions of the people. It would be powerful to have the text read by multiple voices during worship, followed by a brief period of silent reflection. Clarifying the tragic interplay of perspectives elicits deeper insights into the text as it relates to the people of Judah during the time of Jeremiah and as it relates to our contemporary situation.

RESPONSIVE READING
PSALM 113 (RCL); PS. 113:1-2, 4-8 (RC)

This hymn exhorts everyone to praise the name of YHWH from the "rising of the sun to its setting" (113:1–3). Such continual praise is warranted because there is no one like YHWH, who acts on behalf of the poor and needy, raising them to "sit with princes" (113:7–8).

PSALM 138 (BCP)

See Proper 12.

PSALM 79:1-9 (RCL alt.)

In this hymn of the community, people decry the defilement and desecration of the temple. Jerusalem is in ruins, and the "servants" of YHWH are dead (79:1–2). The community prays for YHWH to turn from anger and, in compassion, forgive their sins and save them.

SECOND READING
1 TIMOTHY 2:1-7 (RCL);
1 TIM. 2:1-8 (BCP/RC)

The main body of the letter begins by urging that the community have an active, faithful prayer life. The representative types of prayer identified indicate that many forms of prayer are intended. They are to pray "for everyone" (2:1), of which kings and those in "high positions" are exemplars (1:2). Prayers for leaders were common in both Jewish and Christian worship—an acceptable alternative to the worship of emperors promoted by Roman authorities.

According to the letter, praying for leaders is especially important because the quality of leadership influences the quality of life. Leaders can make it possible to "lead a quiet and peaceable life in all godliness and dignity" (2:2). "Godliness" (*eusebeia*) and "dignity" (*semnotēs*) are not found in the letters with certain Pauline authorship; however, they are common in Greek thought. *Semnotēs* connotes a sober, thoughtful manner than engenders respect. Greek thought emphasized its importance for leaders. Its use is expanded here as an appropriate demeanor for all Christians. *Eusebeia* connotes a life characterized by piety, reverence for God, and dignified behavior consistent with pious reverence. Such godliness is correlated with sound teaching later in the letter (6:3) and emphasized as more important than physical training because it has value for both this life and "the life to come" (4:8).

The value of godliness for the "life to come" is implied in the declaration that "God our Savior . . . desires everyone to be saved and to come to the knowledge of the truth" (2:4). The strong universal note sounded in this letter provides a theological warrant for the exhortation to pray for everyone.

The emphasis on "one God" and one mediator between humans and God, "Christ Jesus, himself human" may suggest a threat from the polytheism of Greek religious traditions and the influence of a Gnostic dualism that pitted the material and spiritual worlds against one another, encouraging docetism, the belief that Jesus was not really human but divine.

The Christological claim made by use of the metaphor of Jesus as a "ransom" (*antilytron*—a buying back of people from slavery or captivity) is placed at the end of the list—Jesus as "mediator . . . human . . . ransom for all" (2:6)—thus emphasizing its importance. Jesus as ransom is used frequently in New Testament texts. The distinctiveness of its use in this text is the emphasis placed on the *universal* efficacy of Jesus' life and death. He was a "ransom for all" (2:6). The reference to this reality being "attested at the right time" is not clear. The point may be that the time is that appointed by God.

This portion of the letter ends with a repetition of Paul's authority. Although his role as an acknowledged apostle is the most important aspect of his authority, in this list his role as "teacher of the Gentiles" is emphasized by its final place-ment. Identifying Paul as teacher implies that he should be listened to rather than opposing teachers. The phrase also reinforces his role as the teacher of the Gen-tiles—an embodiment of the universality of the saving grace of God.

THE GOSPEL
LUKE 16:1–13 (RCL/BCP/RC); LUKE 16:10–13 (RC alt.)

Interpreting the Text

This enigmatic parable is part of the theme regarding wealth and poverty that is introduced in the Song of Mary (1:52-53) and serves as a dominant motif throughout Luke. Taken as a whole, the Gospel of Luke portrays a complex pic-ture of wealth and social relations. In this particular case, a rich man is told that his manager has been "squandering his property" (16:1). He calls the manager in and fires him. The manager makes no attempt to deny the charge or defend himself.

Through a soliloquy we hear the manager's thoughts as he asks himself what he should do. He considers and quickly dismisses the possibility of manual labor or begging. Without revealing any details, he follows his mental "I've got it!" with actions designed to guarantee that when he is no longer manager, people will "welcome [him] into their homes" (16:4). The principle of reciprocity that oper-ated in many first-century cultures undergirds the logic of the manager's actions. When one helped another financially, the person who helped would be in the relationship of a patron to the one assisted. The appropriate response to one's patron would be to grant the person honor and offer hospitality.

In order to take advantage of this dynamic, the dishonest manager summons "his master's debtors one by one" (16:5). In what is quite likely only a represen-tative sample of multiple debtors who benefit from the manager's plan, he asks two of the debtors what they owe. The manager then tells them to take their loan papers and change them. Instead of owing "a hundred jugs of olive oil," a man is directed to write that he owes only fifty (16:6). One who owes "a hundred con-tainers of wheat" is told to write that he owes only eighty (16:7).

Commentators disagree on the interpretation of what the manager did. Some claim that he merely removed his own commission, thus giving up immediate funds for the long-term obligation the debtors would feel toward him. Such a shrewd move might well have been commended by the master. Others disagree, pointing to the specific question the manager asks each, "'How much do you owe my master?'" (16:5), emphasizing that the debt was clearly owed to the master, not the manager. In any case, the amount of the debt that is forgiven in each case is substantial.

Following the parable, several sayings are appended that do not depend directly on the parable for their meaning, although they are related to the theme of wealth. In the first saying, Jesus tells his disciples to make friends for themselves "by means of dishonest wealth" so that the friends "may welcome you into the eternal homes" (16:9). This verse draws on both Jewish tradition and the tradition of reciprocity that characterized friendship in the Greco-Roman world of the first century. One interpretation of the verse is suggested by considering this lection in relation to the parable of the rich man and Lazarus that immediately follows it (see Proper 21). Lazarus was a poor man who lay outside the rich man's house when both were alive, wishing that he might just have the scraps that fell from the rich man's table. After both men die, Lazarus is with Father Abraham, being cared for and comforted, while the rich man is across a wide chasm, suffering in fiery agony with no means of relief.

Luke emphasizes the special care God has for the poor and afflicted. The injustice that permeates social institutions in every culture makes it impossible to accrue wealth without complicity in unjust systems. Therefore when Jesus tells the disciples to make friends for themselves "by means of dishonest wealth so that they may be welcomed into the eternal homes," he may be thinking in terms of his previous admonishment to followers to sell their possessions in order to give alms to the poor (12:33). Befriending those who are poor and considered social outcasts, welcoming them at their table and in their homes, involves violating socioeconomic and religious boundaries. It would mean becoming friends with people like Lazarus, who had nothing during his lifetime. The point may be that such friends will indeed be the ones waiting with Father Abraham to welcome others into the eternal homes.

> LUKE EMPHASIZES THE SPECIAL CARE GOD HAS FOR THE POOR AND AFFLICTED.

The next three sayings build on the concept of being faithful over what is of lesser value, so that one might be trusted with that which is of greater value. The final saying presents two mutually exclusive options: one may *either* serve God or wealth. If we grant economic considerations first priority in the ways we live our lives individually and corporately, wealth becomes idolatry, and we become the ones guilty of apostasy.

Responding to the Text

There is no way to remove the tension of this text and the discomfort it creates in the reader. The narrative violates our expectations. We expect the master to be angry with the manager for taking further advantage of him, yet the master commends the manager for his shrewdness. Further the Lukan Jesus seems to commend the shrewdness of the dishonest manager, even commending such strategies to disciples. What can this mean?

Preachers who suggest possible insights into the meaning of the text are wise to acknowledge as well the conflicted history of interpretation regarding the parable and the unresolvable tension it invokes. Such dissonance can tease our imaginations into action so that we continue thinking about the text long after the sermon is completed—a worthy consequence of good preaching.

SEVENTEENTH SUNDAY AFTER PENTECOST

<small>SEPTEMBER 30, 2001</small>
<small>TWENTY-SIXTH SUNDAY IN ORDINARY TIME</small>
<small>PROPER 21</small>

REVISED COMMON	EPISCOPAL (BCP)	ROMAN CATHOLIC
Amos 6:1a, 4-7 　or Jer. 32:1-3a, 　6-15	Amos 6:1-7	Amos 6:1a, 4-7
Ps. 146 　or Ps. 91:1-6, 14-16	Ps. 146 or 　Ps. 91:1-6, 14-16	Ps. 146:7-10
1 Tim. 6:6-19	1 Tim. 6:11-19	1 Tim. 6:11-16
Luke 16:19-31	Luke 16:19-31	Luke 16:19-31

Many people in today's readings face disastrous events in life or the end of life itself. Most are unprepared for what befalls them. When we are forced to face our mortality, either through advancing age or life-threatening illness, we gain a vantage point that allows us to look with clearer eyes at our lives and assess the wisdom of the choices we made, the paths followed, the paths ignored. If we are dismayed by our assessment, we may die with a profound sense of remorse.

It is worth pondering why a number one book on the New York Times bestseller list for many months was *Tuesdays with Morrie*, the true story of a university professor ravaged by Lou Gehrig's disease. An active lover of life, Morrie becomes a teacher about life and death. If we learned we had only six months to live, how would we spend the time? How would we feel about the life we have lived? Were our priorities the right ones? What would we change? It's a question worth asking. We may be blessed with enough time to live into our answers.

FIRST READING
AMOS 6:1a, 4-7 (RCL/RC);
AMOS 6:1-7 (BCP)

Interpreting the Text

Amos, a shepherd from Judah, prophesied to the rulers and wealthy class in the northern kingdom of Israel. Their lavish lifestyle is presented in detail. With a great—but mistaken—sense of security, the wealthy lounge in sumptuous surroundings, eating the best food, drinking heavily out of bowls, and anointing themselves with pleasant and expensive oils while enjoying music from a harp and other instruments. Even as circumstances begin to turn bad in their country, they do not grieve or turn from their concern for personal pleasure.

After painting a vivid picture of their excesses, Amos announces a brief and ironic condemnation. Those who are the "notables" among the "*first* of the nations" (6:1), who could enjoy the choicest food and wine, will again be first— as they walk in front of all those who will be driven into exile (6:7). The boisterous noise of their festive banquets will be replaced by the silence of their march into exile.

Responding to the Text

The prophetic charge against the wealthy, ruling class is echoed in many of the Lukan passages for this season. Note the close parallel between today's reading from Amos and Luke 6:24-25. Wrestling with the complex realities of economic disparity certainly deserves as much attention in our church teaching and preaching today as it did in the time of Amos.[38]

JEREMIAH 32:1-3a, 6-15 (RCL alt.)

Interpreting the Text

King Nebuchadrezzar has begun the destruction of Judah. Jeremiah is being held in the "court of the guard" in the palace of King Zedekiah of Judah (21:2). It is not clear whether or not Jeremiah was a prisoner or was under protective custody. In verses not included in today's lection, King Zedekiah confronts Jeremiah regarding his prophecy that Judah will be defeated and Zedekiah will be carried off to Babylon. Jeremiah had been advising Zedekiah that he should surrender to Nebuchadrezzar, but other court counselors were opposed to such a plan because of their pro-Egyptian leanings (see Proper 20). Following the encounter, Jeremiah is returned to confinement.

Jeremiah then reports having been told that his relative will soon arrive and ask him to buy his field, which is in Anathoth. The details that follow are quite consistent with the legal requirements for selling property. Relatives had the responsibility to step forward to buy property that someone needed to sell in order to keep land within the family. In light of deeds that have been found in earthen jars in archaeological digs, the deed of sale may have been rolled and sealed in order to assure that no terms of sale would be changed. Then a copy or portion of the deed would be copied onto a second deed that would be rolled around the first but not sealed, giving ease of access for those who needed to know about the sale. This second, outer deed may be what is meant by "the open copy" (32:11). The deed of purchase was signed and witnessed by those present.[39]

The sale of the property was executed with careful attention to community customs and regulations. Each step is noted in the text: the weighing of the silver, the writing, sealing, and witnessing of the deed of sale. It is ironic that this common community event occurs and is reported with such attention to detail in the midst of a foreign military invasion that will destroy the land—according to the very person who is engaged in buying the property. This vignette of family and community life has profound symbolic value precisely because it occurs at just this point.[40]

Despite Jeremiah's accurate prophecy of terrifying disaster, this vignette carries a seed of hope. Jeremiah gives the deeds of sale to his scribe, Baruch, and tells him to put them in an earthenware jar for safekeeping. They must be able to last a long time, for years of exile are imminent. But YHWH will bring the people back sometime in the future. Jeremiah prophesies that "Houses and fields and vineyards shall again be bought in this land" (21:15). There will be a future generation for whom the deeds of sale just consummated will be important.

Responding to the Text

Leaders often fall victim to Zedekiah's weakness: Jeremiah tells him the truth and recommends actions that would help lessen the military disaster, but Zedekiah prefers to listen to those who tell him not to worry, everything will be fine. Too often, leaders punish people who are willing to be the bearers of bad tidings and reward people who will tell them what they want to hear. While this is understandable psychologically—we all prefer good news to bad—it is destructive to the health of any church, institution, community, or country when courageous people who identify problems and speak up for those who are denied social position and status are ignored or silenced. When we have power and status, we tend to find the status quo very satisfying. When change is called for, we are unlikely to see the need—particularly if it means giving up some of our own power, prestige, and comfort. The ancient Hebrews gave a great gift to the world by reporting the words of their prophets and their unwillingness to listen. Though they lived over two thousand years ago, they report human tendencies we have today. How can we learn from their experience and listen more willingly and openly to God's word to us?

> WHEN CHANGE IS CALLED FOR, WE ARE UNLIKELY TO SEE THE NEED—PARTICULARLY IF IT MEANS GIVING UP SOME OF OUR OWN POWER, PRESTIGE, AND COMFORT.

RESPONSIVE READING

209

SEVENTEENTH
SUNDAY
AFTER PENTECOST

SEPTEMBER 30

PSALM 146 (RCL/BCP);
PS. 146:7, 8-9, 9-10 (RC)

This beautiful hymn of praise reflects the life of one whose faith and trust is in YHWH. Others are exhorted not to place their trust anywhere else. Even those with great power and wealth are but mortal and will die. It is YHWH, the creator, the one who is faithful, in whom one should trust and have hope. YHWH loves the righteous, administers justice for the oppressed, frees prisoners, gives sight to the blind, and lifts up those who are "bowed down." Praise to YHWH—whose reign will last forever.

PSALM 91:1-6, 14-16 (RCL alt./BCP)

In the face of all manner of enemies and threats to life, God protects those who take refuge in the shadow of God's protective wings—those who love God and know God's name. To know God's name is to have more than information. Knowledge of God's name refers to knowing the nature of God so that one lives in right relationship with God—an expression of one's love for God.

SECOND READING
1 TIMOTHY 6:6-19 (RCL);
1 TIM. 6:11-19 (BCP);
1 TIM. 6:11-16 (RC)

In the first section of this reading, the proper attitude of a Christian—particularly a church leader—toward wealth is specified. The admonition to be content with food and clothing should not be equated with a rigorous asceticism, which was criticized as characteristic of the opposing teachers. Those who are rich are exhorted not to place confidence in their material wealth but in God. They should do good works and be generous; however, they are not advised to give up everything but food and clothing (6:17-18).

This attitude is contrasted with those who strive after wealth. The danger of being caught up in greed is that one will fall prey to "temptation" and "harmful desires" that lead to "ruin and destruction" (6:9). These realities lead to the famous maxim, "The love of money is a root of all kinds of evil" (6:10).

In contrast to pursuing wealth, Timothy is advised to "pursue righteousness, godliness, faith, love, endurance, gentleness" (6:11). This list of virtues stands in contrast to the list of vices that characterize the effects of the teaching the letter opposes. This section may refer to an ordination liturgy. The phrase "a man of

God" is used in the Old Testament to refer to special leaders such as Moses, David, and Samuel. In the Pastoral Epistles, it is used in 2 Timothy to refer to one who teaches, corrects, and trains others in righteousness (2 Tim 3:16-17).

Following the liturgy, the author returns to the topic of wealth and advises Timothy on what to teach those who have money. They should be advised not to be "haughty" or place their sense of security in their wealth. Their focus should be on generosity and good works that provide true treasure—"a good foundation for the future, so that they may take hold of the life that really is life" (6:19).

THE GOSPEL
LUKE 16:19-31

This parable contrasts an unnamed rich man of fine clothing and sumptuous eating habits with Lazarus, a poor, evidently homeless, man who lays at the gate of the rich man's estate. In place of the rich man's "purple and fine linen" clothing, Lazarus has a body "covered with sores" (16:19-20). Lazarus longs for the scraps that fall from the rich man's daily feast.

Both men die, but only the unnamed rich man receives a burial. In contrast to life on earth, their fortunes are reversed after death. Lazarus is seated next to Abraham—suggesting a seat of honor. The rich man finds himself across a wide, impassable chasm writhing in torment. Both are in Sheol, which is not their final state, but their opposite situations in Sheol are indicative of their judgment.

The unnamed man continues to behave as if his former material wealth defined his status. He calls out to Father Abraham to send Lazarus to give him water to cool his tongue. Apparently he knew Lazarus by name, although he made no effort to help him when he was alive. Abraham reminds the man that, while he had good things during life, Lazarus had "evil things" (16:25). Calling to Father Abraham evokes John the Baptist's warning to people that claiming Abraham as one's ancestor will mean nothing if one does not "bear fruits worthy of repentance" (3:8).

The relationship between the rich man and Lazarus is reversed—exemplifying the eschatological reversal predicted early in this Gospel in Mary's song: God has "brought down the powerful from their thrones" and "lifted up the lowly" (1:52-53). In response to his plight, the rich man begs Abraham to send Lazarus to warn his brothers. Abraham points out that the scripture they have is sufficient. Indeed, though it is not said, Lazarus lying at the rich man's gate embodies a dominant theme of the books of Moses and the prophets—YHWH's demand that the poor and oppressed be treated with justice.

The rich man claims that if only Lazarus would return from the dead to tell others, they would repent. Abraham disagrees. If they do not listen to God's word to them through Moses and the prophets, they will not repent even if one returns from the dead. Jesus' portrayal of Abraham's response is aimed primarily at the Pharisees interpretation of scripture.

Responding to the Text

The complexity of economic realities is reflected in the Gospel of Luke. Although wealth is attacked in some pericopes, in this case the man's sin is not wealth but his refusal to follow the commandments given by Moses and the warnings given by the prophets. YHWH demands that those with wealth pursue justice and provide for the needs of the poor and vulnerable in society. The perspective of this text challenges the Deuteronomic theology that proclaimed a correlation between one's goodness and prosperity, one's wickedness and suffering.

LAZARUS LYING AT THE RICH MAN'S GATE EMBODIES A DOMINANT THEME OF THE BOOKS OF MOSES AND THE PROPHETS—YHWH'S DEMAND THAT THE POOR AND OPPRESSED BE TREATED WITH JUSTICE.

During this part of the Pentecost season, preachers are faced again and again with Jesus' insistent emphasis on the proper use of wealth, the dangers of greed, and the idolatry of placing our faith and hope in money. Yet many pastors in middle- and upper-class churches find their congregations grant them little authority and credibility on economic issues—no matter what the Bible says. Despite the difficulty, it is important to address the idolatrous worship of money that is so prevalent in our society. We need to hear stories of Christian individuals and communities who share generously what they have, engage in Bible study in which we wrestle seriously with the claims the gospel makes on us economically, and search our own hearts and lives in partnership with others to discern the justice and spiritual healthiness of our personal and corporate handling of money.

NOTES

1. Philip Hallie, *Lest Innocent Blood Be Shed* (New York: HarperPerennial, 1994; originally published in 1979).

2. See David Ostendorf, "Countering Hatred," in *Christian Century* (Sept. 8-15, 1999) 861-63, and Frank Gibney Jr., "The Kids Got in the Way," *Time* (Aug. 23, 1999) 24-9.

3. My comments on the Hosea text require me to call attention to a deeply troubling aspect of this story as well. In Gen. 19:8, Lot tries to protect the men whom he has invited into his home by offering to bring out his two daughters to the threatening men, saying they can "do to them as you please." If one reflects seriously on such an offer, it cries out for discussion and condemnation. The issues raised should not be dismissed by pitting the New Testament against the

Old Testament. A more adequate approach is to challenge the theological adequacy of such texts by claiming the more inclusive biblical truth of God's universal dominion in justice and righteousness for all people—women and men. This theological claim is attested in many Old and New Testament texts. Such biblical texts—regardless of where they occur in the canon—provide criteria for criticizing and qualifying the spoken and unspoken claims of texts that are not theologically adequate. For a discussion of this approach to biblical theology, see Rolf Knierim, "Systematic Old Testament Theology," in *The Flowering of Old Testament Theology*, ed. B. C. Ollenburger et. al. (Winona Lake, Ind.: Eisenbrauns, 1992) 465-86.

4. Jehu ordered the death of seventy of King Ahab's sons. Their heads were delivered to him at Jezreel (2 Kings 10:1-11).

5. Abraham J. Heschel, *The Prophets* (Peabody, Mass: Prince, 1999; originally published in 1962) 56.

6. Gale A. Yee, "Hosea," in *The Women's Bible Commentary*, ed. C. A. Newsom and S. H. Ringe (Louisville: Westminster John Knox, 1992) 197.

7. Phyllis Bird, "'To Play the Harlot': An Inquiry into an Old Testament Metaphor," in *Missing Persons and Mistaken Identities: Women and Gender in Ancient Israel* (OBT; Minneapolis: Fortress Press, 1997) 220-21.

8. Heschel, *The Prophets*, 50.

9. Almost one-third of women experience domestic violence in their lifetime. See Adam Edward Jukes, *Men Who Batter Women* (London: Routledge, 1999) 17-27.

10. Hans-Joachim Kraus, *Psalms 60–150,* trans. H. C. Oswald (CC; Minneapolis: Augsburg, 1989) 507.

11. Although most scholars now believe this letter was written by a follower of Paul rather than Paul himself, I will refer to the author as Paul for the sake of convenience.

12. Gershom Scholem, *On the Mystical Shape of the Godhead: Basic Concepts in the Kabbalah*, trans. J. Neugroschel (New York: Schocken, 1991) 20-22.

13. Biblical theologian Rolf Knierim notes the dominance of food as a concern of the Old Testament. On every three pages (NRSV), people eat or drink four times. "They spoke and wrote about it in their prose and poetry, their novels and histories, their legislative works, their preaching and illustrations, their prophecies, and their psalms and proverbs." Rolf Knierim, "Food, Land, and Justice," in idem, *The Task of Old Testament Theology* (Grand Rapids: Eerdmans, 1995) 230.

14. Gary Gardner and Brian Halweil, "Nourishing the Underfed and Overfed," in *State of the World 2000: A Worldwatch Institute Report on Progress toward a Sustainable Society,* ed. L. Stark (New York: Norton, 2000) 60.

15. See C. L. Seow's *Ecclesiastes: A New Translation with Introduction and Commentary* for a detailed analysis of linguistic issues and the history of interpretation of the text (New York: Doubleday, 1997) 112.

16. Ibid., 118.

17. Knierim, *The Task of Old Testament Theology*, 231.

18. Ibid., 438.

19. James Luther Mays, *Hosea: A Commentary* (OTL; Philadelphia: Westminster, 1969) 158.

20. In Margaret Guenther's excellent book *The Practice of Prayer* (Cambridge: Cowley, 1998), the author provides a helpful introduction to the use of the Jesus Prayer, as well as other spiritual disciplines. See also Marjorie Thompson's fine book *Soul Feast: An Invitation to the Christian Spiritual Life* (Louisville: Westminster John Knox Press, 1995) and *Practicing Our Faith*, ed. D. C. Bass (San Francisco: Jossey-Bass, 1997).

21. Bruce J. Malina, *The New Testament World: Insights from Cultural Anthropology* (Atlanta: John Knox, 1981) 83.

22. Bernard Brandon Scott, *Hear Then the Parable: A Commentary on the Parables of Jesus* (Minneapolis: Fortress Press, 1989) 140.

23. The interpretation of *peša'* as "rebellion" is found in S. J. DeVries's analysis of the terms "Sin, Sinners," in *The Interpreter's Dictionary of the Bible* (1962) 4:361–76. The alternative interpretation is reflected in *Handwörterbuch über das Alte Testament*. The change in definition for *peša'* was not noted in Francis Brown, S. R. Driver, and Charles A. Briggs, *Hebrew and English Lexicon* (1906; Peabody, Mass., 1999) 833.

24. This view is developed in detail by George Wesley Buchanan, *Hebrews* (AB 36; Garden City, N.Y.: Doubleday, 1972).

25. The thesis is developed within a vision of reality that suggests both apocalypticism and Platonism. Plato, who lived more than four centuries before the book of Hebrews was written, taught that reality consists of archetypal forms that cannot be seen, whereas what we see and name as reality is but a shadow. Note, for example, the contrast drawn between the heavenly city toward which Abraham looked forward in contrast to his time in the promised land (Heb. 11:9–10, 16). The "heavenly city" embodies reality because its "architect and builder is God" (Heb. 11:10). There is, of course, an apocalyptic aspect to this vision. See Luke Timothy Johnson, "The General Letters and Revelation," in *The Catholic Study Bible*, ed. D. Senior (New York: Oxford Univ. Press, 1990) 541–47.

26. For a picture of the oppressive and violent authority wielded by Roman rulers, see Richard A. Horsley, *Jesus and the Spiral of Violence: Popular Jewish Resistance in Roman Palestine* (Minneapolis: Fortress Press, 1993).

27. For an excellent discussion of the early formation of the Christian community, see Howard Clark Kee, Eric M. Meyers, John Rogerson, and Anthony

J. Saldarini, *The Cambridge Companion to the Bible* (Cambridge: Cambridge Univ. Press, 1997).

28. Morton T. Kelsey, *Psychology, Medicine and Christian Healing* (San Francisco: Harper and Row, 1988) 42.

29. Allen Dwight Callahan, *Embassy of Onesimus: The Letter of Paul to Philemon* (Valley Forge, Penn.: Trinity Press International, 1997) 14.

30. Ibid., 18-19.

31. For a discussion of *doulos* (slave) in early Christian thinking and writing, and the case for Onesimus as Philemon's brother "in the flesh" (v. 16), see Callahan, *Embassy of Onesimus*, 44-56.

32. William L. Holladay, *Jeremiah 1* (Hermeneia; Philadelphia: Fortress Press, 1986) 156.

33. See, for example, David Ray Griffin, *God, Power, and Evil: A Process Theodicy* (Philadelphia: Westminster, 1976); David Ray Griffin, *Evil Revisited: Responses and Reconsiderations* (Albany: State Univ. of New York Press, 1991); William C. Placher, *Narratives of a Vulnerable God: Christ, Theology, and Scripture* (Louisville: Westminster John Knox, 1994).

34. For a good summary of these issues see Jouette M. Bassler, *1 Timothy, 2 Timothy, Titus* (Nashville: Abingdon, 1996) 17-21.

35. Ibid., 43.

36. See Bernard Brandon Scott's discussion of the negative evaluation of shepherds in first-century texts in *Hear Then the Parable* (Minneapolis: Fortress Press, 1989) 412-416.

37. Bernard Scott's analysis of this parable (*Hear Then the Parable*, 99-125) is particularly helpful.

38. One theologian who has been working to bring theologians and economists into conversation is John B. Cobb Jr. His most recent book about concern for the environment, economic policy, and Christian commitments to justice for all people and reverence toward God's creation is *The Earthist Challenge to Economism: A Theological Critique of the World Bank* (New York: St. Martin's Press, 1999). Cobb's *Becoming a Thinking Christian* (Nashville: Abingdon, 1993) is an excellent resource for helping clergy and laypersons engage in theological discussions about significant issues in the church and the world.

39. William L. Holladay, *Jeremiah 2* (Hermeneia; Minneapolis: Fortress Press, 1989) 214. Holladay notes that this section of Jeremiah provides the most detailed information in the OT on the transfer of property.

40. James L. Mays, ed., *Harper's Bible Commentary* (San Francisco: Harper & Row, 1989) 637.

EIGHTEENTH SUNDAY AFTER PENTECOST

OCTOBER 7, 2001
TWENTY-SEVENTH SUNDAY IN ORDINARY TIME
PROPER 22

REVISED COMMON	EPISCOPAL (BCP)	ROMAN CATHOLIC
Hab. 1:1-4, 2:1-4 or Lam. 1:1-6	Hab. 1:1-6 (7-11), 12-13; 2:1-4	Hab. 1:2-3; 2:2-4
Ps. 37:1-9	Ps. 37:1-18 or 37:3-10	Ps. 95:1-2, 6-9
2 Tim. 1:1-14	2 Tim. 1:(1-5), 6-14	2 Tim. 1:6-8, 13-14
Luke 17:5-10	Luke 17:5-10	Luke 17:5-10

This Sunday begins the "countdown" to the end of the church year. Sunday after Sunday there will be a balance between readings that speak of the evils rampant in history and those that exhibit belief in God's ultimate justice with affirmations of hope. This balance leads up to Christ the King Sunday, with its ringing affirmation of Jesus as the *Kosmokrator*, the Lord of the universe.

The challenge for proclaimers is to ring the changes on this constant theme without becoming highly repetitive. One way to accomplish that is to select the fundamental metaphors of one of the lessons and form one's proclamation on its basis.

Pentecost 18 combines a theme of rage over the injustice of Israel's fate (both Habakkuk and Lamentations) with calls for patience and trust in the face of history's evils (Psalm 37). Second Timothy describes efforts of the early church to achieve stability in the face of opposition, while the Gospel for the day stresses the great deeds that faith expects from God.

FIRST READING
HABAKKUK 1:1-4, 2:1-4 (RCL);
HAB. 1-6 (7-11), 12-13; 2:1-4 (BCP);
HAB. 1:2-3; 2:2-4 (RC)

Interpreting the Text

Habakkuk is known to us only from his book, which provides no auto-biographical details. The reference to the Chaldeans in 1:6 implies a date somewhere between 626 and 587 B.C.E., when the Neo-Babylonian Empire threatened Judah. There is no reference to captivity; hence, the prophetic oracles antedate the destruction of Jerusalem.

Habakkuk's work falls into three sections. The first, from which our text is taken, is a dialogue between the prophet and God (1:2—2:5). The second section contains five woes (2:6-20, each in English containing the term "alas"), a commentary on 2:2-5. The final vision (3:1-19), often called "The Prayer of Habakkuk," is hymnic praise of God as Savior (cf. 3:18-19), a powerful evocation of the warrior God who shakes nature and people in care for his people.

Habakkuk questions God's failure to act in the face of confusion, injustice, the breakdown of societal standards, and the ongoing mistreatment of the faithful ("the righteous" in v. 4) by the wicked. A key term for Habakkuk is "violence." It occurs six times in the first two chapters (1:2, 3, 9; 2:8, and twice in 2:17). Habakkuk sets it parallel to destruction (v. 3). The law (Torah), central to Israel's life, recalled to the nation by Hezekiah's reforms, no longer functions because of the violence. Justice is lost, perverted by the "wicked" to their own evil ends. Habakkuk questions God's fidelity to the people, because God seems not to listen to prayer or react to the breakdown of society.

God's first answer is not a word of comfort. Rather, the Chaldeans are God's instrument to punish the wicked (v. 6: "I am rousing . . ."). God describes them as a mighty military force. They will impose justice, but justice according to their own light (v. 7)! That response contains no comfort for Habakkuk. In 1:12—2:1, he expresses his shock that such action will contradict God's own character. Note the titles he applies to God: "O Lord, My God, my Holy One." (1:12)

BECAUSE GOD IS A ROCK, HE CANNOT LOOK ON EVIL AND WRONGDOING AND REMAIN QUIET WHEN THE WICKED DESTROY THE RIGHTEOUS (1:13). AND SO HABAKKUK WAITS FOR GOD'S ANSWER.

Because God is a Rock, he cannot look on evil and wrongdoing and remain quiet when the wicked destroy the righteous (1:13). And so Habakkuk waits for God's answer.

The answer comes in 2:2-5. History moves according to God's plan. Make that clear. Write it in such big letters that a runner can read it on the way past. There is a vision of the end time; wait for it to be accomplished, even if it appears to be slow. Then the righteous who live by faith will be vindicated, not the proud, the wealthy, or the arrogant.

Responding to the Text

"Might makes right." "The end justifies the means." "If it's good for General Motors, it's good for the country." Such slogans run through history from Plato's Greece through contemporary America. And they have been used to justify racism, poverty for sweatshop laborers, and acts of military aggression. The failure of social norms, the prevalence of injustice, the imbalance of economic resources, the pillaging of the resources of developing nations' natural resources by the wealthy north—all these are justified by such slogans.

Over against this, Habakkuk has a powerful theological message: God has power over human history. Write that vision as Habakkuk was to write it in his day. Call God to be faithful to God's own self—and add the consequent call to God's people to trust and be faithful. Another slogan is, "Unless the people have a vision, they perish" (see 2:2-4). The church is a community of vision.

LAMENTATIONS 1:1-6 (RCL, alt.)

Interpreting the Text

Lamentations is a five-poem *cri de coeur* for Jerusalem, destroyed by the Babylonians in 587 B.C.E. The writer laments the tragic fall. The city is desolate (v. 1). Her former allies have become her enemies. Jerusalem, the central location for the worship (cult) of God, is deserted. No one comes for the festivals any longer, while the city gates, normally the scene of intense activity, are deserted (v. 4). The phrase "justice at the city gate," once used to describe good government, is now a mockery. The social fabric is rent, as young women no longer have hope for the future.

What is worst of all, Yahweh has caused all this suffering (v. 5) because Jerusalem and Judea did not keep the covenant. Verse 1:5a, with its reference to "head" (the NRSV translates it "masters"), reflects the conditional covenant blessing of Deut. 28:13, 44. Deut. 28:41 predicts the captivity of Lam. 1:5c. The context in Deuteronomy 28 illuminates the condition of Jerusalem. The reference in Lam. 1:5b to "transgressions" also reflects the breaking of the covenant with God.

Responding to the Text

Abraham Lincoln once referred to the United States as "the almost chosen people." This text, completely dark, invites reflection on the native self-confidence of America as the light of democracy in the world, on its self-assurance and its manifest destiny. God's own people can lose their place—and so can America. We too need to hear the call for fidelity; that is the call that comes in today's Gospel.

RESPONSIVE READING

PSALM 37:1-9 (RCL);
PS. 37:1-18 or 37:3-10 (BCP)

Interpreting the Text

Psalm 37 is a didactic psalm in the wisdom tradition that calls the worshiper to trust in God's protection of righteous people and the judgment of wicked wrongdoers. It is an acrostic psalm (the initial letters of verses follow the order of the Hebrew alphabet), a device to aid memory. Ultimately God is faithful to the covenant. Here is a mature speaker whose experience of God is the basis of his teaching.

The first part (37:1-15) falls into two sections. The first (vv. 1-8) is a sequence of directives to the hearer, while the second (vv. 9-15) stresses the ultimate punishment of the wicked. The series of commands is impressive: Two are repeated: "Do not fret" (vv. 1, 7, 8) because of the success of the wicked (cf. Prov. 24:19-20, another wisdom tradition). Their present good fortune is illusive and temporary (see vv. 2, 9-10, 12-15). The repetition implies that the psalmist addresses one impatient with God's slow judgment, as does the command to "be still and wait patiently" (v. 7). "Trust" (vv. 3 and 5) is the fundamental relationship with God. Trust results in action: "do good" (v. 3), "delight in the Lord" (v. 4), "commit your way to him" (v. 5), "be still," and "wait patiently" (v. 7). Do that, and "you will live in the land" in security (v. 3). Those who "wait for the Lord will inherit the land" (v. 9; cf. vv. 11, 22, 29, 34; Matt. 5:5). The "meek" describes those who know that they depend on God. Vindication is God's action in defense of the people, while justice (*zedekah*) is God acting to save. Vindication will be public, as is the prosperity of the wicked. That is the significance of shining like light at noonday. See Ezek. 36:22-32 for an extensive, detailed parallel to this public action by God.

Responding to the Text

Instant gratification and impatience are taught by television ads every day. Watch the ads on children's programs for marvelous examples of this. Of course, children learn very quickly that such ads deceive. The result is ingrained skepticism, and that carries over into our relationships with God. We become impatient with God's slowness to "reward" goodness and punish oppressors. There is even a slogan in bad Latin that reflects this attitude: *illegitimis non corborundum est.* How does one wait patiently? Trust believes in the face of contrary evidence. That is the burden of Psalm 37. A friend recently returned from a visit to a mountain village in El Salvador that had been destroyed in the civil war in the 80s. He was amazed and humbled by the faith and hope that the villagers had in God's future, which led them to action to realize it.

PSALM 95:1-2, 6-9 (RC)

Interpreting the Text

This psalm is familiar in liturgical churches as part of the Matins (Morning Prayer) liturgy. It is a call to praise God as savior (vv. 1-2). He is the creator God who cares for his people like a king; the king as shepherd of the people is a well-known metaphor applied here to God (cf. Ps. 80:1, 100:3; Isa. 40:11). Such worship means that one does not test God as Israel did at *Meribah* and *Massah.* The reference behind this allusion is Exod. 17:1-7 (cf. Num. 20:1-13), where Israel complained about the lack of water, Moses struck the rock with his staff, and water flowed. The Septuagint (the Greek translation of the OT) translates the two names as *loidoresis* and *peirasmos,* "insult and testing," because Israel there tested God. Jesus refers to this incident in his response to Satan in Matt. 4:7 and Luke 4:12.

This psalm puts our response to God within the context of worship. Worship as faithfulness is a motif that needs stress in our society, where many gauge the value or success of worship by the emotional impact it has on them ("warm fuzzies"). Worship relates to action. That is why some end a Sunday service with the words, "The service is ended, let the worship begin," an intentional pun on the usual language.

SECOND READING
2 TIMOTHY 1:1-14

Interpreting the Text

This text begins a series of four Sundays in which the second lessons are drawn from 2 Timothy. Much modern scholarship holds that the letter reflects a situation much later than the life of Paul, probably slightly post 100 C.E., when the church faced opposition from the surrounding society and threats from divergent Christian teaching. Second Timothy, along with the other two Pastoral Epistles (1 Tim. and Titus), gives instruction about the preservation of the truth ("healthy teaching," 1 Tim. 1:10; "good teaching," 1 Tim. 4:6; "healthy state-ments," 1 Tim. 6:3, etc.). Thus the Pastoral Epistles, including 2 Timothy, offer suggestions for maintaining the faith in a time of crisis. They rethink some of Paul's thoughts for a new time and a new situation.

According to the letter, Paul is in prison (1:8; 2:9), expecting death in the near future (4:6-8). Paul is alone but for Luke, deserted or even harmed by former friends (vv. 10, 14). The letter comes close to a farewell address; it probably should be read as the last word of the Pauline school, the closing of the Pauline corpus.

The brief salutation (1:1-2) is close to that of 1 Timothy (suggesting author-ship by the same writer). The Roman world respected antiquity as a hallmark of a religion, but feared novelty in religion. In 1:3-5, the author suggests a longer history of the Christian faith in two ways. Verse 1:3 ties Paul's service to God to that of his ancestors. The verb *latreō,* which the NRSV translates "worship," has a broader significance, denoting the total service rendered to God (see Rom. 1:9; Phil. 3:3). Second, Timothy's faith continues that of his grandmother, Lois, and mother, Eunice. His faith, not a novelty, should therefore inspire boldness, love, and self-discipline (1:5-7). The latter term, *ōphronismos,* stresses practical self-con-trol, a concept well known in Hellenistic philosophy.

Therefore Timothy should heed a series of admonitions. He is to "stir up the gracious gift (*charisma*) given to him by the imposition of hands. While 1 Tim. 4:14 describes the council of elders as imposing their hands, here the reference is more likely to Paul's baptism of Timothy. Verse 1:7 speaks of the gift of the Spirit, which supports the baptismal reference. Timothy is to confess the faith boldly by joining Paul in suffering for the gospel. Paul's imprisonment is not a cause of shame, but of encouragement to join in suffering for the gospel.

This is supported by the citation of an early Christian tradition in vv. 9-10, a second support for fearless confession. The tradition stresses the priority of God, who revealed in Christ the gift of grace that was his plan from eternity. His res-urrection shows that suffering and death have lost their power. Paul urges Tim-othy to hold on to this tradition just cited to maintain true teaching and conti-nuity with the past.

Responding to the Text

Americans tend to prize independence. "I ain't beholden to anybody." We confess one of the ecumenical creeds each Sunday as a witness that we are "beholden" to the past confessors of the faith. And, like Timothy, we are called to preserve and pass on the faith, for that is one way to meet the variety of expe-riences in life. Vincent of Lerins spoke of that faith as *quod ubique, quod semper, quod ab omnibus creditum est* ("What has been believed everywhere, always, by all"). Second Timothy speaks of the "appearing" (*epiphaneia*) of our Savior Jesus

Christ," using a term appropriate to the manifestation of a divine being. The reference is not to his birth but to his resurrection. Thus, toward the end of the Pentecost season, we are to preach Easter as God's ultimate act of revealing his purpose in history, to show unmerited love (grace). This text is in part an answer to the questions raised by Habakkuk and Lamentations.

The Gospel
LUKE 17:5-10

Interpreting the Text

The text is part of the great travel narrative (Luke 9:51—19:27) in which Jesus and his disciples travel to Jerusalem for the Passion. The long section before this text (Luke 13:22—16:31) contains stories of opposition to Jesus. Luke incorporates much of Jesus' teaching of the disciples into the travel account. In Luke 17:1-4, Jesus comments on the opposition

> THERE IS PERSONAL RESPONSIBILITY FOR WHAT ONE DOES IN HISTORY, EVEN IF ONE IS CONVINCED THAT GOD CONTROLS HISTORY.

to him. Occasions for stumbling are bound to come; history is full of them. These *skandala* (offenses) lead to apostasy by "little ones," i.e., neophyte disciples (cf. Luke 7:23; 10:21). But they are not for that reason to be excused. There is personal responsibility for what one does in history, even if one is convinced that God controls history.

Those who cause offense will be severely judged and punished. In Luke 17:2, Jesus speaks of drowning a man by fastening a millstone around his neck and throwing him into the depth of the sea (certainly the Sea of Galilee). Luke refers to the heavy upper stone from the rotary mill drawn round and round by a mule. Today one can see such upper millstones at Capernaum, excavated by the Franciscans. They are made from black basalt stone, about 3½ feet tall, shaped like a bow tie, and extremely heavy. Perhaps the closest parallel in our time is the cement "boots" that thugs used to drown people in the Hudson or East Rivers.

But judgment is not to come from disciples. They are to forgive, as the Lord's Prayer says (cf. Luke 11:4). The number seven is the number of completeness; hence disciples place no limit on forgiveness.

The disciples respond by asking for greater "faith," *pistis*. The term can also mean "fidelity," which would also fit the context. Luke applies the term "apostles" to the twelve already here. That correlates with the description of an apostle given in Acts 1:21-22: one who has been with Jesus throughout his ministry. Jesus responds with a saying used by Matthew and Mark in the story of the cursing of the fig tree (Matt. 21:21; Mark 11:23). Faith should recognize in him an apocalyptic sign, the arrival of God's saving King. They would tell the mulberry tree to uproot itself and grow in the sea (of Galilee?). Such faith would result in self-denying service, like the service of a slave to the master (vv. 7-10).

Responding to the Text

How should we respond to the jeremiads that characterize many evaluations of contemporary American life and culture? Today's Gospel suggests that we are to pray for strong faith and fidelity. How often our prayers center on asking for help in time of personal need: sickness, poverty, loss of work, and the like. The apostles respond by asking for greater fidelity, not for specific acts on God's part. Jesus' response makes clear that faith/fidelity is shown in forgiveness and service that is self-denying. Rather than moan about our culture and time, we are asked to become its forgiving servants. This applies to any given parish, whether town or country. A proclaimer today must be as much an interpreter of our time as Habakkuk was of Judah's.

NINETEENTH SUNDAY AFTER PENTECOST

OCTOBER 14, 2001
TWENTY-EIGHTH SUNDAY IN ORDINARY TIME
PROPER 23

REVISED COMMON	EPISCOPAL (BCP)	ROMAN CATHOLIC
2 Kings 5:1-3, 7-15 or Jer. 29:1, 4-7	Ruth 1:(1-7), 8-19a	2 Kings 5:14-17
Ps. 111	Ps. 113	Ps. 98:1-4
2 Tim. 2:8-15	2 Tim. 2:(3-7), 8-15	2 Tim. 2:8-13
Luke 17:11-19	Luke 17:11-19	Luke 17:11-19

Leprosy, non-Israelite foreigners, thanksgiving, confession of faith in God and/or Jesus—such are the motifs that run through this Sunday's lessons. These texts stress that awe before God's gracious acts, whether by Israelites or members of hostile or despised nations (Syrians, Moabites, Samaritans), can incorporate one within the sphere of God's merciful sovereignty. This Sunday is ethnically ecumenical. Yahweh is the God of all peoples. For Christians this means recognizing the central role of Jesus in God showing mercy to his people, as the lesson from 2 Timothy makes clear.

FIRST READING
2 KINGS 5:1-3, 7-15 (RCL);
2 KINGS 5:14-17 (RC)

Interpreting the Text

The story of Naaman's leprosy is familiar, but it deserves highlighting. Naaman is a Syrian (2 Kings 5:1-19), a member of a nation that was Israel's political enemy—and a victorious military man at that! The story stresses a number of things. In one sense it is to glorify Elisha as a wonder-working prophet. It is one of a series of miraculous deeds—multiplying of oil for a prophet's widow (2 Kings 4:1-7); the gift of a son to the Shunammite woman and raising him from the dead (4:8-37); a pot of stew (4:38-41); feeding one hundred people from twenty barley loaves (4:42-44)—and is followed by the miracle of the floating ax head (6:1-7). The sequence demonstrates Elisha's extraordinary prophetic powers.

But the story of Naaman interrupts the sequence; it is written to do much more than glorify Elisha. Naaman is a foreigner (Aram = Syria), coming from the nation that had fought against Israel (see 1 Kings 20:1-34; 22:1-40, both in the days of Elijah). Naaman had a Hebrew slave girl, captured in a battle against Israel in which God had given him the victory (5:1)—and he was a leper. She spoke to Naaman's wife of Elisha's healing powers. That led to his coming to the King of Israel with a letter from the king of Syria requesting healing for Naaman. He supports his request with immensely rich gifts to secure that help. But the king of Israel is powerless to help and suspects that Syria's request is merely a pretext for a new war (5:5-70): "Am I God to give life or death?"

What the king cannot do, God's prophet Elisha can, as he tells the king. As God's prophet he does not even personally meet Naaman, but sends a servant-messenger (Gehazi; preparation for the story in 5:19-27) with instructions that Naaman bathe in the Jordan River. Offended at this casual treatment, Naaman is angry and rails against the prophet. But his servants remind him that what Elisha asks is not difficult. He only said, "Wash and be clean!" He bathes in the Jordan and he is cured. God heals an enemy of Israel, without the rites employed by Syria's own priestly healers.

The story stresses the significant role of servants (5:2, 10, 13), including the Hebrew slave girl, Naaman's own servants, and Elisha's servant, Gehazi. These references prepare the auditor for Naaman's ironic personal reversal in calling himself a servant in 5:15.

Naaman begins as a skeptic about the God of Elisha and ends up making a confession of faith and offering a gift of thanks. "There is no God in all the earth except in Israel" (5:15). He offers Elisha magnificent gifts, only to be refused.

NAAMAN BEGINS AS A SKEPTIC ABOUT THE GOD OF ELISHA AND ENDS UP MAKING A CONFESSION OF FAITH AND OFFERING A GIFT OF THANKS.

Instead he ends up asking for a gift for himself: two mule loads of earth to serve as the ground on which to worship the God of Israel in Syria. This earth symbolizes the power of God to act in Syria, Israel's ancient enemy. Naaman cannot give a rich man's gift to the prophet, but takes one home with him. He does not become an Israelite; there is no mention of circumcision or Torah observance. The irony in these reversals in the attitude and status of an enemy of Israel is striking. God saves a non-Israelite.

Responding to the Text

God is not bound by our ethnic or political boundaries, not limited by our limits. Our enmities are not his. Naaman the Syrian found miracle and mercy in Israel. Where are the prophetic Elishas in our time who would heal enemies, whether national or personal? It is striking that the story makes no mention of the purity laws related to leprosy in the Old Testament and does not interpret the two mule loads of earth as meaning that the worship of Yahweh was restricted to the earth of Palestine. Naaman does not become an Israelite in order to fall under God's gracious rule. It is tempting to identify God with our own land.

I recall a conversation with a German pastor in 1963, when memories of World War II were still much alive. In a prisoner of war camp, he was told by fanatical Nazis that when they won the war, people like him would "get it." He commented that he could not pray for the defeat of his people, since he knew what that might mean; and he could not pray for the victory of Germany, knowing what that would mean. And so, he said, he simply prayed. He understood that God is not hampered by our political loyalties. We need to pray like that and know that God is not an American!

RUTH 1:(1-7), 8-19a (BCP)

Interpreting the Text

Much modern scholarship regards Ruth as a short story written in a late period of OT history, when many Jews had become xenophobic. One function of the story is to support faithful non-Jews as worthy of respect as worshipers of the God of Israel.

This is a story of three women, widowed at that. Naomi, a resident of Bethlehem, is an alien in Moab. Ruth, a widow at home in Moab, becomes a resident alien in Bethlehem. Orpah is in many ways the most typical Mediterranean woman: the argument that she would stay with her own ethnic kind persuades her. This is a world in which identity is created by membership in family, place, and race. The first five verses set the backdrop against which the story will play out. Naomi decides to go home to Bethlehem, where she will have family and friends. She urges both Orpah and Ruth, her widowed daughters-in-law who set out for Bethlehem with her, to remain in Moab and find security with new Moabite husbands. She invokes the blessing of Yahweh on them (1:8-9). Eventually the ethnic/family argument persuades Orpah to stay in Moab, but Ruth declares her allegiance to Naomi and her God in powerful poetic language. She goes to become a resident alien in Bethlehem, claiming Naomi's people as her own and Naomi's God as her God.

Responding to the Text

Ruth in many ways makes the same point as the Naaman story, but in a more leisurely and entertaining way. It makes the point that a non-Hebrew could be faithful to Yahweh, be accepted by Yahweh, and therefore should be accepted fully by Hebrews, integrated into their familial structure, as Ruth is. As the end of the story makes clears, she marries Boaz and thus becomes the great-grand-mother of King David (4:18-22). She is one of the unusual women mentioned in Matthew's genealogy (Matt. 1:2-17), along with Tamar, Rahab, and the wife of Uriah (Bathsheba). All are taken into the line of Jesus' ancestors. Not every Israelite is of Israelite ancestry. Not every member of our parishes is European in background. God is the God of all, wildly inclusive in his generosity. God's church can be no less.

JEREMIAH 29:1, 4-7 (RCL/alt)

Interpreting the Text

Jeremiah was a prophet in the middle of social and political upheaval, called by God to deliver a message that often ran contrary to the situation. His great love for God led him to denounce what was happening in Judah and to set himself against prevailing social currents. Think of the visit to the potter (18:1-12) and Jeremiah's interpretation of it, or his wearing of a yoke, indicating exile and slavery when all seemed to be well (28:1-17).

In some respects the present text is also such a counter-popular text. Judah is exiled to Babylon; there her people long for the defeat of Babylon and their return to Palestine and the temple of Yahweh. Some prophets even urged rebellion. Jeremiah had described Babylon's victory over Judah as God's punishment. Now Jeremiah urges these expatriate Judeans to settle down in Babylon, "build houses, plant gardens" (29:5), establish families, and—which must have grated on them—to work for and pray for the well-being of the city of their captivity.

This is an amazingly gracious letter of advice to aliens in a strange land. Aliens throughout antiquity were, in a sense, nonpersons, never quite fitting into the strange society. Jeremiah's directive must have had a great effect. Many Jews remained behind in Babylon at the time of the return from exile. The most extensive collection of traditional Jewish teaching on the Torah and the oral law comes from there, the Babylonian Talmud. Americans found it relatively easy to be gracious to its defeated enemies after World War II (think of the Marshall plan). It is much more difficult to be gracious in defeat. America is still coming to terms with its role in the Vietnam War.

What is true of nations is equally true of denominations, parishes, and families. Jeremiah's advice to Jewish exiles calls for a gracious relationship with those with whom we have been in controversy, even when we have lost.

RESPONSIVE READING

227

NINETEENTH
SUNDAY
AFTER PENTECOST

OCTOBER 14

PSALM 111 (RCL)

Yahweh is an inclusive God, not exclusive. Both Old Testament readings for today call for equally inclusive people. Ethnic identity does not determine theological conviction or faith's God. Psalm 111 praises Yahweh as the creator who feeds his people (v. 5), remembers the covenant with them, and gives them the land (the heritage of the nations in v. 6). God redeemed his people, an oblique reference to the exodus from Egypt, and established an eternal covenant (v. 9). The response to such a God is thanks (v. 1), religious awe (the "fear of the Lord" v. 10), and praise. Psalm 111 calls the hearer to praise God (vv. 1-4) because of his incomparable acts in raising the poor to exalted places (vv. 7-8) and in giving children to parents without hope. One thinks of Hannah in 1 Sam. 2:5. They thus identify Israel in slavery as the poor whom God has raised up and the barren whom he has endowed with children.

We too need to celebrate God's great acts, which means that we need to identify them in our own environment. There should be no abstract, bloodless praise. It would be an interesting exercise to ask parishioners a week in advance to each write down the name of one such evidence of divine mercy that they have observed in their lives. It could also be used as a springboard to a Thanksgiving Day service.

Our prayers often are lists of requests for things or deeds that our world, our society, and we as individuals need. We do not pray prayers of adoration and praise often enough for what God has already done. One would do well to read the *Shemoneh Esreh*, the great prayer of praise of the synagogue, to recall how to bless the name of God. This could be a day to count the blessings.

PSALM 113 (BCP)

Psalm 113 is a hymn lauding God as the helper of the helpless. Verses 1-4 invite Israel to praise the Lord throughout the day, because he is exalted above all the nations. Verses 5-9 detail God's infinite "otherness." Seated on high, God surveys the universe, both heaven and earth. God elevates the poor and deprived from the city dump to sit with the elite of his people and turns the shame of barrenness for a woman by making her the joyful mother of many children.

Psalm 113 is a part of the great "Hallel," Psalms 113–118, psalms that praise God for his mighty acts in Israel's past. Together they form a magnificent outpouring of praise for God. They have become an integral part of the Passover Seder, Psalms 113–114 sung before the meal and Psalms 115–118 after the meal. By using these psalms in this manner, the poor in Israel and the barren woman are identified as God's people whom he saved from slavery in Egypt, thus giving the generic psalm a specific context.

Using this psalm within the context of today's lessons suggests that the poor and barren are the strangers and foreigners in our cities.

PSALM 98:1-4 (RC)

Psalm 98, like the other two psalms in today's lectionary, is an invitation to praise God, here as the warrior king who fights battles on our behalf in faithfulness to his people. We are invited to sing a new song, because God's praise goes beyond what we have sung before.

Some may have problems with the warfare imagery. It is used to support the idea that God is powerful enough to do all that is needed for his people in a public display of continuing support for them.

SECOND READING

2 TIMOTHY 2:8-15 (RCL);
2 TIM. 2: (3-7), 8-15 (BCP);
2 TIM. 2:8-13 (RC)

Interpreting the Text

"Remember Jesus Christ, raised from the dead, a descendant of David." Second Timothy cites a "classical" early Jewish-Christian creed. "Descendant of David" reflects 2 Sam. 7:13-14, the promise of a future Davidic king. "Raised from the dead," recalling Ps. 110:1, recalls that Jesus' resurrection is also his enthronement. (cf. Rom. 1:3-4 for a similar confession).

Timothy is to make this the central focus of his preaching. "To remember" is more than to recall; it makes effective in the present what happened in the past. Thus the Lord's Supper in 1 Cor. 11:24-26 is a proclamation—not just a recollection—of Jesus' death. Paul is a model of how this confession works out in life: he endures imprisonment so that others might be saved. There follows a "sure saying," a citation of a hymnic text known to the author and his readers (vv. 11-13). It stresses the correlation between Christian confession and the action of God in Christ, thus a call to faithful confession. If Timothy proclaims in this manner, he will avoid useless controversy and prove to be a teacher of the truth.

"TO REMEMBER" IS MORE THAN TO RECALL; IT MAKES EFFECTIVE IN THE PRESENT WHAT HAPPENED IN THE PAST.

Responding to the Text

229

NINETEENTH
SUNDAY
AFTER PENTECOST

OCTOBER 14

Timothy provides the christological basis for Christian life and so the basis for the inclusion of anyone into the Christian community. The church is a mouthpiece for recalling and proclaiming the resurrected, regnant Jesus. Timothy makes clear what is implicit in the thanks of the Samaritan leper, anticipated by Naaman and Ruth. Proclamation must correlate this christological importance with confession to and celebration of God; otherwise we so stress the second article of the creed as to omit the first.

THE GOSPEL

LUKE 17:11–19

Interpreting the Text

Jesus is on the road to Jerusalem, traveling most likely down the Valley of Jezreel past Scythopolis to cross to the east side of the Jordan River, then south through the region of the Decapolis to re-cross the Jordan near Jericho (Luke 18:35), and then ascend through the Wadi Qilt to Jerusalem over the Mount of Olives (Luke 19:28). Samaria lay to the southwest of the Jezreel Valley, Lower Galilee to the northwest. This way meant that one could avoid traveling through Samaria.

This is the second narrative about Samaritans in Luke's great travel narrative. In Luke 9:51-56, at the beginning of the trip, a Samaritan village refuses hospitality because Jesus was determined to go to Jerusalem. James and John want punitive fire called down, but Jesus refuses. (This is the most negative portrayal of Samaritans in Luke. The parable of the Good Samaritan, Luke 10:25-37, may reflect an actual event.) Samaritans, descendants of the old northern kingdom, appeared to be neither Gentile nor Jew to the strict Jews and so were often regarded with suspicious hostility.

Luke's narrative is straightforward. As Jesus came to an unnamed village, ten lepers, standing at a distance (cf. Lev. 13:46; Num. 5:2-3), appeal to him for help, saying "Jesus, Master, show mercy to us." The term "master" (*epistates*) appears only in Luke, and always on the lips of disciples (5:5; 8:24, 45; 9:33, 49). Jesus responds by telling them to go to the priests for certification of purity (as directed in Lev. 13:2-8; 14:2-3). When one of them sees that he is cured, he turns back, prostrates himself before Jesus, and thanks him. Prostration is an act of obeisance before a ruler or a divine being. The Samaritan leper draws conclusions about Jesus; his return demonstrates his faith, as Jesus' response in v. 19 makes clear. And he was of a different race (v. 18). This statement of faith is elsewhere made about the sinful woman (7:50), the woman with the flow of blood (8:48), and the blind beggar (18:42; cf. 7:9 on the centurion's faith). In each case, an outsider recognizes Jesus and receives this accolade.

Responding to the Text

This familiar story fits in well with the emphases of the Old Testament readings. Luke does not have a major interest in leprosy per se. This is the only leper cleansing in his Gospel. Lepers are mentioned elsewhere in 4:27 and 7:22. Nor is this story in the Gospel of Luke simply to urge thankfulness, significant as this is. The Samaritan leper's thanks arises out of his insights into the person of Jesus. He sees that Jesus is God's ultimate agent and comes back to act out a confession of faith.

> LUKE DOES NOT HAVE A MAJOR INTEREST IN LEPROSY PER SE. NOR IS THIS STORY IN THE GOSPEL OF LUKE SIMPLY TO URGE THANKFULNESS, SIGNIFICANT AS THIS IS. THE SAMARITAN LEPER'S THANKS ARISES OUT OF HIS INSIGHTS INTO THE PERSON OF JESUS.

TWENTIETH SUNDAY AFTER PENTECOST

OCTOBER 21, 2001
TWENTY-NINTH SUNDAY IN ORDINARY TIME
PROPER 24

REVISED COMMON	EPISCOPAL (BCP)	ROMAN CATHOLIC
Gen. 32:22-31	Gen. 32:3-8, 22-30	Exod. 17:8-13
or Jer. 31:27-34		
Ps. 121	Ps. 121	Ps. 121:1-8
2 Tim. 3:14—4:5	2 Tim. 3:14—4:5	2 Tim. 3:14—4:2
Luke 18:1-8	Luke 18:1-8a	Luke 18:1-8

How does faith express itself as time goes on? That is the issue this Sunday's lessons address. Jacob wrestles with God to get God's blessing. A widow finally gets action from a judge by pestering him until he responds. How do Christians in a new millennium express an expectant faith and seek to hold God to his promises? And how does one use the Bible in the process of encouraging such persistent faith? We no longer stand on tiptoe in expectation of the day of the Son of Man. For what are we waiting and how do we wait? This Sunday helps to answer the second question, but not the first.

FIRST READING
GENESIS 32:22-31 (RCL);
GEN. 32:3-8, 22-30 (BCP)

Interpreting the Text

This narrative is both significant and mysterious, unclear in its details, yet decisive for the career of the patriarch Jacob. It leaves many questions unanswered, yet illuminates the future. Jacob is returning to Palestine twenty years after fleeing from Esau, having secured Isaac's blessing by a ruse. He is called Jacob ("the supplanter") because he twice supplanted Esau, first by getting Esau's birthright (Gen. 25:29-34) and second by securing the blessing Isaac intended for Esau (Gen. 27:36). His name is a constant reminder of his past actions.

He camps at Mahanaim and learns that his brother, Esau, is coming with four hundred men. In fear he prays to Yahweh (Gen. 32:9-12) for deliverance from Esau's anger, prepares rich gifts for Esau, and moves wives and children across the River Jabbok. Left alone, he wrestles all night with a man, who wishes to leave. But Jacob holds him and demands a blessing. He does not get one! Instead, the man asks him his name and replaces it with a new one, Israel, "for you have striven with God and humans and prevailed" (vv. 28-29). The folk etymology interprets the name to mean "the one who strives with God." But when Jacob in return asks the man for his name, he does not learn it but instead gets a blessing (Genesis gives it no content). God's proper name is reserved for Moses in Exod. 3:13-14. So Jacob calls the place Penuel, for "I have seen God face to face, and yet my life is preserved" (v. 30). Jacob had cheated to get his brother's blessing; now, by wrestling with God, he receives a blessing.

> THIS STRANGE, BUT COMPELLING STORY OF JACOB AT PENUEL INVITES US INTO CONTROVERSY WITH GOD FOR THE SAKE OF THE GOSPEL.

Is that blessing his new name? Some hold that it is. Is it his survival, even though lamed? What is clear is that he receives a blessing that may well be the answer to his prayer in 32:9-12. His meeting with Esau leads to reconciliation. But perhaps the etymologies of the names Israel and Penuel are the key. Jacob has also achieved new status as the one whose name became the patronymic for the nation. And he achieved it without trickery or deception, but by holding God to his promise.

Responding to the Text

Jacob is on the road home, after spending twenty years away from the land of promise. In fear he prays to God, wrestles with God. We find this concept strange, but it contains an important insight. One way of showing faith is by arguing with God, by holding God to his word. One thinks of Abraham arguing with God for Sodom and Gomorrah (Gen. 18:16-33). Of course, the answer may inflict pain, as it did with Jacob. Jeremiah complained to God but did not thereby demonstrate lack of faith. Rather, he argued God's love against God's judgment. This strange, but compelling story of Jacob at Penuel invites us into controversy with God for the sake of the gospel. Such controversy and gospel are not contradictory.

EXODUS 17:8-13 (RC)

Interpreting the Text

Moses raises his rod so that Joshua can defeat the Amalekites. Such is the summary of this curious narrative. The Amalekites were a fierce tribe that lived in the vicinity of Kadesh (Gen. 14:7). They are still fighting Israel in the time of David (2 Sam. 30:1-20). Moses asked Joshua to fight them at Rephidim, while he would stand on top of a hill, with "the staff of God in my hand" (17:9). When the battle is joined, if Moses raised his hands with the rod, the one he had used in leading Israel out of Egypt, the battle goes in Joshua's favor. The raised hands were a symbol of strength. But when Moses grew tired and his hands drooped, Amalek prevailed. Aaron and Hur (later mentioned only in 24:14, where he is also associated with Aaron) provide a stone as a seat, then hold up Moses' hands, one on each side. This lasted until the sun set, and Joshua won the battle.

The lection should be extended to include vv. 14-16. There is a prediction of ongoing war with Amalek, to be written in a scroll (vv. 14 and 16). More important, Moses built an altar and named it "The Lord is my banner," a testimony that God was the one who gave the victory. This story introduces Joshua as if he were well known. His Hebrew name means "The Lord saves." (His name in Greek is *Iesous,* the name given to Mary's son.) Was his name given as a result of this battle? God alone knows, but it is certainly significant.

Responding to the Text

This story presents a Moses who is less than adequate by himself. He does not function as the general who defeats the enemy. He cannot by himself even wield the "Rod of God" but requires assistance to carry out his promise to Joshua. This story is precious, for it reveals the humanity and the fragility of Moses' leadership. It is a warning against over-reliance on self, on developing a strong ego, on taking credit for what God really accomplishes. No one person is competent to do what is necessary. "Even Zeus nods," the saying goes. And yet God uses such frail instruments to accomplish his work. No one is so weak or fallible that God cannot use him or her. Someone summarized this in the rather wry comment, "If God can speak through Balaam's ass, he can also speak through you." Joshua, Aaron, and Hur remind us that aid comes from unexpected sources. Hur is really a nobody who makes Moses' actions possible. And such still arise in God's church.

> THIS STORY REVEALS THE HUMANITY AND THE FRAGILITY OF MOSES' LEADERSHIP. IT IS A WARNING AGAINST OVER-RELIANCE ON SELF, ON DEVELOPING A STRONG EGO, ON TAKING CREDIT FOR WHAT GOD REALLY ACCOMPLISHES.

JEREMIAH 31:27-34 (RCL alt.)

Interpreting the Text

Here is one of the purple passages in Jeremiah, a promise that offers hope and expectation. The passage is in two clear divisions. The first, vv. 27-30, promises a change. God has passed judgment on Israel and Judah (pluck up and break down, overthrow, destroy, and bring evil), but now protects those who "build and plant." A proverbial saying had seemed to apply: What the fathers do affects their descendants (this proverb is cited also in Ezek. 18:2 and interpreted in a similar fashion). In the future, one will only be judged on the basis of one's own actions. Thus Jeremiah says that the threat issued in Exod. 20:5-6, "visiting the iniquity of the fathers on the children until the third or fourth generation," will no longer be in force.

The second section, vv. 31-34, speaks of a new covenant, different from that made at Sinai, for it will be accompanied by a transformation of the people so that they will know the law without instruction. That means that they will also know God as the one who forgives their iniquity—and so he will be their God and they will be his people.

Responding to the Text

This is an almost scandalous idea, that the Sinai covenant will no longer be in force, replaced by something better. God will do completely unexpected great things. Years ago, J. B. Phillips wrote a book with the title *Your God Is Too Small*. The title is on target for this Jeremiah passage. God is more gracious than we can really imagine. He trumps the Sinai covenant with something even better. God is a God of surprises. And we should expect God to outdo himself.

RESPONSIVE READING
PSALM 121 (RCL/BCP);
PS. 121:1-8 (RC)

Interpreting the Text

Each of Psalms 120–134 is labeled "A Song of Ascents." The meaning of the title is unclear. It may refer to a form of composition or, more likely, to their use as pilgrim psalms, sung as Israelites went up to Jerusalem for one of the great pilgrim feasts. One should then read them as a collection, taking seriously the order in which they are arranged.

Psalm 121 is a hymn expressing confidence in God as rescuer from evils. The psalmist identifies the Judean hills surrounding Jerusalem as God's throne (cf. Ps. 48:1-3; 87:1-2). He answers his own question by naming God the creator of the universe as his helper. God does not leave his creation defenseless. "Help" is here practically equivalent to "rescue, salvation."

Psalm 121:3-8 changes from first to third person. Now a voice (a priest or a resident of Jerusalem?) amplifies the statement of faith in v. 2. God is always vigilant, even when humans are asleep. He is not like Baal, whom Elijah mocks with the suggestion that he is asleep (cf. 1 Kings 18:27) when he does not answer his priests on Mount Carmel. Therefore neither the burning summer sun nor the moon will harm one. Life is in the hands of the God who preserves from all evil.

Therefore one is sure of access to the temple of God. Psalm 122, which follows, is a statement of joy in coming to Jerusalem. Thus Psalms 120–122 form a sequence assuring the pilgrim of God's abiding protection.

Responding to the Text

Certainty and security are two quite different things. Security is the removal of worry from life. Social Security was initiated to make certain that workers would not have to worry about adequate financial resources in retirement. Security makes us take out life insurance to make the future for children less uncertain. IRA accounts, Medicare and Medicaid, and the like are designed to give security. Security can be problematic in many ways, precisely because it depends on what the government is doing and on the stability of financial resources.

God does not promise security; faith rather has certainty. Certainty is the conviction that God is in control and that God means good. Certainty for a Christian rests in understanding how God acted through Jesus and in Jesus to bring good out of evil, triumph out of defeat. As we move toward the end of the church year, we need to focus on the resurrected Jesus as God's assurance that the future is in God's hands—that he is moving toward salvation.

SECOND READING
2 TIMOTHY 3:14—4:5 (RCL/BCP);
2 TIM. 3:14—4:2 (RC)

Interpreting the Text

The sacred writings of the Jewish people were a major resource for the early Christian church. But the resource also entailed a problem or two. The canon of the Old Testament was not yet fixed during the time of the early church, especially the third part, the Kethuvim (the "writings"). This passage helps Christians disturbed by the discussions in Judaism deal with this uncertainty by describing the function of the Old Testament for the Christian church.

Verse 13 sets the context: there are people disturbing the church. Second Timothy proposes two ways to deal with uncertainty. (1) Respect the tradition you have been taught. (2) The Old Testament can instruct you for salvation as it is correlated with Jesus Christ. Every inspired (i.e., canonical) text will prove to serve that instruction. Note that the Greek text has no verb "is" in this text. One must decide where it is implied. I translate as follows: "Every inspired text is also useful for . . ." instruction, for refutation of wrong teaching, for correction of wrong actions, and for moral education. Whatever the Jewish people decide is part of their scriptures will be useful in this way.

And so these scriptures will be useful in leading the church away from wrong teaching (4:3) as it is used to prepare people to face God (4:1-5). Timothy is to use the Old Testament for such purposes.

Responding to the Text

How does one maintain the faith? That is one of the concerns that drive 2 Timothy. The answer is by preserving the tradition and by using the Old Testament to instruct people about living *sub specie aeternitatis* ("in the face of eternity"). That happens when you relate it to Christ. Here is an essential hermeneutical principle. In 1534, Martin Luther gave his doctoral student Nicolas Medler the following thesis to defend: "If our adversaries argue the Scriptures against Christ, then we will argue Christ against the Scriptures." Second Timothy 3:15 and 4:1 anticipate what Luther said in radical form. And that should guide us in our use of both Testaments still today.

> HOW DOES ONE MAINTAIN THE FAITH? THAT IS ONE OF THE CONCERNS THAT DRIVE 2 TIMOTHY.

THE GOSPEL
LUKE 18:1-8 (RCL/RC);
LUKE 18:1-8a (BCP)

Interpreting the Text

This curious parable of "The Unjust Judge" is Jesus' version of Jacob's wrestling with God. How does one prepare for the trials that are bound to come? The reference to the coming Son of Man in 18:8 ties this parable closely to Luke 17:22-37—instructions to the disciples about waiting for "the day of the Son of Man" (17:24, 26, 30). The parable stresses the importance of persistent fidelity, typified in prayer (18:1), as one waits. Luke treats this theme more than once.

The widow in ancient society had lost the male who could represent her in society; she is a symbol of powerlessness (cf. 7:11-17; 21:1-4). A judge, who should defend the widow, does not do so. But because she makes her appeal to him over and over, finally he will act to get her off his back. See the parallel parable in Luke

> THE PARABLE STRESSES THE IMPORTANCE OF PERSISTENT FIDELITY, TYPIFIED IN PRAYER, AS ONE WAITS.

11:5-8. Jesus (called here by the post–Easter title Lord) makes the application: God also responds to persistent prayer, for that is a sign of faith in the face of the delay of Jesus' parousia. "And yet, when the Son of Man comes, will he find faith on earth?" (v. 8).

Responding to the Text

The issue is not whether you pray often enough but whether you demonstrate persistent faith in the face of God's apparent nonaction.

TWENTY-FIRST SUNDAY
AFTER PENTECOST

REVISED COMMON	EPISCOPAL (BCP)	ROMAN CATHOLIC
Jer. 14:7-10, 19-22	Jer. 14:(1-6), 7-10,	Sir. 35:12-14, 16-18
or Sir. 35:12-17	19-22	
or Joel 2:23-32		
Ps. 84:1-7	Ps. 84 or 84:1-6	Ps. 34:2-3, 17-19, 23
2 Tim. 4:6-8, 16-18	2 Tim. 4:6-8, 16-18	2 Tim. 4:6-8, 16-18
Luke 18:9-14	Luke 18:9-14	Luke 18:9-14

What is true worship? Not simply cult or liturgy, singing and reading Scripture. True worship is tied to life outside the sacred place and time. Jeremiah and Sirach both stress the tie between worship and issues of justice and mercy, while the Gospel describes the inner disposition of the true worshiper.

FIRST READING
JEREMIAH 14:7-10 (RCL);
JER. 14:(1-6), 7-10, 19-22 (BCP)

Interpreting the Text

Israel is suffering a great drought. The cisterns are empty; the land is parched, with the ground cracking. Wild animals even desert their young and pant like dogs. Nature itself seems to be conspiring against Israel. Such is the background for this text. It is, in a sense, a text of almost unmitigated gloom, one in which the prophet must speak against his own people.

The text first raises a lament, a complaint against God (vv. 7-9). It presupposes that the dreadful drought is God's judgment on Israel. In the face of that, the people confess their sins and acknowledge their apostasy (v. 7). Then they make their appeal, addressing God as "the hope of Israel, the savior in time of trouble." They are God's people, called by God's name (14:9). God is among them (v.9). How then can God act as a stranger, a traveler just overnighting in the land, like a confused warrior who gives no help? God protects by his presence (in temple and cult). Therefore their appeal is, "Do not forsake us."

Verse 14:10 is an oracle of God denying their pleas for aid; *they* have wandered away (not God)! Therefore he does not accept their lament and plea and will punish! Verses 11-18, omitted from this reading, detail the punishment: war, famine, and plague. The response from the people is another lament, again confessing their sin, but praying God to respond for the sake of his own glorious throne (the Jerusalem temple), for the sake of his name, that is, his public reputation (vv. 19-22). There the lectionary leaves it, not going on to include another severe rejection of Israel's lament and prayer (15:1-4).

Responding to the Text

Natural catastrophes are no strangers to our land. In 2000, the drought through much of the west of the United States led to massive forest fires, while the east experienced floods, tornadoes, and hurricanes. Nature seems to war against the land and us. Jeremiah suggests that such disasters are divine judgment. This text is only gloom and doom. The hope expressed last Sunday in the Jeremiah passage, the new covenant, is completely absent here. This text must lead to a discussion of the need for an honest appraisal of our personal, denominational, and national regard for justice, equity, and humility. Israel responded to natural catastrophe with repentance, a sort of "put out the fire" view of God and religion. God's response calls for a more fundamental self-examination before catastrophe, in time of prosperity.

> THIS TEXT MUST LEAD TO A DISCUSSION OF THE NEED FOR AN HONEST APPRAISAL OF OUR PERSONAL, DENOMINATIONAL, AND NATIONAL REGARD FOR JUSTICE, EQUITY, AND HUMILITY.

SIRACH 35:12-14, 16-18 (RC);
SIR. 35:12-17 (RCL alt.)

Sirach 35 contains instructions for proper sacrifices in the reconstituted second temple in Jerusalem. The chapter opens by saying that true worship consists of "keeping the law," giving alms to the needy, and supporting justice (35:1, 4, 8-9). Sirach gives practical advice about sacrifice: be generous (v.10), cheerful, and joyful in giving (v. 11), as generous in giving as God has been generous to you (vv. 12-13).

Cultic acts that do not rest on such a life-style make sacrifice to God simply a bribe that he will not accept. God responds to the worship of people who have been wronged, the orphan and the widow.

It is strange to find what looks at first glance like a stewardship text in today's complex of lessons. Sirach is down-to-earth wisdom, practical to the nth degree.

He rejects cultic worship that is *pro forma,* not based in the worship that runs through daily life. In this attitude he carries forward the message of the great eighth-century B.C.E. prophets who, in scathing terms, accused the people of formalistic religion (see Amos 5:21-24; Micah 6:6-8; this is continued in James 1:27 and Rom. 12:1-2). Sirach invites us to consider the relation between our worship and our values, our cult and our life. Worship takes place outside of sanctuary in everyday existence, not just at sacred times and in sacred places.

JOEL 2:23-32 (RCL alt.)

This text from Joel is the counter-balance to the Jeremiah passage above. The passage begins with an invitation to rejoice in God who has poured out rain in abundance (no drought here). The harvests of grain, grape, and olive will be abundant (2:24), for God is repaying Israel for the plague of locusts, the army God sent against them. Given this plenty, Israel can be sure that God is among them (the reversal of the language in Jeremiah is striking!).

But the blessings go far beyond great harvests. God will pour out his spirit so that all Israel (sons, daughters, old men, male and female slaves) will become prophets and see visions. Social status will no longer be a great distinguishing mark. All of this will occur "afterward" (v. 28), "in those days" (v. 29), both phrases referring to eschatological hope for the future. In the light of that future, the apocalyptic events that occur before "the great and terrible day of the Lord" are the prelude that teaches people to call on the name of God.

Peter cites Joel 2:28-29 in his great Pentecost sermon in Acts 2. This great message of hope, according to Peter, has been fulfilled by the work of the Spirit in the church. Hope sustains Israel in the apocalyptic events described in Joel. The Spirit sustains the church as it lives out its faith in a dusty, often hostile world. We might well ask for ways in which the Spirit is fulfilling Joel's prophecy. One certainly is the more universal recognition of the gifts of women for ministry.

RESPONSIVE READING
PSALM 84:1-7 (RCL);
PS. 84 or 84:1-6 (BCP)

Psalm 84 sings the praise of the temple by a pilgrim coming to worship there. The mention of the early rains (v. 6) suggests that the psalm may be related to the Festival of Booths, celebrated in the fall. The early rains usher in the rainy season, give cooling refreshment, and cause the grain to grow (fall is the time to plant grain in Palestine). The pilgrim rejoices as he thinks of coming to the temple (the Lord's house, v. 1). To sing God's praises in the temple is cause for happiness. Verses 5-7 describe the feelings of the pilgrim on the way to Jerusalem. Going through an arid place makes it a place where springs of water gush forth, because pilgrimage to the temple gives strength.

How should one worship? The psalmist says with joy at being in the presence of God. Even the trip to the temple is an occasion for joy. Try that one out on an American family on Sunday morning. It appears idealistic, but the psalmist is sure it is reality. This psalm correlates with the Joel text.

PSALM 34:2-3, 17-19, 23 (RC)

This psalm of thanksgiving celebrates deliverance from trouble. The lectionary selection first focuses attention on God, inviting others to join the psalmist in making God's name glorious; that is, in proclaiming what God has done that elates the humble (vv. 2-3). Verses 17-19 then give the basis for such praise: God rescues the righteous and encourages and lifts up those burdened by life's tragedies. God rescues all the righteous. None of those who flee to God for help will be disappointed.

As on many Sundays, the responsive reading gives a message of hope and joy to counterbalance the stark pessimism of other lessons, in this case Jeremiah.

Second Reading
2 TIMOTHY 4:6-8, 16-18

Interpreting the Text

Some scholars, who do not think that Paul wrote the Pastoral Epistles, argue that the biographical data in 2 Timothy are nonetheless accurate. We may have here historical data about the end of Paul's ministry.

Paul is facing death—and knows it. He has been in prison. But he interprets his death as a sacrifice (libation, offering of liquid). In the Roman world, libations were offered in the family before meals, while generals poured out libations before battle. Paul has finished the battle, keeping the faith (his relationship to Christ). So he anticipates the wreath used to recognize victors. His death is not defeat!

The second part of this lesson shows the source of such power and faith: the Lord who stood by Paul at his trial, which became an occasion for proclamation. And that is why Paul ends with a doxology to the Lord who has "stood by" him.

Responding to the Text

This text contains the final evaluation of Paul in the Pauline corpus. The writer of this text knew that Paul was martyred—and that raised a problem. Why should such an apostle who preached the gospel of God not be defended by God? It was not because the Lord had deserted him, nor was he being left to die alone. Indeed, his trial and impending death become evidence for him that his proclamation of the message (*kerygma,* the term for proclamation to non-Christians) has been a success. Paul's criterion of success is fidelity to the call he had from God, which suggests that a discussion of the success syndrome would be useful in many contexts of the contemporary church.

THE GOSPEL
LUKE 18:9-14

Interpreting the Text

Who is the true worshiper? The parable of the Pharisee and the tax collector gives one answer by providing examples. The story is well known. The introduction makes clear what the lesson is: a self-righteous religious attitude leads to contempt for other people. The two men go to the temple for prayer—presumably individual prayer. The Pharisee prays a self-congratulatory prayer that calls attention to his acts of piety: proper fasting and tithing. He uses this as evidence of his moral superiority over people who engage in overt acts that break the law: thieves, rogues, adulterers, and "this here tax collector" (the Greek implies a derogatory gesture, 18:11). The tax collector gives physical evidence of repentance (cf. Luke 23:48) and asks God for mercy. Verse 14 draws out the conclusion. The tax collector is a true worshiper, because he came without any pieties to offer.

Responding to the Text

What does one offer to God? With what expectations does one worship? Luke's parable stresses that worship is not a form of self-expression or self-congratulation. External acts of worship must reveal the inner disposition of the heart. This parable stresses two points that are significant for anyone thinking about worship. First, worship is not offering our piety to God, but presenting ourselves to God as ones who are empty handed. It puts in narrative form Paul's description of faith in Rom. 4:5: Abraham believed on "the God who justifies the ungodly," and that was justifying faith. Worship is putting one's self before God as the ungodly person who needs mercy. Second, the parable makes clear that worship has social implications. It is not just between an individual and God. Worship that puts down another person is wrong.

> WORSHIP IS NOT OFFERING OUR PIETY TO GOD, BUT PRESENTING OURSELVES TO GOD AS ONES WHO ARE EMPTY HANDED.

REFORMATION DAY

OCTOBER 31, 2001

REVISED COMMON
Jer. 31:31-34
Ps. 46
Rom. 3:19-28
John 8:31-36

Observing Reformation Day is a peculiarly Lutheran (or Protestant) liturgical innovation. It originated as a way to heighten Lutheran identity during the Thirty Years War. As a result it often took on an anti-Catholic bias. That has changed since the renaissance of biblical studies in the Catholic Church, with the decisions of Vatican II and, most recently, with the document on justification signed on October 21, 1999, at Augsburg, Germany, by representatives of the Roman Catholic Church and the Lutheran World Federation. Today we celebrate Reformation Day as a reminder of God's ongoing love for and care of the church by the power of the gospel. Therefore it celebrates the proclamation of the gospel by all churches. It is no longer a triumphalist Lutheran flag-waving day.

The lessons for today bring forward a series of terms that resonated in the Reformation: covenant, law, knowing God, faith, grace, justification, freedom, and God as refuge and fortress.

FIRST READING
JEREMIAH 31:31-34

Interpreting the Text

Jeremiah is one of the few biblical characters who writes out his feelings. He lived through one of the most troubling times for the people of Judah. One great empire, Assyria, came to an end, while another, Neo-Babylonia, arose. Even though Josiah had discovered the "Book of the Law" in the temple and based a reform movement on it, the Kingdom of Judah was doomed. Jeremiah has been called "the weeping prophet," because he had to prophesy against the reigning king, Jehoiakim, against Jerusalem, and even against the temple, the place where God was present with his people. That is the burden of chapters 1–29 of Jeremiah—gloom and doom for Judah—a message that he tried not to deliver.

He appeared to be a contrary person. When everyone else finally despaired, then Jeremiah began to speak and act out a future hope. In spite of submission to the yoke of Babylon (chapter 27), Jeremiah urged the exiles in Babylon to "seek the welfare of the city" (Jer. 29:7) and develop a life there. Jeremiah 30–31 is an expression of hope for the restoration of Israel and Judah in the land. But God's future is more than a simple re-establishment of what once was. Jeremiah 31:31-34 promises a new covenant, superior to the Mosaic covenant at Sinai. Forgiven by God, the law (Torah) will no longer need to be taught by a Josiah; it will be written on the hearts, and all will "Know the Lord" as the God who forgives.

Responding to the Text

Radical newness—that is what Jeremiah promises, but a newness in continuity with the past. We often prize novelty: the latest model computer or car, the newest sound system, the most recent fad. Each season the newest styles of dress are touted. We even call our information programs the "News"!

> JEREMIAH STANDS WITHIN A FIRM BIBLICAL TRADITION WHEN HE TELLS US THAT GOD'S FUTURE IS THE PAST MADE THE WAY IT SHOULD HAVE BEEN.

Jeremiah stands within a firm biblical tradition when he tells us that God's future is the past made the way it should have been. It will be a covenant, but better than the Mosaic. The Torah (which means "instruction") was to teach Israel how to live before God (cf. Deut. 6:4). In the future all will know God. In similar fashion Romans 8 thinks of the created universe as freed from corruption. And the coming Davidic king will be superior to David. The future rests in God, and so is new—not new in kind, but new in realization.

RESPONSIVE READING
PSALM 46

Interpreting the Text

Psalm 46 sings of a faith like Jeremiah's. It is a song that expresses confidence in God's fidelity to Jerusalem and her people in the face of war and oppression. It falls into three sections. (1) Verses 1-3 describe Israel's confidence in God in the face of cosmic upheaval: earthquake and tsunamis. Earthquake was (and is) frequent in the Middle East, a very real possibility. But God controls creation. Sections (2), vv. 4-7, and (3), vv. 8-11, each end with the same refrain: "The Lord of hosts is with us; the God of Jacob is our refuge." They suggest that the psalm may have been written during the time of Jeremiah. The refrain restates the assurance of God's assistance of v. 1. Section 2 expects stability from God in the face of social and political unrest. The city of God is clearly Jerusalem. Section 3 presents God as the warrior king, the "Lord of hosts," i.e., of armies, who triumphs in war and so rules.

Responding to the Text

Psalm 46 is the text from which Luther took off in writing his hymn "A Mighty Fortress Is Our God." Luther's four stanzas interpret the psalm from his own experience of life in a cauldron of troubles. He picks up the motif of the Lord of hosts victorious in warfare, but now identifies him as "Christ Jesus, mighty Lord, God's only Son adored." His fourth stanza is a powerful statement of faith in the face of loss. But the standard English translation obscures one of his important insights. God's Word is identified in Luther's German as Jesus. He fights by our side. Thus Luther models how one transfers what was originally a statement about Jerusalem in the seventh century B.C.E. into a statement of faith about the present. And that is the task of proclamation in every age.

SECOND READING
ROMANS 3:19-28

Interpreting the Text

Romans 3:19-28 is one of the seminal texts for understanding Paul. It is the first restatement of the theme of Romans given in Rom. 1:17-18: The gospel is the power of God that moves toward salvation for every person who believes, regardless of ethnicity, because the gospel is the place where God's *dikaiosyne* (the Greek term can mean "justice" or "righteousness") is revealed "from faith to faith," a citation from Hab. 2:4. These verses introduce key terms that are significant throughout the book: faith, gospel, righteousness, salvation.

The text includes the verse that summarizes Romans 1:18—3:20, in which Paul lays out the failure of all humans to achieve righteousness before God by human accomplishment (Paul's phrase is "works of law," v. 20; note that the term "law" returns in vv. 27-31). Paul regards the law as one of the three great forces that hold people in slavery: sin, death, and the law. (See Rom. 8:2, which sums up Romans 5–7). In vv. 24-26, Paul makes use of and edits a creedal statement formulated by Jewish Christians. The syntax and vocabulary of Rom. 3:24-26 are unusual and striking. Only here does Paul use the term *hilasterion* (translated as "sacrifice of atonement"). The Greek text literally says "through faith in his blood" (note how the translators interpret this). The terms "pass over" and "forbearance" are rare. Add to that the fact that v. 24 actually begins with a participle. A literal translation would be, "For all were sinning and falling short of the glory of God, being justified as a gift by his grace," etc. (English translations clean up the unusual syntax.) Paul inserts two phrases that at first appear redundant ("by grace" in v. 24 and "through faith" in v. 25) to support his proclamation about God's justification.

Paul writes to unite the Roman church, split between Jewish and Gentile Christians. The Jewish Christians cited their creed to argue that Jesus' death was a sacrifice to remove sin, in line with the Old Testament covenant. Gentiles needed to join the Jewish covenant community in order to benefit from it. Thus the Jewish Christians seek to establish their superiority. Paul interprets their creedal statement to underscore that God justifies by grace through faith. Boasting (i.e., priority before God) is excluded. It is not deeds that correlate with the OT law that justify. Romans 3:28 sums it all up: "We draw the conclusion that a person is justified by faith, quite apart from works that conform to the law."

Romans 3:29-31 makes Paul's concern explicit. God is God of all alike, as the Jewish creed "God is one" makes clear. God, in fidelity to the covenant, justifies Jewish people; through faith, God justifies Gentiles who are not people of the OT covenant.

Responding to the Text

God is not a tribal God, not restricted by any of the boundaries we erect to keep our self-images. That is the assertion that Paul makes in Rom. 3:27-31. American society is in danger of fragmenting into ethnic or special interest groups—and the church sometimes falls prey to such special interests. This great passage, which stresses the core values put forward by the Reformation, is a great leveler. The Christian community is not a special tribe, with better access to God; America, which often is described as a "Christian nation," does not have priority over other nations. If the church lives out this understanding of God, it will be a welcoming community (see Rom. 15:7-9) that prizes diversity among its members.

> IF THE CHURCH LIVES OUT THIS UNDERSTANDING OF GOD, IT WILL BE A WELCOMING COMMUNITY THAT PRIZES DIVERSITY AMONG ITS MEMBERS.

This does not mean that democracy is necessarily the best form of government in church or community. It does mean that whatever structure the church adopts (episcopal, presbyterian, democratic), it must strive for equal valuation of all people, a challenge to a society that prizes accomplishments and success, in which people are measured by where they live and what they have.

Luther, it is said, exclaimed on his deathbed, "Wir sind Bettler; das is wahr!" ("We are beggars, that's the whole truth"). That is what grace and faith imply: coming to God with empty hands that God fills.

JOHN 8:31-36

Interpreting the Text

This text is part of a long dialogue between Jesus and the Judeans that begins at John 7:14 and ends at John 8:59. (The story of the woman caught in adultery, John 7:53—8:11, is not an insertion into this Gospel at a later date, as the manuscript tradition suggests.) I use the translation "Judeans" rather than "Jews" to avoid an illegitimate transfer from a historical text to the present day. The dialogue reflects the growing animosity to Jesus that culminates in the crucifixion. This dialogue ends with the Judeans picking up stones to throw at Jesus, because they regard him as a blasphemer. In the dialogue Jesus makes great claims for himself. He brings light (8:12). His Father testifies to him, though they do not know him. He says he is not of this universe (8:23); therefore, the listeners will die in their sins unless they believe "that I am he" (v. 24). He uses the Greek phrase *eg͞eimi,* used throughout this Gospel when Jesus makes claims about his person and work (there is no messianic secret in John).

Jesus then turns (v. 31) to those who believe in him: If you continue in Jesus' *logos,* that is, true discipleship, you will know the truth that makes you free. When the Judeans reply that, as descendants of Abraham, they have never been slaves, Jesus replies that only the son has a secure place in the household. Only if the Son makes one free is one actually free, and not a slave. This enigmatic formulation caps this text. The Son comes from heaven, where his Father is. Even though he is here, the "lifting up of the Son of Man" (v. 28) will testify to his relation to the Father.

Responding to the Text

"Freedom" resonates with Americans. It was a watchword at the birth of the nation. The American Revolution began with an act to free Bostonians from a hated tax. The Civil War was fought, in part at least, to secure freedom for African Americans. Think of the other wars fought since then, and how often Americans died in the cause of freedom. It's a word to conjure with in America. Freedom means being unhindered in doing what one wants to do. Freedom is individualistic, uninhibited, self-affirming.

> JOHN'S USE OF THE WORD "FREEDOM" IS ALMOST UN-AMERICAN. FOR HIM IT IS NOT POLITICAL BUT RELATIONAL.

John's use of the word "freedom" is almost un-American. For him it is not political but relational. The African American spiritual "Oh, Freedom" (No. 208

in *This Far by Faith: An African American Resource for Worship* [Minneapolis: Augsburg Fortress, 1999]) seems close to the Johannine view. Freedom is being freed from slavery to sin, through the Son, who testifies to the truth. That truth is knowing the Son for who he actually is, and that liberates from all egocentrism. For freedom means a relationship with God through Christ.

ALL SAINTS DAY

NOVEMBER 1, 2001

REVISED COMMON	EPISCOPAL (BCP)	ROMAN CATHOLIC
Dan. 7:1–3, 15–18	Sir. 44:1-10, 13-14 or Sir. 2:(1-6), 7-11	Rev. 7:2-4, 9-14
Ps. 149	Ps. 149	Ps. 24:1-6
Eph. 1:11-23	Rev. 7:2-4,. 9-17 or Eph. 1:(11-14), 15-23	1 John 3:1-13
Luke 6:20-31	Matt. 5:1-12 or Luke 6:20-26 (27-34)	Matt. 5:1-12a

All Saints Day celebrates the catholicity of the Christian church, as its members recall and celebrate generations of Christians who have preceded them in confessing the faith and preserving it for generations to come. It picks up those unnamed saints, forgotten by almost all, who did not make it into the ritual calendars of the different communions. It offers the opportunity to celebrate the multitudes of the faithful who, in the face of opposition, persecution, war, pestilence, and famine, have rested their faith and hopes in God.

All Saints Day is a celebration, not a day of mourning. It recalls the victory of those who died in the faith. Many parishes list and recall especially those members who died in the past year. In Germany they also celebrate *Totensonntag* ("Sunday of the Dead"), on which they hold services in cemeteries remembering especially those who died in the year past. It is a lighthouse in the middle of a dark and stormy seacoast. It celebrates the past to illuminate the future—and should be so celebrated

There is an amazing variety of texts to discuss for this day. They offer a bewildering and rich variety of resources.

FIRST READING

DANIEL 7:1-3, 15-18 (RCL)

Interpreting the Text

Daniel 7 opens the second half of this book, the section that is "apocalyptic" by genre. (The first half of the book is "haggadic," that is teaches by telling stories.) Daniel 1–6 stresses stories of fidelity to God, while Daniel 7–12 stresses God's ultimate vindication of his suffering people. The historical setting is the attempt of Antiochus IV Epiphanes (175–164 B.C.E.) to force Greek religion and concomitant culture on Palestinian Jews, beginning with the establishing of a Temple of Zeus to replace the Temple of Yahweh in Jerusalem (167 B.C.E.).

This lectionary text is a strange selection, as much for what it omits as what it includes. Daniel 7:1-3 introduces a dream vision of Daniel in which he sees four beasts come up out of the sea (i.e., from the west). The lectionary then omits the description of the beasts (7:4-8) and the vision of the Ancient One and the coming of "one like a human being" to the throne of the Ancient One (7:9-14). It thus omits the apocalyptic heart of the vision, important both in later Jewish texts, the Gospels, and the Apocalypse of John. Instead, the text moves directly to the interpretation of the vision in 7:15-27, using only vv. 15-18. An angelic being (one of the members of the heavenly court, v. 16) tells him the four beasts are four kings; but their rules are no threat. The phrase "the holy ones of the Most High" could refer either to God's faithful people or, even more likely, to the angelic members of the heavenly court who represent them there (see 8:10-13 for angelic beings; 7:27 may imply a distinction between the people and angelic beings). In either case, 7:18 is the first statement of assurance to a persecuted people.

Responding to the Text

Death is not the end—in spite of our universal fear that it is. An old Latin funeral inscription reflects that fear in a way: *Non eram, eram, non sum, non curo* ("I was not, I was, I am not, I don't care"). Life so often seems meaningless because people are at the mercy of forces over which they have no control: government, mortgage payment, income tax, and management that controls our work career. And death seems only the most certain of such forces. Thus the modern ennui, the feeling of futility that runs through much modern literature. I think here of Samuel Beckett's play *Waiting for Godot,*

THE DANIEL TEXT CLEARLY FOCUSES ON 7:18, WHICH SETS A SIGNIFICANT THEME FOR ALL SAINTS DAY. THERE IS A FUTURE THAT GOD'S PEOPLE CAN EXPECT BECAUSE GOD IS MORE POWERFUL THAN ALL FORCES OF FUTILITY.

which captured a generation's feeling of emptiness in life. People identified with Estragen and Vladimir, who waited for a Godot who never came. What Beckett laughed at in this comedy about unhappiness Jean Paul Sartre treated as tragedy in his *Flies*. His rewriting of Aeschylus suggested that the only way to find meaning in life was to acknowledge guilt and accept responsibility for it. Both plays expressed the deep despair of the post–World War II generation. And they continue to do so today.

The Daniel text clearly focuses on 7:18, which sets a significant theme for All Saints Day. There is a future that God's people can expect because God is more powerful than all forces of futility. Its omission of the apocalyptic imagery of the text makes that verse immediately applicable to our world as it is, as a contradiction of *Waiting for Godot*. The future rests in God's hand.

SIRACH 44:1-10, 13-14 (BCP)

Interpreting the Text

Sirach is an Old Testament deuterocanonical wisdom text, written ca. 180 B.C.E. The author brought together traditional Near Eastern and Israelite wisdom with the Torah and the celebration of the temple.

Sirach 44–50 is a long poem praising the great heroes of Israel's past. It begins with the significant invitation, "Let us now sing the praises of famous men, our ancestors in their generations" (v. 1). Sirach 44:16—49:16 tells the history of Israel through the activities of the great figures of her past. Sirach 50 praises Simon Ben Onias, high priest from 219 to 196 B.C.E., the only contemporary of the author to be praised. Sirach 44:1-15 is the introduction to this extended hymn of praise. In vv. 3-6, he praises a series of unnamed people of the past: unnamed rulers, warriors, wise counselors, prophets, leaders by virtue of their counsel, teachers of folk knowledge, musicians, poets, wealthy people who lived quietly in their homes (vv. 3-6).

Sirach recognizes that some good people, honored in their own time, are no longer remembered; that is equivalent to having never lived at all (v. 9). (Sirach reflects an era when hope for resurrection was not yet strong.) Others will not be forgotten. Buried in peace, their glory will not be wiped out, but their names live on generation after generation.

Responding to the Text

Christians have long celebrated the heroes of faith. But nameless millions have died in faith. Visiting medieval churches in Europe is always an experience in recalling the forgotten, as one surveys the grave markers in the floor even in simple parish churches. Local parishes in our new world still need to devise ways to recall the unnamed local saints. Sirach invites us to mention by name those whose acts or presence have enriched the faith and life of specific parishes. That is what All Saints Day is ultimately about: making a banner with the names of local saints; preaching that tells the stories that can only be known locally. Celebrate life in hope.

SIRACH 2:(1-6), 7-11 (BCP alt.)

Sirach 2 is a call to live in such a manner that one demonstrates trust in God and expectation of his great deeds (2:7-8). Sirach reminds its hearers that such trust is based on the past: "Has anyone trusted in the Lord and been disappointed? . . . persevered in the fear of the Lord and been forsaken? . . . called upon the Lord and been neglected?" (2:10).

In a way that the other two Old Testament lessons do not, Sirach 2 draws a firm line between remembrance of the things past and the life of the living in the present.

REVELATION 7:2-4, 9-14 (RC)

Interpreting the Text

Revelation 7 presents a consolatory interlude between the sixth (6:12-17) and seventh seals (8:1-2). The sixth seal ends with the question, "the great day of their wrath has come, and who is able to stand?" (6:17). Revelation 7 gives an answer in terms of two visions. The catastrophe will not come until the angels have marked God's servants with a "seal on their foreheads" (7:3). Seals were used to mark ownership and thereby protection (cf. Ezek. 9:4-6). The number sealed is 144,000, 12,000 from each of the twelve tribes. (Note that the tribe of Daniel is omitted from the list in vv. 5-8; Manasseh, Joseph's son, fills that empty space. One branch of apocalyptic expected the antichrist to come from the tribe of Dan.)

Revelation 7:9-12 universalizes the first, Israel-oriented vision. Now there is an unnumbered throng from every human people clad in white, the color of heaven (cf. 6:11). They sing a victory song (7:10) to which the members of the heavenly court add their own. God moves through the morass of human history to save his own.

Responding to the Text

Revelation invites God's people to join in cosmic praise of the savior God who moves through history. In Philippi, Paul and Silas sing praises to God when chained in jail (Acts 25). God responded with earthquake, an apocalyptic evil according to Rev. 16:17-18), but also an event that signifies a theophany. History is ambivalent, but invites praise. Some of the greatest hymns were written during the "Thirty Years War." All Saints calls for song!

RESPONSIVE READING
PSALM 149 (RCL/BCP);
PS. 149:(11-14), 15-23 (BCP alt.)

Psalm 149 is a hymn of praise for God's great acts. Verses 1-4 call worshipers to praise the creator God who called Israel into being (v. 2) and rescues the humble (v. 4) with a "new song" (cf. Pss. 33:3; 40:3; 96:1; etc.). This song is more than cerebral: The psalmist calls for dance with tambourine and lyre. Verses 5-9 also call for celebration, but with a jarring note. Here praise is expressed in military vengeance on Israel's enemies (cf. Ps. 137:7-9 for a parallel vindictive hope). Is this language mere ritual or does it anticipate a real eschatological battle? Hard to say. Verse 5, translated in the NRSV as "exult in glory" could also be rendered "exult in the Glorious One," i.e., God. That would correlate well with the implication in v. 9 that the punishment of the nations is determined by a divine decree. Then the psalm calls for exultation arising from God's great acts of deliverance.

Psalm 149 responds to the call for praise in Rev. 7:9-12. Praise God indeed, with organ and strings and sounding brass; let choirs resound; let congregations be encouraged to sing Ralph Vaughn Williams great *sine nomine* setting of "For All the Saints," or the great Scandinavian hymn "Behold a Host Arrayed in White."

PSALM 24:1-6 (RC)

Psalm 24 is a liturgy for entrance into the temple. Verses 1-2 open the psalm with a confession to the creator God who owns the universe as its maker. The reference to the seas reminds one of the taming of chaos in the ancient Near Eastern creation myth. Verses 3-10 are the dialogue that makes up the entrance liturgy proper. Someone (a priest?) asks what the proper characteristics are for one to enter the sanctuary (v. 3). Verse 4 contains the answer: one must be ritually and actually pure, witnessed to by actions of integrity. Such people God will both bless and vindicate, i.e., rescue. The worshipers respond with the call to open the gates of the temple precinct to them (vv. 7 and 9). They so correspond to the criteria for entrance that God the warrior, the Lord of Hosts, i.e., their victorious defender, will enter with them and be present for them.

This psalm offers the occasion to describe the saints in one's own parish as people whose actions have shown their ritual and actual purity, to call the present congregation to live up to them, and to invite them to enter God's gates.

SECOND READING

EPHESIANS 1:11-23 (RCL); EPH. 1:(11-14), 15-23 (BCP alt.)

Interpreting the Text

The author of Ephesians wrote this letter in the name of Paul to the church sometime after 70 C.E. as an appeal for unity when Gentile Christians, now in the majority, tended to disregard or write off the Jewish Christian minority. All English translations obscure the linguistic grandeur of Ephesians. Chapter 1 is made up of two long sentences (1:3-14 and 1:15-23). The text picks up in the middle of the first sentence, which blesses God for his cosmic plan to choose and endow his church with every spiritual blessing in Christ. Then 1:11-13 applies this universal statement to the author and his readers: you heard, you believed, you were sealed. Their experience in the church assures them of their inclusion in this cosmic plan of God.

Ephesians 1:15-23 is a great prayer of thanksgiving and intercession for these readers. It requests knowledge for the readers. (The author of Ephesians loves to heap up synonyms for emphasis; note the preponderance of knowledge language in vv. 17-18.) They must recognize the glorious gift they have received (the term "inheritance" stresses this gift character) in the lordship of Christ. In glorious, exalted language reminiscent of Ps. 110:1, he describes Jesus' resurrection as his enthronement as *kosmokrator,* "Lord of the Universe" ("all things" in v. 22 is the standard phrase for the universe). He rules all the powers of this age (note the four terms for them in v. 21: rule, authority, power, dominion), not just the political powers we all know and fear, but the cosmic forces who inhabit the heavens. He is now enthroned above the heavens (the Greek term *epouranioi,* v. 20, describes the area above the seven heavens). He rules "for the church," his body, which by its existence makes his presence in the universe visible.

Responding to the Text

Entering into Ephesians is like entering a great cathedral. The language is exalted, the thought equally so. This is the first document in Christianity to think of the church in universal, cosmic rather than local terms. That ancient cosmology includes the view that the universe is ruled by powers in the heavens (the basis of ancient astrology). Some years ago, Martin Marty noted that millions of Americans take the daily horoscopes seriously—a view based ultimately on this ancient cosmology. Even the wife of a recent American president was reputed to take the daily horoscopes seriously.

Ephesians thinks of Christ not only in terms of what he has done for humankind, but also in terms of what Christ is doing *now* for the church, delivering it from fear of the powers, whether cosmic or terrestrial. The saints are evidence of that.

There is a mosaic in the mausoleum of Galla Placidia in Ravenna that shows St. Laurence achieving martyrdom by being grilled alive. His martyrology includes the story that, at one point, he asked to be turned over on the grill, because he was being "unequally roasted." Whether historically based or pious mythology, the story reflects that confidence in the rule of the Lord of the Universe.

REVELATION 7:2-4, 9-17 (BCP alt.)

See the notes under the first lesson above.

1 JOHN 3:1-13 (RC)

Interpreting the Text

First John stresses the life of Christians. The *Leitmotif* of his epistle is love which, for the writer, is the main characteristic of life for his community (2:5, 10, 15; 3:11, 14, 16, 17, 18, 23; 4:7, 11, 12, 16, 17, 18, 19, 20, 21; 5:1, 2, 3; this list does not include passages that refer to God's love for people!). As one can see from the many references, John rings the changes on this motif.

Chapter three first stresses that we are God's children because of God's love for us (v. 1). God's love has consequence. What he is determines our future (v. 2) and affects our present, because we purify ourselves as he (Jesus) is pure. Verses 4–10 make clear that this means a rejection of sin in the ongoing life of the child of God. Sinning shows that you are a child of the devil (v. 8). John sees things in stark, primary colors. One either is a child of God or the devil. Children of God (1) do what is right and (2) love their brothers and sisters (v. 10). Thus the primary message (the one heard from the beginning) is that "we should love one another" (v. 11). Hatred à la Cain leads to death and reveals one's evil character.

> JOHN STRESSES PRACTICAL CHRISTIANITY. LOVE HERE IS NOT AN EMOTION OR WARM FUZZIES, BUT AN ACTIVE, EFFECTIVE MODE OF RELATING TO OTHERS.

John stresses practical Christianity. Love here is not an emotion or warm fuzzies but an active, effective mode of relating to others. It is not, in this text, a directive to specific actions but a posture determinative for Christian life. Love is the mode of sainthood. Perhaps the greatest, though not certainly the only example of this is Francis of Assisi. He respected both the world of humanity and the world of nature. In the middle of the war between the crusaders and Saladin, Francis walked fearlessly among the Muslims, respected as a holy man. He gave away his wealth and identified with the poor. He was love in action!

THE GOSPEL
LUKE 6:20-31 (RCL);
LUKE 6:20-26 (27-34) (BCP alt.)

Interpreting the Text

Luke gives the Sermon on the Plain (Luke 6:20-49) a distinctive shape and message when compared with Matthew's Sermon on the Mount (Matt. 5:1—7:28; see the alternate lesson for today). Both begin with beatitudes (Luke 6:20-23; Matt. 5:3-12), but Luke's are more socially oriented (as the parallel "woes" make clear, 6:24-26). *Makarios* ("blessed") is used both in wisdom (Ps. 1:1) and apocalyptic contexts (Sir. 48:11; *Ps. Sol.* 17: 44-45; 18:6) in the Old Testament and Judaism. Both Luke and Matthew use it in apocalyptic contexts to describe the blessings of the end time (cf. Luke 7:23; 10:23; 11:28; 14:15; cf. Matt. 11:6). Note how the "woes" balance the beatitudes.

WE ARE IN DANGER OF BEING THOSE TO WHOM LUKE'S WOES APPLY. HOW CAN ONE BE A SAINT IN A WORLD WHERE RELIGION IS IRRELEVANT?

Luke casts the beatitudes in the second person plural. "The poor" were identified as the pious in intertestamental Judaism (cf. *Ps. Sol.* 10:5-6). Luke stresses the outcast and the marginalized in his Gospel (cf. Luke 4:18). The beatitudes identify the disciples with them and promise a drastic reversal of status for disciples in the future. The fourth beatitude (vv. 22-23) stresses that popularity is not a key to favor with God, looking to a time of persecution. At that time disciples will return a blessing for a curse, pray for their persecutors, and in general trump evil with good. That is what the "golden rule" demands (v. 31). Judaism knew this rule, as Lev. 19:18 and Tob. 4:15 make clear. While Matt. 7:12 makes this rule the summary of the entire Sermon on the Mount, Luke uses it to summarize reactions to active opposition to the disciple community.

There is persecution of Christians in our world, as recent events in Serbia and West Timor have made clear. And they are not isolated cases, as El Salvador and other recent dictatorships demonstrate. Christians clearly abhor fanatic religious hatred that issues in acts of terror. But our country, *deo gratias,* does not experience such direct persecution. Rather, faith is marginalized, ridiculed, disregarded, and privatized in our time. And that makes the stuff of sainthood less dramatically clear. It is hard to be an Oscar Romero in America. Sainthood among us is expressed in our relations to the poor and marginalized, the illegal immigrant, or the political refugee. We are in danger of being those to whom Luke's woes apply. How to be a saint in a world where religion is irrelevant—now there's a theme worth exploring in the light of all the lessons for this day.

MATTHEW 5:1-12 (BCP);
MATT. 5:1-12a (RC)

Interpreting the Text

Jesus sits down on the mountain and summons his disciples (note that he has only four at this time (4:18-22). What follows is a reinterpretation of the Torah and the prophets (cf. 5:17; 7:12). Jesus' posture is that of the teacher of the law (cf. 23:2-3). But this is Moses and the prophets for the disciple community, not a new general social ethic. The beatitudes open Matthew's version of the Sermon on the Mount. (See the discussion of Luke, above, about *makarios.*) The beatitude on Peter in 16:17 illustrates how one is blessed—by a revelation from the Father (cf. 11:6, 25-30; 13:16). The beatitudes fall into two groups. The first four describe disciples as the totally needy (5:3-6). They, the poor in spirit, are under the royal rule of God (v. 3). This picks up the expectation of God as coming king (cf. Isa. 40:9-11) or the Davidic messianic king (cf. 2 Sam. 7:14; *Ps. Sol.* 17:21). The basis for the blessing is given in terms of Israel's expectations: comfort (Isa. 40:1), the inheritance of the land of Palestine, and the liberation of Jerusalem as God's demonstration of his justice (Zech. 9:9). What Israel hoped for and prayed for the disciples receive. The second four beatitudes describe the disciples in terms of their character and activities: merciful, pure in heart, peacemakers, persecuted for the sake of righteousness. Such people are God's family (v. 10).

Responding to the Text

In his commentary on the Sermon on the Mount, Luther said that the beatitudes were a "fine, sweet, and friendly way"

THE DISCIPLES, WHO COME TO GOD WITH EMPTY HANDS, HAVE HANDS FILLED WITH GIFTS FOR OTHERS.

for Christ to begin the sermon. Matthew stresses that the disciples, who come to God with empty hands, have hands filled with gifts for others. His stress on actions correlates well with the great image of judgment in 25:31–46. There the Son of Man does not ask, "What do you believe?" but stresses how the nations have acted toward "the least of these who are members of my family" (25:40, 45). That spells out what Jesus stressed at the end of the Sermon on the Mount, "doing the will of the Father" (7:21–24); not that those rejected there make the correct confession, but that they do not do the will of God. Matthew stresses that faith must be active in love, to cite St. Paul.

TWENTY-SECOND SUNDAY AFTER PENTECOST

NOVEMBER 4, 2001
THIRTY-FIRST SUNDAY IN ORDINARY TIME
PROPER 26

REVISED COMMON	EPISCOPAL (BCP)	ROMAN CATHOLIC
Isa. 1:10-18 or	Isa. 1:10-20	Wis. 11:22—12:2
Hab. 1:1-4; 2:1-4		
Ps. 32:1-7	Ps. 32 or 32:1-8	Ps. 145:1-2, 8-11, 13-14
2 Thess. 1:1-4, 11-12	2 Thess. 1:1-5,	2 Thess. 1:11—2:2
	(6-10), 11-12	
Luke 19:1-10	Luke 19:1-10	Luke 19:1-10

These last Sundays before Christ the King Sunday stress judgment and persecution. They exhibit apocalyptic language in three lessons from 2 Thessalonians and the Little Apocalypse of Luke 21, which emphasize future judgment on behalf of God's suffering people in metaphoric language. The challenge on these Sundays is to proclaim hope in the face of radical evil in society and politics and to call for action on the part of God's people to "redeem the time."

FIRST READING
ISAIAH 1:10-18 (RCL);
ISA. 1:10-20 (BCP)

Interpreting the Text

This passage is both an indictment of Israel's worship and a great promise of forgiveness. It begins with a call for attention (1:10): "listen to the teaching of our God," the first of a series of imperatives in vv. 10-17. The rejection of the sacrifices and cult in the Jerusalem temple follows (1:11-15), based on the hands stained by violence and murder.

Nine imperatives follow (vv. 16-17). Bloody hands require purification, because true worship comes from pure hearts. But purification here is not accomplished by ritual washing. Rather it comes by actions: remove evil, cease evil, learn good, seek justice, rescue the oppressed, defend orphans, plead for the widow. True worship and life dare not contradict one another.

If life and worship agree, then there is forgiveness even for hands made red by blood. But if life and cult contradict one another, sure punishment will follow (1:18-20).

Responding to the Text

How do our worship and God's justice relate to each other? History is not blind; people's decisions do affect what happens. Instead of blaming God for the evils in our world, Isaiah calls us to examine our lives in relation to our cultic practices. Are we communities that welcome outcasts? Do our worship practices and language exclude or include? Are we committed to justice for all? And how do we act out our convictions? Such questions arise from Isaiah. We too are called to "reason together" as we seek forgiveness from God.

> INSTEAD OF BLAMING GOD FOR THE EVILS IN OUR WORLD, ISAIAH CALLS US TO EXAMINE OUR LIVES IN RELATION TO OUR CULTIC PRACTICES.

HABAKKUK 1:1-4; 2:1-4 (RCL alt.)

Interpreting the Text

Habakkuk stresses the power of God over world history that calls people to trust him and be faithful. This lection comes from a dialogue between the prophet and God. It begins with a question that involves a complaint: Why does God not respond to the violence and evil (1:2-4)? "Violence" occurs six times in this book, a major concern for Habakkuk. Justice never wins, the law by which order is to prevail has become slack. In 1:5-11, God responds that worse judgment is to come. Habakkuk responds with another complaint (1:12-17).

The prophet then takes the role of watchman, looking for an answer from God (2:1) And God answers in a twofold way. (1) Make the response (vision) public on a huge stele so that all can read it (2:2). (2) The vision is that history moves according to a timetable; though it is not yet here, it will surely come. What it calls for is faith: "The just shall live by faith" (2:4).

Responding to the Text

The hymn "Watchman, Tell Us of the Night" takes its point of departure from this text. It is a hymn of expectation. God's answer is picked up by Paul in Rom. 1:17 and Gal. 3:11 as fundamental to understanding God's way of making people righteous. And it was this word that led Luther to a breakthrough in his own life in his *Turmerlebinis* (tower experience). God's answer is that "The mills of God grind slowly, but grind exceedingly fine." Faith is waiting on God. In this respect, Habakkuk and apocalyptic literature are in full agreement. Waiting on God needs to be worked out in our time over against the desire to act and to act for immediate accomplishment.

WISDOM OF SOLOMON 11:22—12:2 (RC)

Interpreting the Text

Wisdom 11:1—19:22 is a long discussion showing how God's judgments on the Egyptians had parallel blessings for Israel. The section 11:15—12:2 first describes God's forbearance in punishing the Egyptians. Because they worshiped snakes and animals, God sent mindless animals as punishment to teach them that God punishes according to how one sins (11:15-16); the reference is to the plagues of frogs, gnats, flies (Exod. 8:1-24), and locusts (Exod. 10:3-5). He could have sent terrible animals to destroy them completely but did not (11:17-21).

Wisdom 11:22—12:2 affirms God the creator's awesome power over his creation (v. 22), which he does not use out of merciful love to offer opportunity for repentance to all people. God punishes to correct little by little (12:2), to warn them of their sin, and teach them trust. Wisdom 12:1 seems to breathe a bit of Stoic panentheism when it affirms that God's immortal spirit is in all things.

Responding to the Text

The relevance of this text is clear. God as trainer or teacher through history is a motif that occurs in wisdom literature (Prov. 6:23; 2 Macc. 6:12-17; Heb. 12:5-11, which cites Prov. 3:11-12 from the Septuagint). Discipline comes from a loving parent. One might well make that a theme of proclamation. It correlates well with the lesson from 2 Thessalonians for this Sunday.

RESPONSIVE READING
PSALM 32:1-8 (RCL/BCP alt.); PS. 32 (BCP)

This psalm has a double face: it is a psalm of thanksgiving (vv. 3-7) within the framework of a wisdom psalm (vv. 1-2, 8-10). The psalm opens with a beatitude. "Happy" was translated "blessed" in older translations. That caught the implication that the happiness was a divine gift, seen and wanted by others. The basis of happiness is forgiveness. The psalmist uses three synonyms: transgression, sin, and iniquity. Together they express the depth of depravity in human actions and attitudes.

Given that blessing, the psalmist teaches the significance of confessing one's sins (vv. 3–5). He speaks of the physical effects of hiding one's responsibility for evil: the body suffers from guilt, strength goes. The psalmist may have experienced psychosomatic symptoms or actually have been sick and understood it as the result of his hidden guilt. Certainly the language is more than metaphor, for it leads to the decision to confess his sins and consequent forgiveness.

Based on his own experience, the psalmist urges others to turn to God in prayer (for forgiveness). For God is one who responds to prayer (vv. 6–7). This is the word of instruction he has for all the faithful. (Some scholars regard this as a divine oracle.) What he has learned by experience is the burden of his message. Pray for forgiveness and you will learn that God forgives.

PSALM 145:1-2. 8-11, 13-14 (RC)

A hymn of praise to God for all that he has done and does. The first ten verses are dominated by verbs of speaking: extol, bless, praise, laud, proclaim, declare, celebrate, sing, give thanks. All of them have God and his deeds as object! The psalm begins with an individual vow to praise God, whose nature is beyond knowing (v. 3). The lectionary omits vv. 3–7, which elevate the praise from individual to transgenerational. Verses 8–11 then give the basis and content of the praise, recalling Exod. 34:6. Note the sequence of predications: gracious, merciful, slow to anger, full of steadfast love (*chesed,* a key term that denotes God's unmotivated love that does not change), good, compassionate. His deeds will give thanks (v. 10). The faithful will praise God's royal rule and his power (v. 11). Verses 13–14 reinforce what has been said. God rules forever; and he is the God whose actions do not contradict his words.

This invitation to praise God heaps up word on word to describe what God is like. It is sung here toward the end of the ecclesiastical year. What has God revealed of his character in our lives in this past year? And what does that lead us to expect as we move toward Christ the King Sunday? When Paul describes the order of resurrection, he ends up by saying that Christ will finally be subject to God, "in order that God might be all in all." Put praise of God in as the ultimate goal, even for Christ!

SECOND READING

263

TWENTY-SECOND
SUNDAY
AFTER PENTECOST

NOVEMBER 4

2 THESSALONIANS 1:1-4, 11-12 (RCL);
2 THESS. 1:1-5, (6-10), 11-12 (BCP);
2 THESS. 1:11—2:2 (RC)

Interpreting the Text

Second Thessalonians addresses disheartened Christians who wonder whether God has deserted them when they are being persecuted. Chapter 1, after the letter opening, begins with a prayer of thanksgiving for the steadfast faith of the church at Thessalonica under persecution and afflictions (vv. 3-4). The next section of the prayer, vv. 5-10, reflects on the meaning such troubles have for the Thessalonians. First, they are a sign that God is truly just, because such trials and persecutions work to show that one is worthy of the kingdom of God. They demonstrate endurance in fidelity.

Second, their endurance makes it certain that God will repay the persecutors when Jesus is revealed from heaven. His revelation is described in apocalyptic language. He is accompanied by powerful angels, i.e., with the heavenly court (see Zech. 14:5). Fire is a symbol both of the presence of God (Exod. 3:2; Ezek. 1:4, 27) and of eschatological judgment (Isa. 66:15-16; Luke 3:17). He comes to make a great division, vengeance on the persecutors by excluding them from the presence of God and his glorious might because they "do not know God . . . and do not obey the gospel of our Lord Jesus Christ" (v. 8). But the persecuted will get relief, and they will join all the saints in glorifying him. Others will marvel at them because they believed the witness they heard.

After this "interlude" on the significance of persecution and the ultimate judgment of God, the writer prays that God will make them worthy of his call and will carry out the work that validates their faith.

The alternate reading begins with this final petition and adds 2:1-2 to it, an exhortation not to be disturbed by people who claim direct revelation, or who address them directly or by letter claiming that the day of the Lord is very close.

Responding to the Text

This passage, 1:1—2:2 rings very modern. The bumper sticker that warns, "Look out! This car will be driverless at the rapture!" is only one manifestation of a literalistic interpretation of passages like this one. The function of this apocalyptic message is to strengthen people in time of persecution by interpreting history as under divine control and moving toward a salvific goal. It stresses God's justice as the ultimate thread that makes sense of history and waits for this divine denouement. It does not lay out a program or chronology by which God will act. Indeed, it needs to be set alongside passages like today's Gospel.

THE GOSPEL

LUKE 19:1-10

Interpreting the Text

The story of Zacchaeus is the last event in Jesus' ministry before he enters Jerusalem for his passion. (Luke 19:11-27, which follows, is Jesus' final statement about the present and future aspects of the royal rule of God.) Jesus sees Zacchaeus, the tax collector, and invites himself to his house. The tax collector served the Roman government and so was despised by other Jews as a traitor (cf. 5:30). Luke shows a special interest in tax collectors. They come to John the Baptist for baptism (3:12; 7:29); Levi becomes a disciple (5:27) and celebrates with a dinner to which other tax collectors come (5:29). Later, tax collectors listen to Jesus (15:1). Recall the conclusion to the story of the Pharisee and the tax collector last Sunday (18:9-14). Opponents of Jesus twice accuse him of eating with tax collectors and sinners (5:30; 7:34). Eating together meant blessing the name of God together and so accepting table companions into the religious community.

Zacchaeus is the last in a long series of tax collectors. When Jesus invites himself to dine with Zacchaeus, others gave the old complaint, "He is the guest of a sinner" (v. 7). Jesus' presence in his home changes Zacchaeus: he becomes a benefactor to the poor and promises generous retribution to any he has defrauded (cf. Exod. 22:1; Num. 5:7, which give prescriptions for restitution).

Jesus' response is significant: "Today salvation is come to this house, because he too is a son of Abraham" (v. 9). "Today" has high significance in Luke. It denotes a decisive time in which a significant event takes place (2:11; 4:21; 22:34; 23:43). Zacchaeus's decisions show his response to Jesus' presence; thus, he is a member of the community. The evangelist adds a comment that summarizes the ministry of Jesus: he came to seek out and save the lost. They are the ones society has marginalized. Jesus' last use of "today" assures the thief on the cross of his inclusion, too (Luke 23:43).

> ISAIAH 61:1-2, WHICH JESUS IN LUKE 4:17-21 SAYS HAS BEEN FULFILLED, IS A PROGRAMMATIC DESCRIPTION OF HIS MINISTRY TO THE MARGINALIZED, EXPANDED TO INCLUDE NON-ISRAELITES.

Responding to the Text

In Luke, Jesus opens his public ministry in the Nazareth synagogue, where he cites Isa. 61:1-2 and says it has been fulfilled when he read it to them (Luke 4:17-21). It is a programmatic description of his ministry to the marginalized, expanded to include non-Israelites. This story invites one to recall Jesus' ministry throughout this Gospel: Peter, self-identified sinner (5:8-10), Levi (5:27-28), the widow at Nain (7:11-17), the sinful woman in the house of Simon (7:36-50), women (8:1-3), etc. As his response to Zacchaeus makes clear, Jesus widens the groups included in God's mercy. His ministry is more than words. Sum up this combination of inclusivity, action, and proclamation as a model for the church today.

TWENTY-THIRD SUNDAY AFTER PENTECOST

Revised Common	Episcopal (BCP)	Roman Catholic
Job 19:23-27a	Job 19:23-27a	2 Macc. 7:1-2, 9-14
or Hag. 1:15b—2:9		
Ps. 17:1-9	Ps. 17 or 17:1-8	Ps. 17:1, 5-6, 8, 15
2 Thess. 2:1-5, 13-17	2 Thess. 2:13—3:5	2 Thess. 2:16—3:5
Luke 20:27-38	Luke 20:27(28-33), 34-38	Luke 20:27-38 or 20:27, 34-38

Faith triumphing over adversity is the theme of today's lessons, whether Job or 2 Thessalonians or Jesus confronting the Sadducees. Future hope, whether for vindication or resurrection (2 Maccabees and the Gospel), characterizes all the lessons in one way or another. Faith triumphs! That might well be the theme for the day.

First Reading
JOB 19:23-27a (RCL/BCP)

Interpreting the Text

This text reaches a high point in the book of Job. Job is deserted by his three friends, family, and maybe even by God (19:13-19). He fears that God has become his enemy (19:6, 11-12). In despair Job makes a confession of his faith. In the face of death he calls for his personal confession to be engraved on a stone stele so that it will be a permanent witness to what he believes, a witness that will speak in the future when he himself no longer can. Persians (and later Romans) often cut the outline of letters into the rock and then inserted lead to form the letters.

The content of the message is given in 19:25-27. The Hebrew text is notoriously difficult to interpret in detail, since the text is in many respects uncertain. Job looks for a "Redeemer," a vindicator, in the future. The vindicator was a relative who avenged a death or redeemed from slavery or poverty (Num. 35:19-21; Deut. 19:6). It is not clear here whether Job looks for one to vindicate him against God or whether he looks to God to vindicate him in the future (v. 27a favors the second). He will see God "from his flesh," either clothed in flesh or without flesh. God is a God of life; even after death, Job will know that God has vindicated him.

Responding to the Text

Here is a faith that says *credo* (I believe) against all evidence. *Credo ut intellegam* (I believe in order to understand), Augustine is supposed to have said. Job is an example of faith believing against the physical evidence. He is like Abraham as Paul describes him: "He believed in the God who gives life to the dead, who calls nonexistent things into existence" (Rom. 5:17). He hoped against hope. Job opens up the doors to a discussion of faith in the face of adversity.

HAGGAI 1:5b-2:9 (RCL alt.)

Interpreting the Text

Haggai urges the rebuilding of the temple on the return from Babylon. The people argued that the economy would not sustain the program. Haggai 1:5-11 urges the reverse: failure to build the temple has led to economic problems. Haggai's word of judgment roused the governor Zerubbabel and the high priest Joshua and the people to rebuild the temple. "I am with you" is the Lord's promise (1:12-15). The people's change prompts a change on God's part. The economics will improve.

The new temple, say those who remember Solomon's, is inferior in beauty and glory. But God is present there as he was present in the Exodus (2:5). He will act powerfully to give glory to the temple. "I will fill this house with splendor" (v. 7) is a double entendre. On the one hand, it means that the temple will be filled with gold and silver, will be rich beyond that of Solomon (2:7-9). But it also means that the glory of the Lord will come down and dwell there, as it did in the tabernacle (Exod. 40:34–38) and in Solomon's temple (1 Kings 8:10-11).

Responding to the Text

What gives glory to a house of worship? The presence of God. How do we know if God is present in our places of worship? God is present in his word, in the proclamation of Gospel in Scripture, in homily, in baptism, in the Lord's Supper, in the word of forgiveness, in the recognition of others as sisters and brothers in Christ. God is present when acts are done in God's and Christ's name, when people see God at work through us. So God is present in cathedrals and small clapboard churches. What makes a place of worship a house of God is not its cost but its function.

2 MACCABEES 7:1-2, 9-14 (RC)

Interpreting the Text

Second Maccabees 7 tells the story of the martyrdom of a mother and her seven sons because of their fidelity to the Torah. The first two verses set the stage. The king (Antiochus IV Epiphanes, 7:24) demands, using torture, that they eat pork. One brother replies that they would rather die than break their ancestral law. After torturing the first to death (7:3-7), they kill the other six brothers in turn. Each makes a brief speech expressing his convictions about the future and his faith in God before dying. Verses 9-14 contain the speeches of the second, third, and fourth brothers.

All three confess belief in the future resurrection that will reverse their death at the hands of Antiochus's men. The second says that Antiochus can kill, but "the King of the universe will raise us up to everlasting life" (7:9). The third says that God will restore the hands that they have cut off (7:11), while the fourth states that one will choose to die at the hands of mortals in the hope that God will raise him again. But there will be no resurrection to life for the oppressors (7:14).

This hope of future life for the righteous—but not for the unjust—agrees with the view expressed in Dan. 12:1-3. The righteous will shine like the stars in heaven.

Responding to the Text

The hope of the resurrection in this passage is not based on some innate quality of human beings (immortal soul), but on the power of God. Second Maccabees develops a theology of martyrdom that contrasts present suffering with future resurrection, present evil rulers with the King of the Universe, fidelity with conformity. This insight is developed further in 4 Maccabees 8–18. It is not surprising that these martyrs were incorporated into later Christian martyrologies, since they model sustaining belief in the power and justice of God. Proclaim such a victorious faith.

RESPONSIVE READING

269

TWENTY-THIRD
SUNDAY
AFTER PENTECOST

NOVEMBER 11

PSALM 17:1-9 (RCL);
PS. 17 or 17:1-8 (BCP);
PS. 17:1, 5-6, 8, 15 (RC)

This seems to be a nighttime prayer that asks for God's judgment and deliverance ("visit me by night," v. 3; "when I awake," v. 15). The speaker is being persecuted by enemies, as vv. 9-12 make clear (omitted from the lectionary to generalize the application in liturgical use). The psalmist is convinced of his own innocence in this persecution. He calls on God to hear his "just cause" (v. 1). The phrase suggests that he is coming to God as judge, asking him to see that justice (vindication) is done for him.

He asserts his innocence, calling on God to check him out (vv. 3-5). He has remained faithful to "your paths," a claim to have lived within the covenant prescriptions of the Torah. Therefore he calls on God with confidence (v. 6) to listen, show his love, guard him, and hide him from the wicked. Verse 15, which concludes the psalm, is a statement of confidence that the prayer for vindication and defense will be heard.

Holding God to the covenant is what this psalmist does. He claims God's actions for himself, not as an act of arrogance, but a plea for the recognition of his faithfulness to God's own promises.

SECOND READING
2 THESSALONIANS 2:1-5, 13-17 (RCL);
2 THESS. 2:13—3:5 (BCP);
2 THESS. 2:16—3:5 (RC)

Interpreting the Text

In this section of 2 Thessalonians, the writer addresses the major problem confronting this church: the excitement over the supposed revelation of the imminent parousia (return) of Christ. He deals with the problem in two ways. He first warns against that belief by denying that he holds it. The day of the Lord cannot come until the apostasy ("rebellion" in the NRSV) comes first, led by a false messiah. This is a stock idea in early Christian apocalyptic literature (Matt. 24:23-24; Jude

RECOGNIZE THAT GOD HAS CHOSEN YOU FOR SALVATION THROUGH FAITH IN THE TRUTH AND THROUGH THE SANCTIFYING ACTIVITY OF THE SPIRIT. HE DID THAT THROUGH THE PROCLAMATION OF THE GOSPEL. THEREFORE, DO NOT BE DISTURBED BY FALSE ANNOUNCEMENTS.

17-19). This false messiah is called the "man of lawlessness," who breaks the Torah by claiming deity, taking his seat in the temple, and claiming worship. This description is based on Dan. 11:21-45 and Ezek. 28:1-10 and on the actions of the Roman emperors Caligula and Nero in the first century.

How then do you live as you wait for this revelation of evil? Recognize that God has chosen you for salvation through faith in the truth and through the sanctifying activity of the Spirit. He did that through the proclamation of the gospel. Therefore, do not be disturbed by such false announcements; rather, hang on to the tradition that you have been taught This reference to maintaining the tradition, repeated in 3:6, indicates a later period in the first century. The lesson ends with a prayer for hope, comfort (or exhortation), and strength from the Lord Jesus and from God.

Responding to the Text

Maintain the tradition. *In dubito, pro tradito* (in a problematic matter, hold to the tradition). We are not the first to believe; the faith has been tested in time by the generations before us. This text holds that God moves according to plan. Evil must be unmasked before God will act decisively. We might wonder whether that face of evil has not been revealed; this text warns against over-hasty conclusions.

THE GOSPEL
LUKE 20:27-38 (RCL/RC);
LUKE 20:27 (28-33), 34-38 (BCP);
LUKE 20:27, 34-38 (RC alt.)

Interpreting the Text

The question from the Sadducees is the third question put to Jesus by religious leaders in the great courtyard of the Herodian temple. Sadducees were leaders in the priestly caste and religious conservatives in early Judaism. According to Josephus they accepted only the Torah, the five books of Moses, as authoritative Scripture. As Luke notes, they rejected the Pharisaic teaching that affirmed a future resurrection. They pose a question that they feel reduces the idea of resurrection to an absurdity. If a woman, following the law of levirate marriage (Deut. 25:5-6), marries seven brothers in succession, whose wife will she be in the resurrec-

> THE SADDUCEES ASSUME THAT RESURRECTION MEANS THAT FUTURE AGE IS LIKE THE PRESENT AND THEREFORE WILL REQUIRE HUMAN PROCREATION TO ENDURE.

tion (Luke 20:27-32)? The Sadducees assume that resurrection means that future age is like the present and therefore will require human procreation to endure.

Jesus first contradicts their assumption that life in the age to come will be just like life in the present age. Sex and procreation will not be part of the new age. Jesus' next response meets them on their own turf by making his case from the Pentateuch. Underlying his answer is the conviction that God is a God of life. In Exod. 3:6, God identifies himself to Moses as the God of the patriarchs Abraham, Isaac, and Jacob. But God is the God of living people, not dead ones; hence the patriarchs must be alive, hence raised from the dead

Responding to the Text

This story in context certainly has the function of showing Jesus' superiority to the religious leaders in Israel. But this specific story also speaks about future resurrection. And there it gives two significant indications of how one should speak of the resurrection. The first is that any talk about the future rests first of all in our conception of God, not in a theory about the human soul, immortality, or the like. The second is that resurrection is not resuscitation to life as we now know it. As with talk about God, so with the resurrection. We can say what it is not, but we cannot give any description of what it will be. And that is why we can only begin, as Jesus does, with consideration of what God is and how God deals with us.

TWENTY-FOURTH SUNDAY AFTER PENTECOST

November 18, 2001
Thirty-third Sunday in Ordinary Time
Proper 28

Revised Common	Episcopal (BCP)	Roman Catholic
Mal. 4:1-2a	Mal. 3:13—4:2a, 5-6	Mal. 4:1-2a
or Isa. 65:17-25		(Engl. numbering)
Ps. 98	Ps. 98 or 98:5-10	Ps. 98:5-9
2 Thess. 3:6-13	2 Thess. 3:6-13	2 Thess. 3:7-12
Luke 21:5-19	Luke 21:5-19	Luke 21:5-19

This Sunday's lessons combine a realistic view of life with an exuberant hope for the future (Malachi and Isaiah). The lessons all teach us to be expectant of the creator God's actions for us and call us to realistically look at our time and hold out a vision of what will be.

First Reading
MALACHI 4:1-2a (RCL/RC); 3:13—4:2a, 5-6 (BCP)

Interpreting the Text

Malachi wrote after the return from exile, when the temple was rebuilt (see the critique of temple worship in Mal. 1:6-14, 2:11). The prophet's name, Malachi, may be descriptive, because it means "my messenger," and Malachi is indeed a messenger with a powerful message.

The returnees have not learned from past history. The worship in the rebuilt temple is once again not what it should be. And the faithful are disillusioned. What good does it do to serve God faithfully (vv. 13-15)? The righteous ought to prosper and the wicked be punished, as Psalm 1 says (cf. Prov. 28:13). But this conventional wisdom is false!

Malachi 3:16-18 is God's response. The faithful people are recorded in a book of remembrance, whom God will claim as his own (Israel as God's special possession is one of the great titles; cf. Exod. 19:5-6; 1 Pet. 2:10; Rev. 1:5-6). The time will come when the conventional wisdom will prove true. Malachi closes by mentioning the two great prophets who shaped Israel: Moses gave Israel the Torah, the teaching by which they are to live (4:4). Elijah is the prophet who will prepare the people for the judgment. This motif is picked up in Sir. 48:10-11 and the New Testament (Mark 1:2; Matt. 17:10-13). Both went to heaven without dying, according to later Jewish tradition. Both appear at Jesus' transfiguration, and both are regarded as witnesses to Jesus in Rev. 11:3-11.

Responding to the Text

Malachi provides a strong link to the New Testament. His interpretation of Elijah determines the description and role of John the Baptist. These two witnesses, both preeminent prophets, witness to Jesus' coming death at his transfiguration. Malachi's vision of hope is thus tied to Jesus in the New Testament. His words, as used in the New Testament, point to Jesus as the one who claims a people as God's own possession.

ISAIAH 65:17-25 (RCL alt.)

Interpreting the Text

This text is an exuberant description of the joyful future that stretches out before the people of God. It celebrates God the creator (65:17-18). There will be a new heaven and new earth, i.e., a whole new created universe (the motif is picked up in Rev. 21:1 in another ecstatic vision of the future). The past will be forgotten.

There will be a new Jerusalem (cf. Gal. 4:26-27; Rev. 21:11-27), a city as it should be, full of joy. Children will live to old age. There will be peace, as people live in security, enjoying their crops. The population will be blessed by God. The natural world will also be changed. Wolf and lamb live in peace together, and the lion is no longer carnivorous (cf. Isa. 11:6-9). In short, the creative will of God is brought to fulfillment.

Responding to the Text

"If the people have no vision, they perish." This text provides a vision for the church. Third Isaiah stresses that God is still creating, making new things in our world. God was not uncaring for Israel in her problems (v. 24), and God is not unaware of ours. In his fourth Eclogue, Vergil paints a picture of the future with remarkable similarities to Isaiah. The birth

THE CHURCH DARE NOT BE A CARETAKER OF THE STATUS QUO; IT MUST HOLD UP THE POSSIBILITIES FOR PEACE IN A NEW WORLD—AND IN THIS OLD ONE.

of a child will inaugurate a golden age when lion and lamb live together in peace. It is not surprising that he was regarded as a prophet by the medieval church.

What vision do we hold up before the modern church and society in general? That is the question this text from Third Isaiah raises for us at the beginning of a new millennium. The church dares not be a caretaker of the status quo; it must hold up the possibilities for peace in a new world—and in this old one.

RESPONSIVE READING

PSALM 98 (RCL/BCP);
PS. 98:5-9 (RC); PS. 98:5-10 (BCP alt.)

Psalm 98 praises God as mighty warrior who defends his people. It calls on the entire creation to join in this praise. And it looks for the same actions by God in the future. The psalm opens with an announcement of God's acts of victory.

This Sunday's Gospel is strongly apocalyptic in character. It speaks of the birth pangs of the new age as natural and historical upheavals that will try the faith of the very elect. Psalm 98 is the counterbalance to this Gospel, because it speaks of the assurance that God's future coming will bring equitable judgment.

SECOND READING

2 THESSALONIANS 3:6-13 (RCL/BCP);
2 THESS. 3:7-12 (RC)

Interpreting the Text

Second Thessalonians 3:6-16 addresses the issue of Christians' lifestyle as they wait for God's action. Christians are encouraged not to fall into disorderliness and idleness. They should live "according to the tradition" received from Paul (v. 6). This use of tradition shows the later origin of this letter; enough time has passed for a standard form of teaching on behavior to develop. They will follow the tradition and imitate Paul, who worked night and day while he lived and preached among the Thessalonians (the language is borrowed from 1 Thess. 2:9). He did this to give them an example (v. 9), a somewhat pedestrian reason when compared with Paul's words in 1 Cor. 9:11-18. He encourages everyone to work, to earn his or her own livelihood, and not get weary of doing so.

Responding to the Text

275

TWENTY–FOURTH
SUNDAY
AFTER PENTECOST

NOVEMBER 18

Read this very practical advice in the context of today's Gospel. Common sense is often not common. St. Francis, so the story goes, was asked what he would do if he knew the world would end the next day. "Plant an apple tree," was his response (some tell this story of Luther). This passage suggests that the best way to prepare for the Lord's return is to live daily life in faith and confidence, without suddenly doing unusual things as acts of preparation. Live daily life in the expectation of the end.

THE GOSPEL
LUKE 21:5-19

Interpreting the Text

This long reading opens the apocalyptic discourse in Luke. This discourse is presented as public teaching in the temple itself. (In Matthew and Mark the discourse is spoken only to disciples on the Mount of Olives, from where one could survey the temple from the east.) The text has a clear outline. The introduction (vv. 5-7) begins with Jesus' prediction of the destruction of the temple, with the hearers' response asking for the date and the sign that indicates the nearness of that event. The sermon that follows gives an extensive response to the request for a sign, but only a brief, enigmatic response about the date (21:29-33).

Jesus responds with an exhortation to those who called him "teacher" (vv. 8-9): "Look out for" false messiahs who present themselves as prognosticators of the end. And don't be terrified by what is to come. Next he predicts both political and natural disasters: war, earthquake, famine, plague, and cosmic upheaval (vv. 10-11). These correlate very well with the four horsemen in Rev. 6:1-8, an indication that the sermon contains many elements from Jewish apocalyptic tradition (cf. Isa. 19:2, Jer. 4:13-22; Ezek. 38:19-23 for war and cosmic events as God's agents of judgment).

The third section of the discourse (vv. 12-19) predicts the bleak-sounding future of the disciples, a description of post-Easter events (Matt. 10:16-23 places these words in the discourse sending out the twelve to preach the gospel): arrest and trials because of their faith (v. 12), rejection by family and friends, execution and hatred by all (vv. 16-17). Jesus also gives assurance. Persecution will be the occasion for witness, a witness in which Jesus will supply wisdom and words. Fidelity will ultimately be vindicated; the disciples will be preserved.

The apocalyptic discourse has two main foci: (1) the destruction of Jerusalem because of the rejection of Jesus (19:7—21:4) and (2) the ultimate vindication of the persecuted disciples by the regnant Son of Man. The lectionary omits the section of the sermon that carries out the latter program. Apocalyptic language is dangerous language, as the recent furor over Y2K made clear. It is most relevant to people in time of persecution; its concern with the future leads to strange speculation among literalists.

Apocalyptic language is highly metaphorical. Its ultimate aim is to comfort oppressed Christians. In 1947, Bishop Hans Lilje said that you did not need to persuade Germans (after Hitler and WW II) that they were living in the last times. Twenty-five years later he spoke again in America, after the economic miracle of postwar Germany. No one in Germany was any longer concerned with the last times.

America is so comfortable with personal religion that overt persecution does not exist. Rather we are faced with disregard of religion. Lessons like this Gospel call for proclamation that makes clear the relevance of faith in such a world.

> APOCALYPTIC LANGUAGE IS DANGEROUS LANGUAGE, AS THE RECENT FUROR OVER Y2K MADE CLEAR. ITS CONCERN WITH THE FUTURE LEADS TO STRANGE SPECULATION AMONG LITERALISTS. APOCALYPTIC LANGUAGE IS HIGHLY METAPHORICAL. ITS ULTIMATE AIM IS TO COMFORT OPPRESSED CHRISTIANS.

LAST SUNDAY AFTER PENTECOST / CHRIST THE KING

NOVEMBER 25, 2001

Kosmo Keator

REVISED COMMON	EPISCOPAL (BCP)	ROMAN CATHOLIC
Jer. 23:1-6	Jer. 23:1-6	2 Sam. 5:1-3
Ps. 46	Ps. 46	Ps. 122:1-5
Col. 1:11-20	Col. 1:11-20	Col. 1:12-20
Luke 23:33-43	Luke 23:35-43 or 19:29-38	Luke 23:35-43

Christ the King Sunday is, in one sense, the culmination of the church year. Its focuses on a description of the present regnant Lord of the Universe. It celebrates the final outcome of the work of Christ and is, at the same time, the basis of Christian hope for the future. Its great themes are royal, Davidic, cosmic, and surprisingly cruciform.

FIRST READING
JEREMIAH 23:1-6 (RCL/BCP)

Interpreting the Text

In this passage Jeremiah looks forward to the restoration of Israel after the exile. In the section just before this text, Jeremiah exhorted the royal house of Judah to do justice, but predicted its demise (Jer. 22:1-9). He then addressed the sons of Josiah: (Jehoahaz (22:10-11), Jehoiakim (22:13-19), and Jehoiachin (22:24-30). Jeremiah sums up this denunciation by describing the kings as shepherds who scatter and ruin the people, their flock. The image of shepherd for king was prevalent (see 2 Sam. 5:2; 1 Chron. 11:2; Num. 27:17; Jude 11:19; 2 Chron. 18:16; Matt. 2:6, 9:36; 1 Pet. 2:25). Jeremiah describes the people as God's flock, not the king's. Therefore God will attend to these kings, who have not attended to the flock (note the wordplay on "attend.")

God is not simply a God of punishment but a God who will bring the remnant of his flock back from exile. They then "will be fruitful and multiply," an allusion to the promises made to Abraham and Jacob (Gen. 17:1-8, 20; 28:3) and to the command to Adam and Eve in Gen. 1:28. God's plans for creation and the children of Israel flow together.

The future includes proper kings (v. 4), whose rule will not cause fear. The text leads to the prediction of a "righteous branch " raised up for David, a future Davidic king who will act in wisdom and righteousness. "Branch" appears to be a messianic, i.e., royal title (as in Zech. 3:8 and 6:12). His name will be "Yahweh Zidkenu" ("the Lord is our Righteousness"). Names often reflect character in the Bible—and that is certainly the case here. "Righteousness" in relation to God implies God's fidelity to the covenant. This king will bring God's will for Israel and the created world to reality.

Responding to the Text

History is a confusing business. It is often only long after an event that one begins to make sense of what happened—if one can. In the middle of this ambiguity, Jeremiah assures his community that God is in ultimate control. History remains confusing. It's "just one damn thing after another," as someone put it in modern times. Confessing the rule of God in the face of political, social, or economic disorder reveals one's concept of God.

> CONFESSING THE RULE OF GOD IN THE FACE OF POLITICAL, SOCIAL, OR ECONOMIC DISORDER REVEALS ONE'S CONCEPT OF GOD.

Jeremiah challenges us to conceive of a God great enough to be in control.

2 SAMUEL 5:1-3 (RC)

Interpreting the Text

This is, at first glance, a bare-bones account of David's coronation as king. But several motifs are significant. David, a Judahite, had waged a guerrilla war against King Saul. His succession was by no means certain, as the assassination of Saul's son Ishbaal makes clear (2 Samuel 5). Now the leaders of the twelve tribes acknowledge their kinship to David and accept him as their king because of God's word. He is to be the shepherd of God's people, that is, a king who leads and protects with care. David makes a covenant with them, committing himself to his responsibilities in return for their loyalty. This took place at Hebron, where the tombs of the patriarchs were thought to be located. And the rule was successful: it lasted for forty years, the biblical number of completion or for a full generation.

This lection stresses the relationship between king and people. The people identify with the king; the king commits himself to the people. There are massive social and political implications for the contemporary world in all of this. Christ the King Sunday can appear to be romantic futurism, but the future is, in part, a responsibility that all people are to realize.

RESPONSIVE READING
PSALM 46 (RCL/BCP)

Interpreting the Text
See the discussion of this Psalm at Reformation Day, above.

Responding to the Text

The focus on Christ the King Sunday elicits a different response from Psalm 46 than a Reformation observance does. In this context one stresses the priority of God in history as a resource for faith. God is present in history as refuge and protector. There is a saying that "God is in the details." That is true also of our daily life. God is present in the problems that make up our lives, whether natural disasters, social unrest, or wars. In that sense God is democratic, not elitist, concerned with the stuff of everyday life and not just the great events.

PSALM 122:1-5 (RC)

Psalm 122 is probably a "pilgrim psalm," sung as people went up to Jerusalem for one of the great feasts. Jerusalem is the place of God's presence, concretized in the temple on Mt. Zion ("the house of the LORD"). The psalm summons its singers to give thanks to God because Jerusalem was a city that was secure, where the kings ruled in justice.

Praise of Jerusalem is the theme of this psalm, but not of its architecture or its location. Rather it calls for praise. The city evoked a sense of awe in its pilgrims. That is a reaction that seems foreign to modern worshipers, who tend to think of God as friend. Moses was told to "Come no closer! Remove the sandals from your feet, for the place on which you are standing is holy ground" (Exod. 3:5). Today one can and should call for awe before the God of history.

SECOND READING

COLOSSIANS 1:11-20 (RCL/BCP); COL. 1:12-20 (RC)

Interpreting the Text

Colossians 1:15-20 is a carefully written prose hymn deriving from the Colossians, cited and interpreted by the author of Colossians. Unfortunately, neither NRSV nor REB prints it as poetry; NAB does indicate its poetic structure. The hymn is in two stanzas. The first, Col. 1:15-18a, is paralleled in structure by the second, 1:18b-20. Both begin with a relative pronoun ("Who"), not reproduced in English translations, followed by a predication ("image of the invisible God" and "the beginning"), a statement about being "the firstborn" (of the entire universe and from the dead), and a statement giving the basis for the predications. Both stanzas describe the subject in relation to the universe (the phrase "all things" is a standard formula in ancient philosophy for the universe).

Stanza one pronounces Christ the creator of the universe, including the things in heaven and on earth. The phrase "whether thrones or dominions or rulers or powers" are terms that describe the seven beings in the heavens (five planets, sun, and moon) that ancients thought of as living beings that controlled human fate. Stanza one states that these supposed divine beings are creatures made by the one who is "the image of the invisible God." This phrase at first sounds like nonsense! How does one create an image of what cannot be seen? He is God's image because he creates. And therefore he also is superior to them and holds the creation together (Col. 1:17), and therefore is creation's head.

Stanza two speaks of the significance of the resurrection from the dead (Col. 1:18b). The created universe has become an enemy of God and must be pacified. The resurrection takes place in order that he might "come to have first place" in the universe. He is the way in which God is present in the universe, for by him God reconciles the rebellious powers and makes peace. Thus the hymn celebrates the cosmic Christ who both creates and reconciles the universe to God.

The author of Colossians provides an introduction to the hymn in 1:12-14 and applies the hymn in 1:21-23 (unfortunately, not included in the lectionary). The introduction makes clear that the one who rules is the Son of God's love, who removes us from the authority of darkness. This suggests that the hymn may have been used in a baptismal context. The writer also interpolates two phrases into the hymn that show how he takes the Colossians' hymn and folds it into his own theology. (1) In Col. 1:18a, he identifies the body of which he is the head as "the assembly," the church. Christ rules directly only in the church, not in the universe. (2) In Col. 1:20, he inserts the phrase "through the blood of his cross." The significance of this is clarified in Col. 2:11-15, where Jesus' crucifixion is interpreted as a victory trophy and his resurrection as a triumphal procession in which he leads the defeated enemies as captives in a public spectacle.

Finally, Col. 1:21-23 applies the hymn to the Colossians. It calls for constancy and fidelity, confession and commitment. What the hymn proclaims in third-person reportorial style must be realized in the present life of the church, whose head Christ is.

Responding to the Text

Reading and meditating on Col. 1:15-20 is like walking into a great cathedral on a very hot day. The great Byzantine churches present Christ as the *Pantokrator,* the Lord of the Universe, either in the central dome or in the apse. One enters to be amazed by the brilliant colors coming through the stained glass, by the height of the arches, the length of the nave, and the glory of the apse and altar. Colossians provides a major entry into discussing what it means that the entire universe is subservient to God in Christ. Joseph Sittler used this text at New Delhi to introduce the idea of Christian responsibility for ecology and creation. One must move from the glorious cathedral out into the plaza before it, into the marketplace of the everyday world. And Colossians does that as it moves into day-to-day life in chapters 3–4.

> COLOSSIANS PROVIDES A MAJOR ENTRY INTO DISCUSSING WHAT IT MEANS THAT THE ENTIRE UNIVERSE IS SUBSERVIENT TO GOD IN CHRIST.

THE GOSPEL
LUKE 23:33-43 (RCL/BCP);
LUKE 23:35-43 (RC)

Interpreting the Text

Luke's account of the crucifixion was included in the Gospel for Passion Sunday earlier this liturgical year. Luke's narrative has many unique features. (1) Luke reports the word of Jesus, "Father, forgive them, for they don't know what they are doing" (v. 34). In a manner different from Mark and Matthew, Jesus is not forsaken by God but is in communion with him. He intercedes on behalf of his executioners. That makes credible the centurion's confession at his death, "This man was righteous (*dikaios*)," the term that was applied to Zechariah and Elizabeth back in Luke 1:5. It recalls the fact that Pilate three times pronounces Jesus innocent in the Roman trial. (2) The people (*ho laos*) do not mock Jesus in Luke (23:35). Rather, the rulers mock him. This prepares for the people's action at his death: they return to Jerusalem "beating their breasts," a sign of repentance. (3) The *titulus* put on the cross in Luke reads, "This is the King of the Jews" (Luke

23:38). It is an announcement of his identity, not an accusation. (4) It is only in Luke that one of the crucified robbers testifies to Jesus' innocence and asks for his aid. Jesus' response, "Today you will be with me in Paradise," like the response to the crucifixion detail, shows him still carrying out his ministry to the marginalized and outcasts.

The text breaks off in the middle of the crucifixion account, omitting the third word from the cross, "Father, into your hands I place my spirit," a citation from Ps. 31:5. He dies in full communion with his Father.

THE OFFICE HYMN FOR GOOD FRIDAY IS *VEXILLA REGIS PRODEUNT,* "THE ROYAL BANNERS FORWARD GO." IT SINGS OF THE CROSS AS THE THRONE FROM WHICH CHRIST REIGNS. IN THAT RESPECT COLOSSIANS AND LUKE COME TOGETHER. THE CROSS IS NOT A DEFEAT, BUT THE TRIUMPH OF THE CRUCIFIED OVER HIS FOES AND OURS.

Responding to the Text

The crucifixion as Christ the King Sunday text? It seems ridiculous at first glance—but not on closer examination. The office hymn for Good Friday is *Vexilla regis prodeunt,* "The Royal Banners Forward Go." It sings of the cross as the throne from which Christ reigns. In that respect Colossians and Luke come together. The cross is not a defeat, but the triumph of the crucified over his foes and ours. The very fact that the crucifixion is taken as the text provides a starting point for tying the reign of Christ to the events of Passiontide. And from there one can move into the rule of Christ in the midst of our lives.

LUKE 19:29-38 (BCP alt.)

This lection is the account of Jesus' entry into Jerusalem. Luke presents it as the parousia of a king, acclaimed by the crowds (see their actions in Luke 19:36). The acclamation makes it explicit. "Blessed is the king who comes in the name of the Lord!" Neither Mark nor Matthew are as explicit (John is). And Luke has them follow it with, "Peace in heaven, and glory in the highest heaven" (v. 38), a reprise of the angelic choir in Luke 2:14. These phrases have long been recognized as formed in opposition to the Roman ruler cult, as expressed in the great calendar inscription from Priene in Asia Minor.

How does one welcome a king? In the ancient world, city officials went out in procession to escort a king or emperor or his representative into the city. So the Jerusalemites welcomed Alexander the Great in 332 B.C.E. How does one welcome the Lord Christ today? I would be tempted to create some form of welcoming ritual if I preached on this text. It would be an interesting exercise to involve a worship committee or an adult forum in planning the symbolism of such a welcome rite.

APRIL 2001

Sunday	Monday	Tuesday	Wednesday	Thursday	Friday	Saturday
1	2	3	4	5	6	7
8 Palm Sunday Passover	9	10	11	12	Maundy Thursday	13 Good Friday	14
15 Easter 1 Easter Evening	16 Easter Monday	17	18	19	20	21
22 Easter 2	23	24	25	26	27	28
29 Easter 3	30					

MAY 2001

Sunday	Monday	Tuesday	Wednesday	Thursday	Friday	Saturday
		1	2	3	4	5
6 Easter 4	7	8	9	10	11	12
13 Easter 5 Mother's Day	14	15	16	17	18	19
20 Easter 6	21	22	23	24 Ascension Day	25	26
27 Easter 7	28 Memorial Day	29	30	31		

JUNE 2001

Sunday	Monday	Tuesday	Wednesday	Thursday	Friday	Saturday
					1	2
3 Pentecost	4	5	6	7	8	9
10 Pentecost 1 Holy Trinity Sunday	11	12	13	14	15	16
17 Pentecost 2 Body and Blood of Christ Father's Day	18	19	20	21	22	23
24 Pentecost 3 Nativity of St. John the Baptist	25	26	27	28	29	30

JULY 2001

Sunday	Monday	Tuesday	Wednesday	Thursday	Friday	Saturday
1 Pentecost 4	2	3	4 Independence Day	5	6	7
8 Pentecost 5	9	10	11	12	13	14
15 Pentecost 6	16	17	18	19	20	21
22 Pentecost 7 St. Mary Magdalene	23	24	25	26	27	28
29 Pentecost 8	30	31				

AUGUST 2001

Sunday	Monday	Tuesday	Wednesday	Thursday	Friday	Saturday
			1	2	3	4
5 Pentecost 9	6	7	8	9	10	11
12 Pentecost 10	13	14	15	16	17	18
19 Pentecost 11	20	21	22	23	24	25
26 Pentecost 12	27	28	29	30	31	

SEPTEMBER 2001

Sunday	Monday	Tuesday	Wednesday	Thursday	Friday	Saturday
						1
2 Pentecost 13	3 Labor Day	4	5	6	7	8
9 Pentecost 14	10	11	12	13	14	15
16 Pentecost 15	17	18	19	20	21	22
23 Pentecost 16	24	25	26	27	28	29
30 Pentecost 17						

OCTOBER 2001

Sunday	Monday	Tuesday	Wednesday	Thursday	Friday	Saturday
	1	2	3	4	5	6
7 Pentecost 18	8 Columbus Day	9	10	11	12	13
14 Pentecost 19	15	16	17	18	19	20
21 Pentecost 20	22	23	24	25	26	27
28 Pentecost 21	29	30	31 Reformation Day			

NOVEMBER 2001

Sunday	Monday	Tuesday	Wednesday	Thursday	Friday	Saturday
				1 All Saints Day	2	3
4 Pentecost 22	5	6	7	8	9	10
11 Pentecost 23	12	13	14	15	16	17
18 Pentecost 24	19	20	21	22	23	24
25 Pentecost 25 Christ the King Sunday	26	27	28	29 Thanksgiving	30	